The Mufti of Jerusalem

Muhammad Amin al-Husayni (1895–1974)
by John Mattar, Guelph, Canada.

The Mufti of Jerusalem

Al-Hajj Amin al-Husayni and the
Palestinian National Movement

Revised Edition

Philip Mattar

Columbia University Press

NEW YORK

Columbia University Press
New York   Oxford
Copyright © 1988 Columbia University Press
Printed in the United States of America

Library of Congress Cataloging-in-Publication Data

Mattar, Philip
  The Mufti of Jerusalem : Al-Hajj Amīn al-Husaynī and the
Palestinian National Movement / Philip Mattar.—Rev. ed.
      p.   cm.
  Includes bibliographical references and index.
  ISBN 0–231–06462–4
  ISBN 0–231–06463–2 (pbk.)
  1. Husaynī, Amīn, Grand Mufti of Jerusalem, 1893–1974.
2. Palestinian Arabs—Biography.   3. Politicians—Palestine—
Biography.   4. Jewish-Arab relations—1917–1949.   5. Palestine—
History—1917–1948.
DS125.3H79M37   1992
956.94'04'092—dc20
[B]   92–793
                                                       CIP

Book design by Ken Venezio

Clothbound Columbia University Press editions are Smyth-
sewn and printed on permanent and durable acid-free paper.

Printed in the USA.

c 10 9 8 7 6 5 4 3 2 1
p 10 9 8 7 6 5 4 3 2 1

To my mother

Contents

Illustrations   ix

Preface to the Revised Edition   xi

Preface   xiii

1. The Making of a Palestinian Nationalist: The Formative Years   1

2. Rise to Religious Power   19

3. Political Struggle Over the Western Wall, 1928–1929   33

4. The Politics of Moderation and the General Islamic Congress   50

5. The Arab Revolt: The Challenge   65

6. The Arab Revolt: The Response   73

7. Iraq's Quest for Independence, 1939–1941   86

8. The Nazi Years   99

9. Diplomacy and War, 1946–1948   108

10. Decline of Power   135

11. An Overview and Assessment   140

Notes   155

Bibliography   177

Index   187

Notes   155
Bibliography   177
Index   187

Illustrations

Frontispiece: Muhammad Amin al-Husayni (1895–1974) by John Mattar, Guelph, Canada.

These illustrations appear as a group after page 80.

As an Ottoman officer in 1917.

Two of the Mufti's aides: Jamal al-Husayni (right) and Emile al-Ghuri (left), London, 1947.

Al-Hajj Amin al-Husayni (right) and King Faysal of Iraq (left), Jaffa Harbor, 1925 (W. Khalidi, *Before Their Diaspora*).

The Arab Higher Committee, formed April 1936. Front row, left to right: Raghib al-Nashashibi, al-Hajj Amin al-Husayni, Ahmad Hilmi, 'Abd al-Latif Salah, and Alfred Roch. Second Row, left to right: Jamal al-Husayni,

Dr. Husayn al-Khalidi, Ya'qub al-Ghusayn, and Fu'ad Saba (W. Khalidi, *Before Their Diaspora*).

The Mufti (far right, front row) standing with Musa Kazim al-Husayni (center) and Raghib al-Nashashibi (left) as members of the Palestinian delegation, London, April 1930 (W. Khalidi, *Before Their Diaspora*).

In Lebanon in 1949.

With Jamal 'Abd al-Nasir, President of Egypt (right) and Shukri al-Quwatli, President of Syria, Cairo, 1958.

The Mufti with King Husayn of Jordan, Amman, 1967.

In Beirut, June 1974, weeks before the Mutfi's death.

Preface to the Revised Edition

The publication of this edition has given me an opportunity to add a chapter covering 1946–48 and to expand two others. Since the first edition went to press in 1987 two biographies of the Mufti and a number of useful books and monographs about the end of the Palestine mandate have been published.

The new chapter 9 discusses the Mufti's role within the Arab League, rivalry with Abdullah, involvement in the 1948 war, and the establishment of the All-Palestine Government. Chapter 10, concerning his decline, and chapter 11, which is an overview and assessment, are expanded, as is the select bibliography.

I wish to thank a number of friends and colleagues for their assistance:

Kate Wittenberg, editor in chief of Columbia University Press, for giving me the chance to enlarge this biography;

Linda Butler, for her wise comments and editorial help;

Neil Caplan, for his generous and critical advice;

Kathy Christison, for her comments and encouragement;

Anne Curley and Charlie Zenzie for typing the new material with patience and good cheer;

Ben Joseph and Bill Young for their speedy and meticulous Hebrew and German translations, respectively;

And, as always, my wife for her patience and continuous encouragement.

Preface

Muhammad Amin al-Husayni (1895–1974), the Mufti of Jerusalem, was the principal leader of the Palestinian national movement and a popular personality in the Arab world during most of the years of British rule over Palestine (1917–1948). Yet the accounts of his life are barely adequate. The absence of a balanced consideration of al-Husayni's political career is not remarkable in view of the passion his name has always inspired.

The biographers of the Mufti, also known as al-Hajj Amin, often told us more about themselves than about the Palestinian leader. They were written by Jewish nationalists, such as Moshe Pearlman, Joseph Schechtman (a Revisionist Zionist), and Eliahu Elath who attempted to vilify him and discredit his movement; by Arab nationalists, such as Zuhayr al-Mardini, who lauded him and his cause; or by German national socialists who portrayed him as the Muslim leader seeking to liberate the Arab and Islamic lands from British oppression. The accounts were so partisan and polemical that the historical al-Husayni and the movement he led were scarcely discernible.

These works were flawed further by their meager use of oral and unpublished primary sources, and by the lack of familiarity with the Mufti and his politics. Schechtman's *The Mufti and the Fuehrer*, which is the best known biography in English, relies on, and strongly echoes the words of, Moshe Pearlman's *The Mufti of Jerusalem*.[1] Pearlman's work is an expanded version of *The Mufti Over the Middle East*, by Moshe Waters, who is none other than Pearlman. Both biographers rely on the Western press for details about the Mufti. Both lack an elementary familiarity with al-Husayni, Palestinian society and politics, Islam, and Arabic.

Their illustrations of the Mufti tell us, again, more about themselves than about their subject. Waters' (i.e., Pearlman's) early work shows, on the cover, a drawing of a hook-nosed, grotesque man ironically resembling an anti-Semitic caricature of a Jew, with blood dripping from the fingernails of his hand. Schechtman's photographic portrait of the Mufti, on the frontispiece, is that of a straggly bearded figure with a turban who, despite the claims of the caption, is not al-Husayni at all.

Similarly, the best known Arab biography of the Mutfi, al-Mardini's *Alf Yawm ma'a al-Hajj Amin* (A Thousand Days with al-Hajj Amin), is also flawed. It reads like a self-serving memoir of an official who made all the judicious decisions but was overwhelmed by the conspiracies of his enemies. In fact, most of Mardini's biography is based on, and quarried from, one source, the Mufti's memoirs.[2]

Such were the accounts about the Mufti until the early 1970s. By then documents pertaining to the early years of the British mandate became accessible to researchers at the Public Record Office, the Institute for Palestine Studies, the Palestine Research Center of the Palestine Liberation Organization (PLO), Israel State Archives, and the Central Zionist Archives.

The first scholarly account, based on a wealth of such primary sources and on Palestinian works, was by the historian Yehoshua Porath, who published an article in 1971 about the rise to power of the Mufti in the 1920s. Despite the constraints of his focus and his Israeli (liberal) views about Palestinian politics, Porath's extensive use of sources and nonpolemical and nonpartisan language helped raise Western and Israeli standards of scholarship about the Mufti. Majid Khadduri followed in 1973 with a brief and critical study, based on Arabic sources, showing a deeper understanding of the Palestinian leader and his politics.[3]

Several studies since then have contributed somewhat to our knowledge about the Mufti. Yehuda Taggar, a former Mosad agent, wrote a well-researched dissertation about the political activities of the Mufti from 1930 to 1937; Shlomo Ben-Elkanah, an Israeli policeman who compiled evidence against the Mufti during the Eichmann trial in 1961, described the Mufti's career in the 1920s, but was handicapped by his partisan Israeli views; and Taysir Jbara, utilizing Arabic secondary works, wrote a study, marred by factual errors, about the religious activities of the Mufti until 1937. None of these works, however, constituted a biography of both detail and scope.[4]

My purpose was to write a succinct political biography, covering the Mufti's entire life, based on oral and unpublished sources. I have tried to transcend the cultural and political constraints of both the sources and the secondary works by writing a detached narrative, free of political and academic theory, except for the last chapter, the assessment. There I present a revisionist view about the role of the Mufti in Palestinian history. This view emerged after a year of research, while a Fulbright fellow, in London, Jerusalem, Beirut, and Cairo.

I am grateful to the following for their help in making this work possible:

The Board of Foreign Scholars, Office of Education of HEW for the Fulbright-Hays fellowship in 1978; the Grants Committee of the American Center in Egypt for an ARCE fellowship in 1979; and the Diana Tamari Sabbagh Foundation, especially Hasib Sabbagh, for their financial support.

The friendly and efficient staffs of Sabri Jiryis at the PLO's Palestine Research Center and P. A. Alsberg at the Israel State Archives, in particular Josepha Taslizky and Michael Plotkin.

At Columbia University, Richard Bulliet, my adviser, who was a generous guide and friend; J. C. Hurewitz, my academic mentor, who, while director of the Middle East Institute, provided me the opportunity, as Visiting Scholar, to revise the dissertation in 1982–1983; Rabbi Arthur Hertzberg, for his views on the Mufti and the Axis; and Laurie Brand, for her research on the late Ottoman Empire. At Columbia University Press, executive editor Kate Wittenberg.

Friends and colleagues who read parts of the manuscript, including the following: Laurie Brand, Neil Caplan, Walid Khalidi, Martin Kramer, Ann M. Lesch, Muhammad Muslih, Barry Rubin, Frederick Seidel, Reeva Simon, Jeanette Wakin, James Webb, Jr., Constantine Zurayk. Also, Linda

The Mufti of Jerusalem

1. The Making of a Palestinian Nationalist: The Formative Years

 CENTURIES OF control of the most important political and religious posts in the city of Jerusalem rendered the Husayni family a wealthy and influential elite whose power and status enabled it to play the critical role of intermediary between the local population and their foreign overlords, first the Ottomans and later the British. The conservatism born of economic position and the experience of working through and with the Ottoman system continued to guide the Husaynis in their dealings with the British after 1917. Muhammad Amin al-Husayni was a product of the political and economic environment of the traditional Jerusalem power elite. Because of its importance for understanding later developments in Palestine in general, and in Amin al-Husayni's life in particular, the pre-1917 socioeconomic context merits greater examination.

The Late Ottoman Setting. Before World War I, Palestine was theoretically controlled directly from Istanbul, seat of the Ottoman Empire. In practice, however, the area was dominated by local *a'yan* (notables) comprising an urban elite. The second half of the nineteenth century in Palestine was characterized by the gradual transformation of the urban elite from notables and religious functionaries to landowners and senior bureaucrats educated in the modernized Ottoman government schools.[1]

The divisions that existed between the cities and the countryside in Palestine were exacerbated in the nineteenth century by new Ottoman policies of reform and centralization which served to strengthen the urban elite at the expense of its rural counterpart. Land was increasingly concentrated in the hands of the urban elite, and consequently the power of individual village leaders was undermined. The process whereby the urbanites gradually assumed regional and district apparatuses led to increasing resentment of the elite on the part of the rural leaders.[2]

The historian Albert Hourani contends that the urban politics of the Ottoman Empire can best be understood as a "politics of notables." Politics of this type develops when three conditions exist: society must be ordered according to relations of personal dependence; it must be dominated by great families residing primarily in the cities from which they draw their strength and because of which they are able to dominate a rural hinterland; and the notables must have some freedom of action. Under the Ottoman Empire, this last condition meant a situation in which the city was subject to monarchical power but in which the urban population was able to exercise some influence over or impose certain limits on the power of the central authority.[3]

The notables must have access to authority and they must possess social power of their own independent of the ruler. Access to authority enables the notable to act as a local leader, while the possession of his own sphere of power in society renders him useful to the central authority. In such a situation the notable must act with care: he must not be perceived as merely an instrument of the central authority, nor must he challenge the authority too strongly lest he risk being deprived of his access.[4]

Ottoman governors and officials generally did not come from the area they administered, nor did they speak the language, or remain in a single post long enough to develop ties to the area. They commanded troops, but their numbers were generally not sufficient to allow them to impose their authority unaided. Thus, of necessity, the Ottomans chose not to crush but to preserve useful local structures. In a situation where authority can maintain its position only with the assistance of local figures, a politics of notables may flourish. The notables are "those who can play a certain political role as intermediaries between government and people, and—within certain limits—as leaders of the urban population."[5] As a result, the notables generally defended the social order and the status quo by supporting the government. Political stability helped ensure the preservation of their positions of influence and power.

In Istanbul the notables were an official group, but in the provinces—apart from the *qadis* (judges)—they came from leading local families. The religious notables, such as *muftis* (Muslim experts who give nonbinding legal opinion [*fatwa*] on the sacred law [*shari'a*]) and *naqibs* (doyens of the descendants of the prophet), generally derived their influence not only from the positions they held, but also from their family's religious reputation, the connection of the local *'ulama'* (Muslim religious experts) with the palace, family wealth (usually based on the custody of *waqfs* or religious endowments), or a traditional connection with the commercial class.[6] In addition, there were those who were "secular notables"—individuals or families whose power derived from political or military tradition, from the memory of a particular ancestor, or from the control of agricultural production through the possession of *malikanes* (hereditary tax farms) or the supervision of waqfs.[7]

Whatever the source of their power, the notables' political behavior was much the same. The families or their representatives were members of the governor's council, which provided them formal access to Ottoman power. Locally, building upon their own power, they formed coalitions with other notable families, the *'ulama'*, leaders of the armed forces, as well as organizations in the general population, such as the guilds. The coalitions extended beyond the city into the surrounding rural areas. In such a situation, there is a tendency toward the formation of two or more coalitions roughly balancing each other. Such coalitions are by nature volatile: forces drawn into one notable's orbit may just as easily be drawn into the orbit of another, or opt to rely directly on the government.[8]

The politics of notables was present in its purest form in holy cities such as Jerusalem. Ottoman authority there had to be real because "its legitimacy in the eyes of the Muslim world was bound up with its control of the Holy Cities and the pilgrim routes."[9] In these cities the notables were members of an ancient aristocracy, some of whom were heirs to a long religious and learned tradition.[10]

Although the Ottoman reforms (the Tanzimat) worked in Cairo and Istanbul to strengthen the power of the government, in the Arab provincial cities they worked initially to strengthen the urban notables. In the first place, the distance of the provincial cities from the center meant that the hand of the government was less heavy. Moreover, as time passed, it came to be regarded as alien. Just as important, however, the long tradition of the 'ulama' and a'yan was too strong to be broken. Although Ottoman control in each of the provinces was sharply imposed or reimposed, the power base of the old ruling families was not completely destroyed. During the nineteenth century, in many cases "families of Turkish or Mamluke military origins . . . blend[ed] with those of Arab and religious origin to form a single class with social prestige."[11]

When the new governors came to enforce the Tanzimat in the provinces, they needed the notables more than ever because of the opposition which the new policies elicited. Without the cooperation and knowledge of the elite, the governors would have been hard-pressed to raise conscripts or new taxes. In most provincial centers, the *majlis* (local council) came to be controlled by the notables. For their part, the local population was also more in need of the notables than before as intermediaries with the government in matters such as conscription, new legal codes, and new methods of collecting taxes. As a result, the notables were able to strengthen their control over both the urban areas and the countryside, where they became patrons of villages and established alliances with village leaders.

As European economic interest and power in the area increased, and with it the European diplomatic presence, many groups within the population sought out European consulates for protection. The rise of the consulates, therefore, threatened the power of the notables. "While the old trading system declined, the growth of the European trade gave wealth and economic power to Christian or Jewish merchants who were for the most part either formal protégés of one or the other consulates or attached to it."[12]

One of the major thrusts of the Tanzimat was the creation of a more direct relationship between the government and the citizen. Therefore, in general, the notables tended to work against the reforms because the reforms ran counter to their interests by undermining their power as intermediaries. Under the Sultan 'Abd al-Hamid, notable families began to send their sons to Ottoman professional schools from which they entered the civil or military service. By joining the Ottoman "aristocracy of service," they saw an opportunity to preserve their power positions.[13]

With the policies of the Young Turks and later of the British, many notables adopted Arab nationalism as a new instrument of resistance. The deposition of the Sultan 'Abd al-Hamid and the subsequent establishment of an Ottoman Parliament dealt a severe blow to the power of the Arab notables. The Young Turks viewed them with suspicion because they had served the previous regime, and many of the notables were dismissed from their posts. Yet a more important factor was at work. The most basic goal of the Young Turk Committee of Union and Progress was to strengthen and unify the empire through a policy of Turkification. In practice, this meant that Turkish was imposed as the official language, particularly in education and administration, throughout the empire; and there was an apparent change from Pan-Islam to Pan-Turanism (a movement to unify the Turkish-speaking peoples).

The notables were not the only ones opposed to Turkification. The liberal intellectuals objected to it on the grounds that the Parliament did not provide for equal rights or the type of political representation they sought. Meanwhile, the 'ulama' balked, as they often did, at any proposal which smacked of reform. These groups joined the Arabist opposition forces which had begun to emerge in the provinces. Nevertheless, until the outbreak of World War I these groups stressed the need for reform within the Ottoman Empire through Arab autonomy and not through secession.[14]

Until 1914, the aims of the Arabists were not substantially different from those of the Ottomanists. However, after 1917, the opposition diverged. Arab nationalist demands reflected the "interest of a growing number of politically active members of an urban absentee landowning and bureaucratic class that had failed to achieve power and influence commensurate with their expectations."[15] Thus, there were essentially two groups, generationally based. The older notables derived a great deal of power from positions in the Ottoman bureaucracy. Unwilling to relinquish their influence, they supported local autonomy, but within an Ottoman framework. The Arabists, on the other hand, were generally younger and from more diverse educational backgrounds. Some came from families which were not socially prominent. Those who were from notable families tended to belong to less wealthy or influential branches, had rarely secured public office, and therefore had little at stake in preserving the empire.[16] It was they who supported the idea of the unification of Palestine and Syria. Some would even travel to Damascus to serve in Faysal's provisional government (1918–1920).

In general, however, few Palestinian notables supported the 1916 Hashimite Revolt, nor did they consider Faysal their representative. The unity of Palestine and Syria would have meant Faysal's usurpation of their power. They therefore preferred to remain loyal to Istanbul until the Allied occupation in 1918,[17] at which point they sought to make deals with either the British or French, depending upon where their interests lay.[18] After the establishment of the mandate, the older generation continued to regard themselves as the natural political leadership. The notables' behavior toward the British paralleled their behavior toward the Ottomans. They exercised caution in expressing discontent with mandate policy so as not to anger their new occupiers.[19]

Despite the efforts of the elite, the British gradually undermined the political position of the notables, although the latter continued to maintain their dominant social and economic status. As their power waned, their realm for political activity narrowed.[20] Nor was the young Palestinian elite capable of taking their place. The failure was particularly significant because the next challenge to the leadership was Zionism [the movement for the return of the Jewish people to Palestine], which sought, through Jewish immigration and colonization, to administer and control and, ultimately, establish a state in Palestine.[21]

Muhammad Amin al-Husayni was born in A.D. 1895/A.H. 1313 in Jerusalem,[22] a scion of one of the most prominent Muslim Arab families in Palestine. The Husaynis consider themselves *ashraf* (descendants of the Prophet Muhammad). The traditional great-grandfather of the family, Muhammad al-Badri, traced his origins to Husayn (hence the family name), son of the fourth caliph 'Ali ibn 'Ali Talib and his wife Fatima, the daughter of the Prophet. Al-Badri's ancestors lived for about two hundred years in Wadi al-Nusur, a small village southwest of Jerusalem, before one of them moved to Jerusalem in A.D. 1380/A.H. 782.[23]

Little is known of the early history of the Husayni family. However, at the beginning of the seventeenth century, the post of mufti of Jerusalem was held by 'Abd al-Qadir ibn Karim al-Din al-Husayni, who died leaving no male heir. The post of mufti went to other families: the 'Alamis and the Jarallas. However, 'Abd al-Qadir's female descendants were able to retain the Husayni name and the sharifi (singular of ashraf) lineage. The Husaynis held a number of religious posts such as *Naqib al-Ashraf* and *Shaykh al-Haramayn* (keeper of the two Jerusalem mosques, al-Aqsa and Dome of the Rock). Then, at the end of the eighteenth century, the Husaynis recaptured the office of the mufti, which they held, with few interruptions, well into the twentieth century.[24]

The family had become landed aristocrats wielding considerable political power by the end of the nineteenth century. Together with the Khalidis, 'Alamis, Jarallas, and Nashashibis, they constituted the ruling elite of the Ottoman administration in Jerusalem. Members of the Husayni family occupied such positions as delegate to the Ottoman Parliament, district governor, mayor, as well as the religious posts. Amin's father Tahir succeeded his father Mustafa as Mufti of Jerusalem, and expected that one of his sons—Kamil, Amin, or Fakhri—would succeed him.[25]

Amin grew up in Shaykh Jarrah, a district of Jerusalem where the Tahir branch of the Husaynis lived. He was close to his quiet and pious mother, Zaynab, who devoted much time to his spiritual and ethical upbringing. Zaynab was Tahir's second wife and the mother of Amin and Fakhri. Amin had seven half sisters and a half brother, Kamil, who were children of his father's first wife. Tahir, who was elderly and demanding, often took Amin to the Haram al-Sharif (the third holiest shrine of Islam, containing al-Aqsa mosque and the Dome of the Rock) where he had an office. In order to familiarize his three sons with his duties as Mufti, he encouraged them to sit in on informal discussions at his office and home concerning the religious, legal, and political problems of the day. These included the increasing Jewish immigration from Eastern Europe.[26]

In the early 1880s, when Jews began arriving in large numbers, Palestine had a population of about 500,000 of which 80 percent were Muslims, 15 percent Christians, and 5 percent Jews. Under the Ottoman Empire, religious diversity was tolerated and each religious community had jurisdiction over its own religious and community affairs. The empire had witnessed nothing like the pogroms and religious persecution of Eastern Europe. However, Palestinians became alarmed in the 1880s with the rise in Europe of Zionism. Palestine was one of several areas suggested as a possible site for a "homeland" for the Jewish people, and immigration increased. To the Palestinians, the immigrants were Europeans and, therefore, foreigners. What most alarmed the Palestinians was the Zionist claim of a historical right to Palestine on the grounds that their ancestors had lived there two millennia before. Moreover, the Jews seemed to have enough money with which they were able to buy Palestinian land, settle on it, and cultivate it.

Tahir and several other Palestinian leaders complained about the situation to Ottoman officials in Istanbul. The Turks tried to impose restrictions, but the European powers invoked the capitulations (economic and
diplomatic privileges given to friendly non-Muslim states) on behalf of
their Jewish subjects, and the Jews bribed Turkish and Palestinian officials
to evade Ottoman restrictions on immigration and land sales. However,
Arab dissatisfaction led the Ottomans to set up a commission headed by
Tahir to monitor land sales to Jews. This was in 1897, the year Theodor
Herzl founded and presided over the World Zionist Organization. Tahir's
commission was effective in halting land sales to Jews for several years.
However, its jurisdiction was limited to the *sancak* (district) of Jerusalem,
which included most of Palestine and its major cities.[27] Furthermore, when
the Mufti Tahir died in 1908, he was replaced by his eldest son Kamil who
was apolitical, amiable, and cooperative. According to the historian Yehoshua Porath, he "went out of his way to aid the British occupation
authorities."[28] His participation in the ceremony of laying the foundation
of the Hebrew University was an example of his friendly attitude toward
the Zionists.[29]

Amin was then too young and lacked the extensive religious education
required for the job of Mufti. In addition to religious lessons at home, he
attended a local Muslim elementary school (*kuttab*) that emphasized Islamic history, theology, Arabic, and literature, and he is said to have mem-
orized by age ten a portion of the Qu'ran. Later at a government Turkish
school, he became fluent in Turkish, and also studied French at Frères, a
local French school. Amin was short and frail, and self-conscious as a result
of a lisp. Perhaps because of these physical characteristics, he was reserved
and laconic. Yet he had a distinctive appearance: reddish hair, blue eyes,
and fair skin. He also stood out in intelligence and maturity. By the age
of sixteen he was ready for higher education, and his mother and half-
brother Kamil were eager for him to begin preparation for a religious office,
such as that of Mufti.[30]

In 1912, Kamil sent Amin to Cairo with a cousin, Ya'qub al-Husayni,
to study at al-Azhar University, the thousand-year-old center of Islamic
and Arabic studies. There, he took courses in Islamic law, theology, phi-
losophy, and Arabic. The sources do not indicate how good a student he
was, but his interests appear to have extended beyond theology. In addition
to al-Azhar, Amin may have attended the Faculty of Arts and Sciences of
the University of Egypt (now Cairo University) as a student of literature.[31]

He also studied at the Dar al-Da'wa wa al-Irshad (House of Prayer and Guidance), the school of Rashid Rida (1865–1935), the Muslim Arab reformer and a precursor of Arab nationalism. Rida often stayed with the Husaynis when he visited Jerusalem, and as a good friend of the family, he took special interest in Amin and frequently invited him to his home in Cairo.[32] Because of the great influence he had on Amin, it is useful to discuss briefly some of the reformer's ideas.

Rida was a follower of the Islamic reformers Jamal al-Din al-Afghani and Muhammad 'Abduh. Like them, he was aware of the need for reform in the Islamic world. Although he taught his students that Muslims could borrow within limits from European science and civilization, he also emphasized the need to revive the Islam of the Prophet Muhammad and his immediate followers. Implicit in his teachings was the need for a reinvigoration of Arab culture, power, and unity, which he believed the Turks impeded. Rida had supported the Ottoman Turks until shortly after the Revolution of 1908, when the Young Turks imposed their Turkification policies upon the Arabs. As a result, he joined the Decentralization party, which sought British aid to set up a united and independent Arab state.[33]

Thus, Amin was introduced to Islamic reform and Arab revival by one of the intellectual founders of the movement. Rida's ideas were progressive for the time and were a potent force among the Arab intelligentsia that came to study in Cairo. Amin did not accept everything Rida taught, or, if he did, he did not act upon it. He apparently did not fully appreciate the extent of the technological, political, and economic gap that existed between the native Palestinians and the Zionist settlers. Indeed, had the Palestinians been more aware, they might have been more effective in their power struggle with the European Jewish immigrants.

Fundamentally, Rida's interest in an Arab renaissance was as a means to an Islamic revival and he only belatedly and grudgingly supported the Arab nationalists in their reaction against Turkish policies and British imperialism. Amin, too, was a devout Muslim who believed that the role of Islam was inseparable from politics and that religious symbols should be used to unite the Arabs. But in contrast to al-Ikhwan al-Muslimun (the Muslim Brothers), who adopted Rida's emphasis on conservative religion, Amin emphasized political change and, later, independence.[34]

While in Cairo, Amin helped organize a Palestinian society to oppose Zionism. The idea may have originated with a Christian Palestinian who offered his house as a meeting place, but it was Amin and his roommate,

'Abd al-Rahman al-'Alami, who gathered together about twenty Muslim and Christian Arabs in the aim of "awakening the people" to Zionism when they eventually returned to Palestine that summer. The headquarters, however, was to remain in Cairo.[35]

According to a friend, Kamil al-Dajani, the society did not survive for very long. But Amin's participation is revealing about his ideas at the time. He was one of the first to identify Zionist claims and Jewish immigration (which increased Palestine's Jewish population from 25,000 in 1882 to 85,000 in 1914), rather than Turkish rule, as the primary antagonist. He realized the need for Muslim and Christian cooperation in defense of Palestine. However, despite Arab sources which exaggerate his accomplishments and talents during this period, there seems to have been nothing remarkable about Amin's organizational skills. On the contrary, a contemporary remembers that while his friends admired him for his intelligence and good breeding, they were not impressed with his leadership qualities.[36]

Amin left Cairo in the summer of 1913 to accompany his mother on the *hajj* (the pilgrimage to Mecca), whereby he earned the honorific title al-Hajj often attached to his name. Instead of returning to Cairo to continue his studies, he went back to Jerusalem with his mother.[37] The sources do not adequately explain why, but it is possible that his brother Kamil, who had become head of the family, disapproved of Amin's political activities in Cairo.[38]

While in Cairo, Amin had learned that political education could be translated into a "spirit of revolt," and that the best forums for disseminating this spirit were the press, the mosques, and the schools.[39] Immediately upon his return to Jerusalem, he began writing articles about the threat of Zionism. He also accepted a part-time teaching job at a religious school, Rawdat al-Ma'arif al-Wataniyya, where he interjected politics into his courses on Islam. He does not seem to have been an effective lecturer, for according to one of his students, he lacked confidence and authority in the classroom. Furthermore, his youth and diminutive appearance caused some students not to take him seriously.[40] Perhaps this is one reason why he stopped teaching after only a few months and decided to train for a military or administrative career at the Military Academy in Istanbul. But his education was interrupted by the outbreak of World War I, when he entered the Ottoman army.

The Turks were reluctant to send Arabs to fight in Arab provinces, so

Amin never participated in battle during the war years. Nonetheless, life in the army, which he described briefly in his diaries, was harsh; and Amin suffered from the cold, lack of food, and sleep. In August 1916, he became an officer and served in the Forty-Sixth Division, first as an aide to a Turkish commander in Izmir, a port in western Turkey, and then as an artillery officer in strategic locations near the Black Sea. Apart from occasional artillery exchanges with the Russians, he did not see much action. But army training, hardship, and deprivation toughened him physically and emotionally. His role as an officer commanding mostly Palestinian and Syrian draftees changed him from a shy teacher who could not command respect in the classroom into an assertive leader.[41]

Amin's loyalty to the Ottomans was based on feelings of identification with Islam. That is, he believed it was his duty to defend his fellow Muslims against the Christian armies of Britain, France, and Russia. However, several factors served to erode his loyalty.

First, the policy of Turkification in the Arab provinces was instituted at the expense of the Arab language and culture. Second, the Turks increasingly followed an apparent policy of secularization by de-emphasizing Islam. Third, the Turks, perceiving a threat to the empire, dealt harshly with Arab nationalists, executing twenty-two in mid-1916. When both the religious and the political bases of his allegiance to the Ottoman Empire were undermined, Amin joined a secret Arab society which sought decentralization in the empire.[42]

While in Turkey, Amin was constantly aware of his attachment to Palestine. During the war he carried with him a short poem, perhaps his own, indicative of his political sentiments: "This [Palestine] is my country and the country of my ancestors—I will sacrifice myself for the sake of its sons."[43]

Indeed, his diary was filled with poems and notes about his love for his country. In an essay composed during the war, Amin wrote about the bonds between the Palestinians and the Syrians, yet it was clear that he considered them separate people. Of all the people in Palestine and Syria, he most admired the Jerusalemites, who, he boasted, were honest, self-sacrificing, sharing, courteous, inseparable, and loyal to one another. It is obvious from this and other private papers that the criteria by which he judged people—Turks, Palestinians, Syrians, Jews, Catholics—were the Islamic ideals he learned during his childhood, which he constantly tried

to emulate. His tendency to boast and to reminisce about fellow Jerusalemites also demonstrates that he was homesick during the war. In another
poem he began: "Whenever I mention Jerusalem my tears flow."[44]

It is useful, at this point, to summarize and put in perspective Amin's
loyalties to the seemingly contradictory ideologies of his day: Ottomanism,
Islam, Pan-Arab (or Pan-Syrian) nationalism, and Palestinian nationalism.
Like most Arabs, Amin was an Ottomanist (loyal to the Ottoman state)
based on his feelings of identification with fellow Muslims within the
empire. Between 1912 and 1917, his loyalty weakened under the impact
of Turkification, the influence of Rida's ideas of reform and decentralization, and his own experiences in the Turkish army, as is evident in his
diaries of 1915 and 1916. But political loyalties took time to crystallize,
and a few years of friction with the Turks were not sufficient to make him
abandon Ottomanism for a clearly defined ideology such as Pan-Arab nationalism. When Amir Husayn declared the Arab Revolt in mid-1916,
Amin (and other Palestinians) saw it as an opportunity to thwart Zionism,
over which he had been deeply concerned for years, by seeking to reunite
Syria and Palestine. When the occasion presented itself, he abandoned the
Ottoman army (and Ottomanism) and joined the Arab Revolt.

Early Political Activities. After a four-hundred-year rule over Palestine, the
Turks were driven out by the British and the Arabs. Promises by Britain
and its allies led Arab nationalists like Amin to believe that if they helped
liberate Palestine from the Turks, they would be permitted to set up an
independent Arab state. Amin wanted to be part of that historic struggle
and, after having been hospitalized, returned to Jerusalem in February 1917
on sick leave. He arrived physically sturdy and more aggressive. A pho-
tograph from the period shows a determined and self-confident man, wear-
ing a rifle and cartridge belts. He sported a new uniform, having discarded
the Ottoman uniform for that of the Arab army of Faysal, who was then
fighting with the British to drive the Turks from Palestine. Amin, described
in a British report as "very pro-British," became a recruiting officer for
Faysal's army and worked with Captain C. D. Brunton.[45] He encouraged
Ottoman-trained Palestinians to volunteer for the Arab army, and he
toured the occupied part of Palestine to help organize a force of about 2000
Palestinians. The new recruits were told that they would be fighting for
an independent Arab nation. Amin and his recruits were sent to Transjordan to fight during the last few months of effort against the Turks.[46]

Despite his commitment to Palestine, Amin's participation in the national struggle alongside the British caused him some concern. As a practicing Muslim he found it difficult to turn against fellow Muslims to support a Christian power. Also, beneath his exterior was a shyness that made him reluctant to become an activist; he told a friend that he hated politics but felt he had to be a part of the crucial events that were taking place in Palestine.[47]

Whatever hesitations he may have had, within months of his return to Jerusalem, Amin became one of the leaders of the nascent Palestinian nationalist movement. He was elected president of a literary and political organization, the Arab Club (al-Nadi al-'Arabi), which, together with the Literary Club (al-Muntada al-Adabi) and the Muslim-Christian Association (al-Jam'iyya al-Islamiyya al-Masihiyya), was formed in 1918 to champion the Palestinian cause. The three organizations were united on one idea: the Palestinians were the rightful inhabitants of Palestine and had owned the land for at least 1300 years, and therefore the Zionists had no legitimate claim.[48]

In this early stage, Amin's group differed from the other two in its national objective. The Literary Club, composed of young members of the Nashashibi family, was anti-British, probably because of the family's connection with French agents, and sought complete independence for Palestine. On the other hand, the Muslim-Christian Association, a united front composed of the older generation of the urban elite who sought to preserve their positions of leadership, expected autonomy under the British. Amin's club was composed of a younger generation of educated Husaynis, such as his brother Fakhri (who had become a lawyer) and his cousin's son Ishaq Darwish, as well as members of other families. The Husaynis and their allies were Pan-Arabists whose objective was the unification of Palestine with Syria as a means of saving Palestine from Zionist claims.[49]

Amin used his position as president of the Arab Club to educate Palestinians about the national cause, as he and his friends in Cairo had pledged to do years before. He campaigned among the urban class as well as among the *fallahin* (peasants), something few Arab aristocrats did. When the first Palestine National Congress was held between January 27 and February 9, 1919, he and his colleagues actively encouraged attendees to adopt a Pan-Arabist line. Amin's message had two themes: Palestinian unity with Syria and anti-Zionism.[50]

As was pointed out above, Amin's hostility toward the Zionists had begun in childhood. His father Tahir had been one of the first Palestinians to oppose Jewish immigration. Moreover, two experiences which he later related to his colleagues profoundly affected his attitude toward Zionists. The first was an account he had heard while in Istanbul of the visit of Theodor Herzl to the Ottoman capital in 1896. Herzl had just published *The Jewish State*, in which he proposed to settle the "Jewish problem" by establishing a Jewish state, possibly in Palestine. Herzl proposed to the Sultan 'Abd al-Hamid that he give Palestine to the Jews in return for financial aid, or, as Amin understood it, in return for a bribe.[51] The Sultan's reply was: "I cannot sell even a foot of land, for it does not belong to me, but to my people. . . . Let the Jews save their billions. When my Empire is partitioned, they may get Palestine for nothing."[52] The words were indicative of the degree of fragmentation already plaguing the empire, and the Sultan could not further alienate his Arab subjects by courting foreign interference in the guise of European Jews.

Amin was struck both by Zionist plans for Palestine as well as Zionist wealth. However, what he did not know was that Herzl's offer was in part a bluff; the Zionists possessed little in 1896. Their interest in Palestine, however, was real and was confirmed a year later when they established the World Zionist Organization.

The second event was as significant for Amin as it was for most educated Palestinians. Britain stated in the Balfour Declaration of November 2, 1917, that it would "view with favour the establishment in Palestine of a national home for the Jewish people . . . it being clearly understood that nothing shall be done which may prejudice the civil and religious rights of the existing non-Jewish communities in Palestine." Amin was thereby convinced that Britain, the greatest power in the world, was under the influence of the Zionists, and his notion of Zionist wealth and power was reinforced. Since it appeared futile for the Arabs to oppose British rule, Amin believed the only practical approach was to attempt to change the British Balfour policy by organizing mass support for reuniting Syria and Palestine, which would then work together against Zionism.[53]

Amin attempted to spread his political ideas in other ways as well. He became a teacher in and possibly part owner of Rawdat al-Ma'arif al-Wataniyya, the school in which he had taught before going to Istanbul. Under the direction of Muhammad al-Salah, the school became a center for Arab nationalists.[54] Some sources indicate that he also held part-time teaching positions at al-Rashidiyya in Jerusalem, and that he was a translator and writer for *Suriyya al-Janubiyya,* a nationalist paper edited by his friend 'Arif al-'Arif. However, it appears that his second attempt at teaching and writing did not last long.[55]

Amin then became a clerk in the British military administration, in the office of Gabriel Haddad, a Christian Arab adviser to Ronald Storrs, the military governor of Jerusalem. He was soon transferred to the Department of Public Safety in Qalqilya. When Haddad was appointed commissioner of public safety in Damascus, Amin eagerly accompanied him and was made a "detective agent." While in Damascus, Amin established connections with the Arab nationalist supporters of Faysal, and served as a liaison official in June and July of 1919 between the Syrian committee that was preparing for the General Syrian Congress and the Palestinians invited by Faysal.[56] The congress was held in July 1919, and under the influence of the Palestinians resolutions were passed opposing Zionism and Jewish immigration to Palestine.

Damascus was the heart of the Arab nationalist movement, and it must have seemed to Amin that Rida's vision of Arab independence and unity was about to be achieved. But the excitement soon faded. Faysal sent Haddad to London, and Haddad's successor Ahmad Lahun did not retain Amin.[57] The British withdrew their forces from Syria, thereby leaving the country open to French conquest, and what President Woodrow Wilson described as "the whole disgusting scramble" for the Middle East was accomplished. The British Foreign Secretary Arthur Balfour admitted that although "we had not been honest with either French or Arab . . . it was now preferable to quarrel with the Arab rather than with the French."[58] The Arabs were, after all, too politically naive to be suspicious of Britain, whose self-interest took precedence over its promises, and they were in no position economically, politically, or technologically to counter it.

In response to the political development in Syria, Amin organized protest demonstrations through al-Nadi al-'Arabi. He and his fellow members of the organization may have cooperated with al-Fida'iyya in the protests of 1919, when the King-Crane Commission (the American fact-finding team whose subsequent report ascertained that the Palestinian people wanted independence or, short of that, an American mandate) visited Palestine.[59]

Amin then helped organize processions in Jerusalem, Jaffa, and Haifa on February 27, 1920, to protest the chief administrator's proclamation that the British government intended to enforce the Balfour Declaration. As 2500 Arabs in Jerusalem passed a Jewish school, the Zionists decided to play their anthem ("ha-Tiqvah"), but the march proceeded without incident.[60]

Amin also helped organize demonstrations throughout the country on March 8, 1920, the day Faysal was proclaimed King of Syria. Some of the most prominent members of the community participated, including two *pashas* (a Turkish honorific title): Musa Kazim al-Husayni (mayor of Jerusalem) and 'Arif al-Dajani. The demonstration in Jerusalem was orderly, and later a written protest was submitted to the Palestine government. Signed by representatives of the three nationalist organizations, including Amin, it demanded Syrian independence and the unification of Palestine with Syria. It also stated its opposition to Zionism and Jewish immigration. The British, alarmed at such a show of national unity, banned future demonstrations.[61]

Amin and other young Palestinians managed to get around the British prohibition by turning a religious celebration in April into a vehicle for political protest. The April incident became violent and marked a turning point in popular perceptions of Amin. The Zionists came to hate him as a Muslim fanatic leading an anti-Jewish pogrom, while Arab nationalists viewed him as a Palestinian patriot leading a revolt against British imperialism and Zionism. Both these polemic versions misrepresented the man, because he was neither a fanatic nor the leader of the revolt. Neither the later Arab writers who praised him, nor the Zionists and Westerners who vilified him had access to sufficient information about his role in the April violence, but assumed a larger role on the basis of his subsequent history and importance. It is necessary, therefore, to reconstruct the facts about the event which enabled him to begin his stormy political career.

By coincidence that year, Passover, Easter, and the Muslim holiday al-Nabi Musa all took place at the same time in early April. Amin and his colleagues galvanized Christian and Muslim Palestinians to use the Easter and al-Nabi Musa celebrations to demonstrate support for Faysal, who had just been crowned King in Syria, and to express opposition to the idea of a Jewish national home. Amin returned from a month's visit to Damascus with the curious notion, perhaps reinforced by General Waters-Taylor, the chief of staff, that Britain did not oppose handing Palestine over to Faysal. Amin shared this perception with his comrades on April 1.[62] The atmosphere before the violence was therefore one of expectation concerning Syria and Palestine but apprehension concerning Zionism.

The few basic facts known about the events of April 4 are found in the interim and final Palin reports of the British military team that investigated the riots in Jerusalem. The Nabi Musa procession on April 4 halted on Jaffa Street in front of the balconies of the Arab Club and the Municipality Building. The crowd was offered lemonade while they listened to anti-Zionist speeches by Musa Kazim, 'Arif al-'Arif, Amin, and others. Amin's speech is not recorded, but he apparently held up a portrait of Faysal and shouted: "This is your King!" to which the crowd responded: "God save the King!" Then, while the speakers were still outside the city walls, a spontaneous disturbance began in the Jewish quarter of the old city. Some sources claim that Jews provoked the outbreak, but there is no doubt the violence was a result of Arab hostility. The Arabs attacked Jews, killing three and injuring many others. Then an armed Jewish group, organized by Zeev Jabotinsky (founder of the Zionist Revisionist movement which opposed the political line of the World Zionist Organization), retaliated by killing and wounding demonstrators as well as Arab bystanders. The British police finally subdued both Arabs and Jews, after contributing to the final death toll of five Jews and four Arabs.[63]

The Palin Commission Report concluded that there were several political causes for the violence: first, Arab disappointment in not being given independence, which was promised them by the British; second, Arab fear that the Balfour Declaration would deny their right to self-determination; third, support for the unity of Palestine and Syria under the newly proclaimed King Faysal.

The British authorities were surprised by the intensity of the violence. The reaction of Ronald Storrs was to dismiss Musa Kazim al-Husayni as mayor, while the British police arrested 'Arif al-'Arif and Zeev Jabotinsky. They also looked for Amin, but he had been informed of the search and went into hiding. The police, who believed he had taken refuge with his brother the Grand Mufti, entered the house and searched it. Later, several men dressed in British army uniforms, possibly Zionists, attempted to assassinate Kamil's son. The Grand Mufti was incensed over the two incidents and returned the British medal he had been awarded for his cooperation in maintaining law and order.[64]

Meanwhile, Amin escaped across the Jordan River and eventually went to Damascus. His friend 'Arif, released on bail, escaped to Transjordan. Both were sentenced to ten years in absentia.[65] Jabotinsky received fifteen years, although his sentence was commuted to one year.

Why a ten-year sentence for a speech and for holding up a picture of a

British ally, Faysal? Perhaps the British military court wanted to show the "natives" that they would severely punish any Arab or Jewish trouble-maker.[66] No other explanation accounts for the stiff sentences of al-Husayni, 'Arif, and Jabotinsky, nor the arbitrary treatment of the mayor and the Grand Mufti.

In Damascus Amin once again became active in the court of Faysal, the only Arab nationalist leader, in his view, who could save Palestine and unite the Arabs. When the French invaded Syria in July 1920 and expelled the new King, his government, and his Arab nationalist supporters, Amin returned to Transjordan where he took refuge among bedouin tribesmen and resumed his political activity among them on behalf of Palestine.[67]

Amin, who had worked for Pan-Arabism for over three years, now shifted his focus to Palestinian self-determination and independence. This does not mean that he abandoned the Arab nationalist idea in July 1920 or shortly thereafter. Indeed, for him Pan-Arab and Pan-Islamic ideas coexisted with Palestinian nationalism without contradiction throughout his career. But in Transjordan, it was Palestine that attracted his attention.

By the age of twenty-five, Amin had matured personally and politically. He had left Jerusalem eight years before, a bright but inexperienced youth. He had received a higher education in Cairo and Istanbul, more than most Arabs could hope for at the time. Moreover, he had been converted to the cause of Arab nationalism by one of its intellectual founders, Rashid Rida, and by its chief political architect, Faysal. Disciplined by military training in Turkey and political experience in Palestine and Syria, Amin had acquired the ability and confidence to become a strong leader. He was honest and sincere enough to inspire admiration and loyalty, yet shrewd enough to know how to acquire political power. But Palestine was occupied by the British and promised to the Zionists, and Syria was in French hands. Amin and his strong ambitions seemed doomed unless something or someone could rescue him from the political obscurity of the Transjordanian desert.

2. Rise to Religious Power

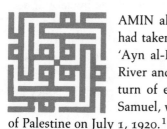 AMIN al-HUSAYNI, a fugitive from British justice, had taken refuge in mid-1920 with a bedouin tribe in 'Ayn al-Huwari, a desert region between the Jordan River and Amman. He was saved from his exile by a turn of events and by a British Zionist, Sir Herbert Samuel, who had become the first High Commissioner of Palestine on July 1, 1920.[1]

The Pardon. On August 20, 1920, Samuel went to al-Salt to formally take over the territory of Transjordan, which was also under his jurisdiction, and to reassure the region's *shaykhs* (village and tribal leaders) of British concern for their welfare. An Arab notable related how an excited young British officer interrupted Samuel and his retinue of soldiers, who were having dinner, shouting: "Hajj Amin and Arif al-Arif are in town. Strap on your side arms and let's go and get them."[2] But the Jerusalem notable pleaded with the officer: "We have come here to protect the representative of the King of England. . . . There are several thousand Bedouin rifles in and about town, and we are the bottom of a deep valley. . . . These two men have sought asylum here. By Bedouin custom they should protect them at the risk of their lives."[3] The officer called off the raid.

The next morning Samuel, dressed in a diplomatic uniform adorned with medals, was preparing to make a speech to the shaykhs when some of them approached and asked him to pardon Amin and 'Arif. He replied that both men would be pardoned and that they could return to Palestine. Within minutes 'Arif emerged on the shoulders of Arab youths.[4] Amin may have been in the crowd but refused to acknowledge the pardon. He did not feel that he was a criminal in need of forgiveness. A few months later, however, when his brother Kamil al-Husayni became ill, Amin decided to accept Samuel's pardon and returned to Jerusalem.[5]

There are a number of theories as to why Samuel pardoned Amin. According to the Zionist writer Schechtman, it was because the High Commissioner, as a Jew, was "haunted by the fear of appearing too pro-Jewish," and therefore suffered from an "impartiality complex."[6] According to the Palestinian historian Darwaza, Samuel wanted to balance the power of the Nashashibis, who now controlled the mayoralty of Jerusalem, with that of the Husaynis, so as to rule more effectively over a divided people. But neither of these theories is supported by any hard evidence, and the Husayni-Nashashibi rivalry antedates British rule by several decades.[7]

The key to understanding Samuel's pardon and, for that matter, his other actions toward Amin and the Palestinians, has little to do with notions of a Jewish complex or dividing the Palestinians. Rather, it has to do with Samuel's view of his role as High Commissioner and the policy he should follow. He was obviously aware that, in addition to his prominent position in the Liberal party, he had been appointed because he was a Zionist Jew to carry out Britain's pro-Zionist policy in Palestine. But as he stated in his report on his first year in office, he was "not commissioned by the Zionists but in the name of the King."[8] He criticized Zionists "who forget or ignore the present inhabitants of Palestine," and those Zionists who are so zealous that when they "learn with surprise and often with incredulity" that there are a half-million Arabs who oppose them, they want to "ride rough-shod" over them.

Although Samuel was a Zionist going beyond the minimum requirements of British policy in his personal advocacy of a Jewish state or commonwealth in Palestine, he was a pragmatist as well. Moreover, as a British administrator he could not disregard the second aspect of Britain's obligation as stated in the Balfour Declaration and incorporated in article two of the mandate: that while supporting the establishment of a Jewish national home, the government also had to safeguard the civil and religious rights of the "non-Jewish population"—more than 90 percent of the country. Needless to say, given the overwhelming numerical superiority of the Palestinians, the British could not abide by the principles of self-determination, and the need to consult the population while framing the organic law had to be postponed until Jewish immigration and land purchases increased. But in the meantime, Arab sensibilities had to be taken into account.

Samuel knew that the Palestinians were apprehensive about their future. He therefore suggested that the Zionist program not be pushed too far too fast, and that the Zionists and the British should meet Palestinian economic, religious, social and minor political needs.[9] He considered the pardon question a minor concession to the Palestinians, which is why he announced a general pardon of political prisoners a week after he took office, on July 1, 1920.[10]

But the pardon had not included Amin and 'Arif, presumably because they were not prisoners but fugitives from British justice.[11] Several appeals were made to Samuel on their behalf by such notables as Musa Kazim al-Husayni, the former mayor of Jerusalem, and Kamil al-Husayni, the Grand Mufti of Jerusalem and Amin's half brother. Samuel could not ignore the help Kamil had given the British, nor indeed Amin's own role in the effort against the Turks and his employment in the British military administration in Jerusalem. According to a Zionist source, 'Abdullah of Transjordan had also asked Samuel to pardon the two Jerusalemites. It is therefore likely that the High Commissioner made up his mind to pardon Amin and 'Arif "for political reasons" even before the appeal of the Transjordanian shaykhs at al-Salt on July 25, 1920.[12]

Return to Jerusalem. It was Kamil's illness that brought Amin back to Jerusalem during the winter of 1920–21. The Grand Mufti was not expected to recover and, according to an Arab source, he designated Amin as his successor.[13] Amin began to prepare himself for the office, even thought it was not entirely certain, when Kamil died on March 21, 1921, that Amin would succeed him. The office was not a hereditary one, and while the Husaynis were eager to retain the Muftiship, they did not all favor the young and impetuous Amin. The British, meanwhile, although eager to follow tradition, did not want a mufti opposed to their rule, and while Amin had generally been cooperative he was known to be against their

Balfour policy. The most serious obstacle to Amin's candidacy, however, came from the Husaynis' rivals, the Nashashibi family and their support- ers. One of the Nashashibis, Raghib, had been appointed mayor of Jerusa- lem the previous year, replacing a Husayni, Musa Kazim. Sensing an opportunity to further expand their power at the expense of the Husaynis by wresting from them the office of mufti for one of their supporters, they mounted a formidable opposition to Amin. This rivalry for the succession to the position of Kamil goes beyond the formal definition of the role of Mufti.

The Mufti of Jerusalem had been a minor official in Palestine until modern times when the increased status of Jerusalem and of the urban mufti in general enhanced his importance. He remained, however, subor- dinated to Shaykh al-Islam in Istanbul, and restricted in jurisdiction to Jerusalem until the British occupation of Palestine in 1917–18. The link with Istanbul was then severed, and the Mufti of Jerusalem, who was then Kamil al-Husayni, became preeminent in Palestine.[14]

Kamil's position was further enhanced by the British military adminis- tration. In exchange for his cooperation with the British, he was given control over the Shari'a Court of Appeal in Jerusalem, thus combining the office of qadi and mufti. This was in addition to his position as head of the Central Waqf Committee, which controlled Muslim religious foundations in Palestine. Then the British bestowed on him the new title of Grand Mufti (al-Mufti al-Akbar), which they probably borrowed from Egypt. By making him the chief representative of Islam in Palestine, they made him in essence the Mufti of Palestine.[15] The increase in his power and prestige was not only a reward but, no doubt, an attempt to spread his pro-British influence throughout Palestine.

Kamil's increased status made his replacement a crucial issue. The Pal- estine government was faced with both legal and political problems. The Ottoman regulations, which the British maintained, had required an elec- toral college to nominate three candidates from which Shaykh al-Islam chose one. Shaykh al-Islam was now replaced by the High Commis- sioner.[16] When an electoral college could not be found, the government chose some Muslim leaders to hold an election, which was set for April 12, 1921.

The Campaign. Amin seems to have been ready to replace his brother at least a month before Kamil's death. The first thing he did was to replace his *tarbush* (a hat worn by the Ottoman official class) with an *imama* (turban), and start to grow a beard.[17] These superficial changes, which made him look older and more religious (thus reinforcing the effect of his title of al-Hajj), helped remind the public that he expected to succeed his brother. When Kamil did die, it was Amin, rather than Kamil's older son, Tahir, who officially accepted the condolences of the government.[18] A day later, his political and cultural club, al-Nadi al-'Arabi, began collecting signatures for *mazbatas* (petitions) which insisted on al-Hajj Amin as the successor.[19]

Amin was not really the ideal choice. He could not claim the religious titles *'alim* (singular of 'ulama') or shaykh because he did not have sufficient religious education and training. Also, he was too young, progressive, and political for some of the older and more traditional members of the Husayni family. But since the Husaynis wanted to keep the office in the same branch, they were limited to three candidates: Kamil's son Tahir, Amin's younger brother Fakhri, and Amin. Tahir, though extremely eager to replace his father, was considered too eccentric to be chosen; his bitterness at having been bypassed led him to become a Zionist informer, providing inside information, of dubious usefulness, about Amin's activities. Fakhri, according to family sources, was more interested in pursuing a secular career. This left Amin, who in any case was the most familiar with the duties of the office, as well as being experienced as a leader, bright, and well educated for his day. Once chosen by the family, he and some prominent Husaynis began to gather support throughout Palestine.[20]

The Husaynis were landed aristocrats, but by early 1921 had been weakened politically by a series of setbacks during the war years. Sa'id al-Husayni, foreign minister under King Faysal of Syria, lost his post and suffered a nervous breakdown. Muhammad Salih al-Husayni, an officer at the Ottoman *awqaf* (Muslim endowment), and Isma'il al-Husayni, director of education until 1918, also lost their posts.[21] In April 1920 Musa Kazim was ousted as major of Jerusalem and replaced by the Husaynis' main rival, Raghib al-Nashashibi. Now Kamil was dead. the Husaynis therefore had to retain the office of the Mufti if they were to maintain power in Palestine. They turned to their relatives and friends for support.

The most enthusiastic supporters of the Husaynis were, not surprisingly, those with a vested interest in their power. the office of the Mufti under Kamil, as we have seen, controlled shari'a court and waqf lands. This explains why dozens of religious dignitaries and notables gave their support. The Husaynis, after all, were the incumbents who had been and continued to be generous to their clients and supporters. There were, however, more powerful social and political factors which helped Amin.[22]

There was a tradition going back to pre-Islamic Arabia in which a leader was chosen for his Arab descent and ability. Unlike most Palestinians, who descended from an indigenous population which traced its origin to the Canaanite period and who were Arabized after the Arab invasion of Palestine in A.D. 638, the Husaynis claimed descent from Arab aristocracy and lineage going back to the Prophet Muhammad. With few interruptions, the Husaynis had held the office of the Mufti of Jerusalem since the seventeenth century, which is why many Palestinians expected the religious tradition to be followed. This tradition provided Amin with religious legitimacy, the disregard of which by a Christian power would be resented by Muslims.[23] Of even more significance for his fellow Arabs, Amin since 1918 had shown himself capable of organizing and uniting Palestinians on popular political issues. His involvement in the April 1920 political violence, considered a *thawra* (revolt) by many Arab writers, made him popular among the people. He was now a proven nationalist leader. Palestinian political frustrations in late 1920 and early 1921 widened his popularity among Muslims and Christians, moderates and militants, peasants and urban classes. So in April 1921 Amin was supported not only because he was a Husayni but also because he was considered a nationalist.

Petitions poured in between March 21 and April 12, 1921, stating that Amin was the "people's choice." Some of the petitions came from ordinary people, others from prominent officials. The qadi of Jerusalem, Muhammad Abu Sa'ud al-'Awri, wrote the district governor, Ronald Storrs, informing him of Kamil's death and, as if to state a legal inevitability, declared: "His brother Hajj Amin effendi is his successor."[24]

The popularity of the Husaynis, however, was not reflected in the Palestine administration or in the Jerusalem district, where the power had tilted in favor of the Nashashibis. Sensing their new power, the Nashashibis felt they could defeat the young Amin and his weakened family, and backed one of their supporters, Husam al-Din Jaralla. Jaralla came from a patrician family, and was a graduate of al-Azhar and an 'alim. He was also a moderate and therefore acceptable to the British and the Zionists. There were two other candidates: Khalil al-Khalidi, a distinguished Muslim scholar who had been appointed acting president of the Shari'a Court of Appeal shortly after the death of Kamil; and Musa al-Budayri, a graduate of al-Azhar, a qadi, and technically more qualified than Amin.[25]

The Election. The Muslim committee put together by the Palestine government met on April 12 to elect three out of the four candidates. Jaralla received the most votes, followed by Khalidi and Budayri. Since only the top three candidates were considered, Amin was shut out.[26]

The Husaynis were indignant at the outcome of the election. Jamal and Isma'il al-Husayni in particular immediately began organizing opposition to influence the High Commissioner, whose duty it was to select one of the three candidates, presumably Jaralla, who had received the highest vote. The Husaynis attacked the election as invalid because the committee was neither the college of electors required by the Ottoman law nor an approximation of one and did not, therefore, represent the Muslims of Palestine. Jamal invited a large number of 'ulama' and notables from throughout Palestine to his home and asked them to organize opposition in towns and villages. The response to the Husayni campaign was considerable. Petitions with hundreds of signatures were sent to the Palestine government. Support came not only from the Muslim 'ulama' and notables, but from the leaders of the Christian communities and, according to a Zionist source, from King Faysal and his brother Amir 'Abdullah.[27]

The election results deepened Arab suspicion and increased support for Amin. Support for him came from every district, including those that did not usually back the Husaynis, and from every religious and political persuasion. Rumors spread to the effect that the mayor of Jerusalem, Raghib al-Nashashibi, the government of Palestine, and the Jews had manipulated the elections. Five copies of an anti-Jewish poster were posted in the old city of Jerusalem on the night of April 19. The poster warned Muslims that the Jews were trying to place in office a "traitor" who would accept Zionism, help kill the Palestinian national spirit, sell the Abu Madyan waqf (a property near the Wailing [Western] Wall), and hand over Haram al-Sharif so that the Jewish Temple could be rebuilt, as urged by the Zionist leaders Alfred Mond and M. D. Eder. The five posters could not have been effective because their authorship was unknown and they were removed the next morning. They do reflect, however, prevalent political suspicion and frustration, national moods from which Amin benefited.[28]

This nationalist sentiment became apparent to the Palestine government in April. Ronald Storrs, the district governor of Jerusalem, who thought he understood the "natives," forwarded to Samuel the many petitions he received with comments to the effect that Amin was the popular choice. Ernest T. Richmond, the High Commissioner's adviser on Arab affairs, translated some of the Arab petitions and interpreted their implications for British policy. Richmond was so sympathetic to the Palestinian nationalists and to Amin's candidacy that historians such as Elie Kedourie credit him with influencing Samuel in favor of Amin.[29] But there is no documentary or oral evidence to show that he influenced Samuel any more than did the two Zionists in Samuel's administration, Wyndham Deeds, the civil secretary, and Norman Bentwich, the legal secretary and a relative of Samuel. Both of these officials were personally closer to Samuel than Richmond, and both were against Amin's candidacy.

Promise and Appointment. Samuel must have expected the popular Amin to win. He spoke with Amin on April 1 and again on April 11 to sound him out on his candidacy. Amin made certain promises to Samuel, in the presence of Bentwich. According to Bentwich's account, Amin declared:

> his earnest desire to cooperate with the Government, and his belief in the good intention of the Government towards the Arabs. He gave assurance that the influence of his family and himself would be devoted to maintaining tranquility in Jerusalem and he felt sure that no disturbances need be feared this year. He said the riots of last year had been spontaneous and unpremeditated. If the government took reasonable precaution, he felt sure they would not be repeated.[30]

What are we to make of this pledge? Bentwich and other officials thought, in retrospect, that Amin must have been sincere because Palestine was peaceful between 1922 and 1929. His Zionist and Arab critics accused him of cooperation with the British for purely personal aggrandizement. It is true that he was a very ambitious man. But his pledge was neither insincere nor a compromise of his political beliefs. Amin's public view was that the Palestinians should not revolt against the British rule, which was too strong and, in any case, ephemeral; instead, they should concentrate on opposing the Zionists, who were the main threat to the Palestinian nationalists.[31]

Al-Hajj Amin's pledge was put to the test within a fortnight, at the Nabi

Musa celebration. He shrewdly assumed Kamil's place at the head of the procession on April 25. Unlike the previous Nabi Musa, when he had delivered a political speech that was followed by violence, the celebrations were peaceful. Afterward, Amin had invited Samuel to a luncheon which was prepared to conform to Jewish dietary laws. Samuel's presence and Amin's gracious hospitality and friendliness implied that Samuel was ready to accept Amin, and that Amin was prepared to cooperate with the British.[32]

Samuel was pleased with Amin's attitude, which was not unlike that of Kamil. Obviously he was aware of Amin's political past, but he may have assumed that once the young nationalist was absorbed into the administration he would become as pacified as was 'Arif, who was given a job in Nablus. Samuel expected Amin to use his family's prestige and influence to maintain tranquility, which would result in a reduction in British troops and expenditures, and a peaceful rule. It was what an imperialist upper-class ruler expected from the native aristocracy.

Within days of the Nabi Musa celebrations, however, an Arab-Jewish clash took place, not in Jerusalem but in Jaffa. The clash on May Day began between Communist Jews calling for a Soviet Palestine and Zionist socialists of the Poale Zion. It spread spontaneously to Muslim and Jewish quarters in Jaffa, leaving 48 Arabs and 47 Jews dead and 219 people wounded. The violence reinforced Samuel's view that Arab grievances should be met. He wrote the colonial secretary on May 8 that the Arabs considered the Palestine government autocratic and wanted to be represented. Perhaps it was no coincidence that he informed Amin shortly thereafter that he would select him as Mufti.[33]

Samuel searched for a legal way to appoint Amin. He asked Ronald Storrs, district governor of Jerusalem, to persuade Raghib al-Nashashibi to drop his support for the unpopular Jaralla. Against the advice of many members of his family, the mayor withdrew his support and persuaded Jaralla to drop out. This enabled Amin to qualify as one of the three candidates. Sometime in mid-May, Samuel picked Amin to succeed Kamil as Mufti.[34] Apparently, there was a lingering doubt about Amin's loyalty, because he was appointed not Grand Mufti, but Mufti of Jerusalem. Also, he never received an official letter of appointment, and his new position was not announced in the official gazette.[35] Still, the appointment of Amin to the office of Mufti gave him religious and moral authority throughout Palestine.

Supreme Muslim Council. Important as the office of the Mufti was, it did not compare with the power of the president of the Supreme Muslim Council, which controlled religious schools and courts, orphanages, mosques, and funds of awqaf. During Ottoman times, religious institutions and awqaf were headed by Shaykh al-Islam in Istanbul and administered by the Ministry of Awqaf. The British occupation of Palestine cut off all ties with Istanbul, and these institutions were placed under British officials.

The Muslim community was alarmed at the prospect of their religious affairs being controlled by a Christian government led by British Zionist Herbert Samuel as High Commissioner and of their most important religious institutions, shari'a courts and awqaf, being under the control of another British Zionist, Norman Bentwich, as legal secretary (later called attorney general). Muslims complained of religious discrimination and demanded control over their affairs. Samuel assured the Palestinians that the "Government does not want to take the place of the Sheikh ul-Uslam," and suggested that the Muslim secondary electors to the last Ottoman Parliament choose a higher body.[36] A committee of this body drew up draft regulations for a Supreme Muslim Council with control over Muslim affairs. The High Commissioner accepted all provisions except the power to dismiss qadis.

Samuel urged the Colonial Office to approve the regulations: "For political reasons it is urgent that Moslem opinions be satisfied as soon as possible."[37] According to the historian Porath, Samuel, who was anxious lest the May 1921 disturbances recur, considered the establishment of a council the best way to "placate" Palestinian opposition to the Zionist part of the mandate. The Colonial Office accepted this rationale, and in retrospect, the head of its Middle East Department, John Shuckburgh, later expressed his satisfaction with their policy: "The institution of a Supreme Muslim Council in 1921 has, on the whole, been one of the most successful moves in Palestine. It practically gave the Mohammedans self-government in regard to Moslem affairs. The arrangement has worked smoothly and has no doubt done much to reconcile Mohammedans to the Mandatory regime with its unpopular Zionist flavour."[38] That is, by pacifying the Palestinian elite over their religious affairs, Samuel and the Colonial Office were able to defuse Palestinian opposition to British policy favoring Jewish nationalism.

This was the same spirit and policy that motivated Samuel to facilitate the election of al-Hajj Amin as *Ra'is al-'Ulama'* (head of the Muslim community), to serve as permanent president of the council, on January 9, 1922. Despite a challenge by the Opposition (al-Mu'aridun), headed by Raghib al-Nashashibi, the vast majority (40 out of 47) of the secondary electors to the last Ottoman Parliament who voted elected Amin and, on a district basis, four council members for terms of four years each.[39]

The election gave the Mufti considerable authority. He controlled the shari'a courts, the hiring and dismissal of court officials, the religious schools and orphanages, and waqf boards and funds. The council's budget in 1922 was Palestine (P)£50,000. While the Mufti and the council's religious activities during the mid-1920s are not the focus of this biography, it is important to discuss briefly how the Mufti consolidated his religious power, enabling him to increase his political influence.

The Mufti's religious initiatives during the 1920s stimulated an Islamic revival throughout Palestine. He established a Muslim orphanage of 160 girls and boys, supported schools such as Rawdat al-Ma'arif (which had 250 students with a scout organization attached to it), repaired the Nahawiyya School building within the Haram al-Sharif and established a library and museum there, imported 50,000 trees to plant on waqf land, expanded welfare and health clinics, and renovated numerous local mosques and other buildings.[40] The most impressive project that he undertook, however, was the renovation of the two mosques in the rectangular area of the Haram, the third holiest shrine of Islam and the center of Muslim worship in Palestine. The mosques were in a state of disrepair and near collapse when the Mufti assumed office. The physical condition of the buildings was only one of the reasons why their renovation became the focus of the Mufti's time-consuming effort, the other reason being that he sought to revive the importance of Jerusalem in the Muslim and Arab worlds and to reassert its centrality within Palestine.

The extensive need for renovation required a massive fund-raising campaign. A delegation to Hijaz was sent in July 1923 (during the hajj), raising P£12,000 and to India in October, raising another P£22,000. Delegations in 1924 to Hijaz, Iraq, Kuwait, and Bahrain raised the total sum to P£84,000. Contributing to this success were King Fu'ad of Egypt, who gave P£10,000, Nizam al-Haydarabad of India, who contributed P£7,000 and King Faysal of Iraq, who gave about P£6,000. In addition, the High Commissioner, after obtaining a written promise that the Mufti would not get involved in political activities, assisted his efforts by sending letters of support to British authorities in Egypt and India to facilitate fund-raising. The restoration activities proceeded under the direction of the Turkish architect Kamal al-Din and with the assistance of Ernest Richmond. Both mosques were renovated, and by the end of the decade the Dome of the Rock was plated with gold.[41]

The delegations and restoration of the mosques reaped a number of significant political benefits. The effort focused Arab and Muslim concern for Palestine, especially since the Mufti and his colleagues appealed to fellow Muslims to defend Palestine against the Zionists, and the Haram in particular against the Jewish threat to regain the area of the site of the Jewish Temple. The fund-raising activity also enabled the Mufti to establish contacts with heads of state and politicians and to become recognized as a Palestinian leader and Muslim figure. His recognition was enhanced in November 1925 when he headed a Syrian Relief Committee to assist victims of the Syrian revolt, and in 1926 when he participated in the Caliphate Conference in Cairo.

Within Palestine, the Mufti's prestige increased. He consolidated his power in some regions, such as Jerusalem, Jaffa, and Nablus, while neglecting centers where the Opposition was strong, such as Hebron, Haifa, and Acre. Gradually he was able to fill key positions throughout Palestine with *khatibs* (preachers), imams, qadis, and other officials who either supported his policies or were Palestinian nationalists. Conversely, critics of Amin's policies found it difficult to produce jobs or to retain positions they already had. Members of the Opposition who challenged the Muftis's policies or ideology, because of interelite rivalry or Zionist bribery, found it virtually impossible to obtain jobs in regions where his influence was strong. This was also true for those advocating more revolutionary tactics. The Syrian-born Palestinian shaykh 'Izz al-Din al-Qassam, for instance, who wanted the Mufti to spend money on arms rather than on mosque repairs, was denied a preaching position in areas controlled by Amin in the mid-1920s, and preached in Hebron until he was killed by the British in 1935.[42]

While the Mufti used his religious position to support, morally and materially, the Palestinian national cause, he was not primarily active in the politics or diplomacy of Palestine. The political affairs of the Palestinian community were managed by the Palestine Arab Executive under the leadership of the former mayor of Jerusalem, Musa Kazim al-Husayni. When Samuel proposed the formation of a Legislative Council in 1922 (and a similar Advisory Council in 1923), the Palestinian nationalist leaders firmly opposed it: they feared that acceptance of the council was tantamount to acceptance of the British mandate (which was approved in July 1922 by the League of Nations) and support for the Jewish national home. They also considered unfair the council's composition, which reserved only 43 percent—10 out of 23 positions (11 British, 2 Jewish)—to the Arabs, who then constituted 88 percent of the population. Finally, they felt that the council was legislatively powerless, especially regarding such constitutional matters as Jewish immigration. But the opposing leaders were led by Musa Kazim and the Arab Executive, not the Mufti. Although Amin backed the Executive, as he did throughout the 1920s, his support was not crucial. In addition, he was too preoccupied with his new duties and religious projects and with the Opposition.

The Opposition, headed by Raghib al-Nashashibi, conducted a bitter campaign against the Arab Executive and the Supreme Muslim Council and its presidents between 1923 and 1928. The rivalry between the Husaynis and Nashashibis, while based on an interelite struggle for power that began in the late nineteenth century, was exacerbated by Raghib's replacement of Musa Kazim as mayor on the one hand and the Husaynis' ascendancy to the highest political and religious positions on the other. Raghib once told a friend that he would oppose any position that the Mufti took, which helps explain why in 1923 the Opposition attacked al-Hajj Amin for opposing the Legislative Council, and reversed itself in the late 1920s and accused him of collaborating with the British. It should be noted that the concept of loyal opposition was rarely practiced by either side. The historian Porath points out that in its eagerness to undermine the executive and the council, "the majority of the prominent personalities of the opposition benefited from financial support from the Zionists" for their personal needs and for setting up their parties. Moreover, of those Palestinians who sold land to Jews, the majority were members of the Opposition.[43]

The Opposition succeeded in gaining strength in the mid-1920s. This was due partly to the decline of the Arab Executive and the Zionist movement, which suffered a temporary setback in Palestine in 1926–27. In municipal elections, the Opposition scored victories throughout Palestine. It appeared to many Palestinians that the nationalists had exaggerated the threat of Zionism. Yet these were short-term victories. Calls for reforms of the council never materialized, and the accusations of corruption and embezzlement proved to be false. The British officials who examined the council's ledgers could find no evidence that the Mufti was anything but incorruptible. By 1928 both factions rallied behind the executive. The Opposition did not capitalize on its political victories, and its members were suspected of collaboration and land-selling to Jews. Besides, the Zionist threat had become real again with the increase of Jewish immigration and the expansion of the Jewish Agency. According to the High Commissioner, support for the Opposition declined to an estimated 20 percent by the mid-1930s.

By 1928 the Mufti had consolidated his religious power while increasing his influence in politics, but never at the expense of his agreement with the British. In return for the establishment of the council, which gave the Palestinians a large measure of control over their religious affairs, and for his appointment as head of the Muslim community, the Mufti was expected to acquiesce and cooperate with the British mandatory government in keeping the peace. He had promised to uphold law and order. While he verbally attacked Zionism and, more cautiously, British policy, he refrained from organizing or participating in demonstrations, and made sure that the potentially volatile Nabi Musa celebration, in which he was the central figure, remained orderly and peaceful. No two individuals were in a better position to know whether the Mufti kept his promise than those to whom it was made: Bentwich, who believed that the Mufti kept the peace between 1921 and 1928, and Samuel, who considered him a moderate man.[44]

3. Political Struggle Over the Western Wall, 1928–1929

 A DISPUTE in September 1928 over Jewish religious rights at the Western (Wailing) Wall, which was a Muslim waqf property, led to a disturbance in August 1929 that cost the lives of 133 Jews and at least 116 Palestinians. It was the worst violence between Jews and Arabs in Palestine in modern times.[1]

Amin al-Husayni emerged from the political violence both famous and infamous. He had become the Palestinians' most popular political leader, for most believed he had taken an active stand against Jewish claims to Muslim holy places and, ultimately, against Zionist designs on Palestine. By the same token he had become the most hated Arab in the Yishuv (the Jewish community in Palestine), for the Jews held him responsible for having turned a minor dispute in September 1928 into a political struggle and for inciting his "fanatical" Muslim followers to attack them in August 1929. Glorification and vilification of the Mufti have continued since the 1929 disturbances, consequently obscuring the events themselves and his role in them. Did he turn a trivial dispute into a political confrontation? How much did he contribute to the tension over the Wall and why? Did he organize the Palestinians and plan the August 1929 attacks on Jews? Before answering such questions, one must first understand how the dispute began in September 1928 and then analyze how the political struggle evolved.

Religious quarrels have always marred the "holy" city of Jerusalem. In modern times the disputes had arisen among Christian groups over control of parts of the Holy Sepulcher or some other shrine, and were usually precipitated by a priest putting a venerable lamp on a contested lamp stand, or saying his prayers in a contested spot. Religious squabble often advanced secular interests and led to riots, violence, and political struggles. In the 1850s such a quarrel was an artificial casus belli for the Crimean War.[2]

The Jews and the Muslims also had their religious quarrels, at the Western Wall in the old city of Jerusalem. The Wall, known to Jews as ha-Kotel ha-Ma'aravi (Western Wall), is a remnant of the western exterior of the Temple of Herod, which was built on the site of the Temple of Solomon. Jews had come to it since the Middle Ages to pray and to mourn the destruction of the Temple and the loss of the glory of ancient Israel.[3] The Wall is also the western wall of the Haram al-Sharif, Islam's third holiest shrine, a rectangular area enclosing al-Masjid al-Aqsa and the Dome of the Rock, from which, Muslims believe, the Prophet Muhammad ascended to heaven on a nocturnal journey.[4] For the Arabs, the Wall is also called "al-Buraq," after the name of the Prophet's "fabulous steed," which he tethered there. The surrounding area was known as the Maghribi quarter and the property of al-Ghuth Abu Madyan waqf. A religious contest over the Wall was virtually inevitable.

Before World War I, the disputants were unevenly matched. The Muslims not only formed the overwhelming majority of the population but also dominated the administrative positions under the Sunni Muslim rulers. In disputes over the Wall, the Ottomans often decided in favor of their coreligionists. These disputes arose from Jewish demands to be allowed to bring to the pavement in front of the Wall such appurtenances as chairs and benches for the elderly, an ark, and a screen to divide men from women. The Muslims feared that if they acquiesced, the pavement would become an open synagogue and, therefore, a Jewish possession. The Jews would then be able to restrict the use of the pavement, considered part of the Haram and for some Muslims the only access to their houses.

The Muslims thus routinely protested Jewish innovations and the Ottomans generally upheld the status quo.[5] There were occasions when the

Maghribi leaders did allow the Jews to bring appurtenances,[6] but these were secret and informal agreements and neither altered the Wall's status nor changed the restrictions which eighteen centuries of anti-Jewish laws and customs had established. The Jews had to endure the restrictions until World War I, when Britain assumed the Palestine mandate and promised to help establish a Jewish national home in a predominantly Muslim country. With the backing of the greatest power and the recognition of the League of Nations, and with the installation in Palestine of a Zionist High Commissioner and legal secretary, the Yishuv grew in size, power, and daring. During the 1920s the status quo at the Wall was increasingly challenged, with the Jews demanding possession of the Wall and the surrounding areas. The Palestinians were suspicious of Jewish intentions and resisted their demands. By the late 1920s, the two communities were heading for a showdown.

The Incident and Reactions. On September 23, 1928, the eve of Yom Kippur, an Ashkenazi *shammas* (beadle) brought to the Wall a larger ark than was ordinarily used, some mats and lamps, and attached a screen to the pavement in preparation for the religious service the next morning. The Muslims were notified, reportedly, by a Sephardi shammas who was unhappy over the Ashkenazi's refusal to share a tip.[7] The *mutawalli* (guardian) of the Abu Madyan waqf immediately complained to Edward Keith-Roach, deputy district commissioner of Jerusalem, that the items were innovations, and that in any case the screen was blocking the public thoroughfare along the narrow (eleven-foot-wide) lane used by the Maghribi residents and their donkeys. Keith-Roach ordered the shammas to remove the screen, and the latter assured him he would do so. But the next morning the screen was still there, and the mutawalli again complained. The British police were sent for, and members of the congregation were ordered to remove the screen. The orthodox Jewish worshipers refused to "work" on this holy day. They apparently did not want others to do so either, for when the police proceeded to remove the screen, the worshipers held on to it, and an elderly woman attacked a policeman with her umbrella. All injuries were minor.[8]

The predominant view in the historiography of Palestine is that the Mufti transformed this minor religious and legal dispute into a political struggle. 'Izzat Darwaza writes that the Mufti used the affair to reactivate the national movement.[9] Yehoshua Porath says that the Mufti and his associates exploited what "seemed to them a Jewish provocation, in order to intensify the struggle against the Jews."[10]

Writers such as Darwaza and Porath virtually ignore the six days that followed September 24. During these days, the Yishuv and world Jewry expressed their outrage and indignation. The incident had taken place during a prayer, Shmoneh Esrei, on the holiest day of the Jewish year, Yom Kippur, and at the holiest site of Judaism, the Western Wall. As if that were not enough, the Jewish leaders and press exaggerated the incident, and charged that the British police had beaten the elderly worshipers, thereby causing serious injuries.[11] The Zionist Organization along with Chief Rabbis Kook and Meir, protested to the British government and the League of Nations.[12] Jews organized a demonstration against police brutality, a Jewish mob in Jerusalem sought out the police officer who had removed the screen, and a strike was held on September 27.[13] The Jewish press was equally agitated. *Davar* quoted from a speech by the poet Hayyim Bialik describing the lane along the Wall as a "public latrine bespatted with dung of man and animal"; had it been a small synagogue, "no swine would dare desecrate it."[14] *Do'ar ha-Yom* implied that the Muslims were worse than the hooligans of the Russian pogroms.[15] Most of the articles called for "redemption" or "expropriation" of the Wall. The Officer Administering the Government (OAG) of Palestine, Harry Luke, concluded, "Jewish public opinion in Palestine has quite definitely removed the matter from the purely religious orbit and has made it a political and racial question."[16]

In short, it was the six days of strong Jewish reaction, however understandable, that transformed the September 24 incident into a political matter. The Mufti was involved neither in the incident nor in the events of the following six days. It is true that during and after October he made up for that low profile. How much did he contribute to the tension which led to the violence of August 1929? Porath states that "his agitation concerning Jewish rights at the Wailing Wall . . . resulted in the disturbances of August 1929."[17]

This thesis fits in nicely with the general Zionist view that the Mufti was responsible for most of the violence in mandatory Palestine, and with the view of many pro-Mufti Arabs that he aggressively resisted Zionism throughout the mandate. The thesis is compelling particularly because Amin and the nationalist movement were the prime beneficiaries of the August violence. But a closer examination of the Mufti's role in the conflict shows that writers have either ignored or assumed too much in an effort to tailor the facts to fit their theses. They ignored the sequence and sources of provocation on both sides, and assumed that the Mufti had the intention and the ability to orchestrate events and to sustain them for eleven months.

The Mufti entered the fray because of the Jewish reaction to the Yom Kippur incident and demands concerning the Wall. As president of the Supreme Muslim Council he was ultimately responsible for all waqf property, including the Wall. It was natural for him to defend it against other claims. He submitted two memoranda to Harry Luke outlining the Muslim position concerning Jewish attempts to take possession of the Wall, its vicinity, and (according to Muslim allegations) the Haram as well. The Mufti seemed unusually alarmed by Jewish propaganda abroad, the object of which, he wrote, was to pressure the British to turn the Wall over to the Jews.[18] He used the occasion to emphasize Muslim ownership of the Wall in the Husayni newspaper *al-Jami'a al-'Arabiyya* on October 1 and 8, 1928. He may have also had a hand in organizing a Committee for the Defense of the Buraq al-Sharif. The committee issued a statement on October 25 in which it claimed to represent the Arab population in its defense of the mosque of al-Aqsa from the Jews.[19]

Jewish leaders apparently realized that they had to refute the Mufti and allay Arab apprehension. On October 10 the Va'ad Le'ummi (National Council of Jews in Palestine) published an open letter to the Muslim community in which it declared that "no Jew has ever thought of encroaching upon the rights of Moslems over their own Holy Places,"[20] and that all the Jews wanted was to worship freely at the Wall. The letter called on "reasonable" Arab leaders to accept this "sincere" gesture and warned the Arabs that "the Jewish people are not ready to make any concession" at the Wall; any "interference or restriction" of Jewish "natural rights" would be regarded as "a serious offense and a grave insult against the Jewish Nation."[21] But the implication that the Jews merely wanted unimpeded worship was inconsistent with other utterances and actions. In a letter to the League of Nations, Colonel Frederick H. Kisch, chairman of the Palestine Zionist Executive, which represented the Zionist Organization in Palestine, requested the British to promote a sale of the Wall and its vicinity or expropriate the area.[22] In another letter, the Va'ad Le'umi urged the Palestine government to expropriate the Abu Madyan property, as it had the Karm al-Shaykh land a few years before.[23]

Thus, intentionally or not, the Zionist leaders contributed to the subsequent events through their statements of intent. Chaim Weizmann, president of the Zionist Organization, wrote to the Yishuv in *The New Palestine*, the official organ of the American Zionist Organization, that "the only rational answer" to the Wall dispute "is to pour Jews into Palestine." We must, he continued, "reclaim" our "homeland" and the Wall, even though the latter may take a year or two.[24] Such language may have been designed to pacify an angry Jewish community, but it also intensified the suspicion and hostility of the Palestinians and helped turn the minor dispute into a major political struggle.

Al-Buraq Campaign. The dispute could not have developed into such a conflict, however, without the counteractions of the Mufti. After weeks of Zionist demonstrations, strikes, and protests, Amin decided to take the initiative by conducting what became known, from the Arabic name for the Wall, as the Buraq campaign. It was not only the intensity and duration of the Zionists' reaction that alarmed the Mufti, but also their use of Jewish influence in London and Geneva to achieve their aims at the Wall. He knew they were the strongest in these capitals and that the Arab voice there went unheard. Here was where the Zionists had won their battles over Palestine: the Balfour Declaration, its incorporation into the British mandate, the appointment of a British Zionist as the first High Commissioner in 1920, the concession given by the British in 1921 to Pinhas Rutenberg to develop electricity in Palestine, the denial of proportional representation in the proposed Legislative Council in 1922 and in the Advisory Council of 1923.

The Mufti believed that the Jews had the ear of the British because they were represented in every layer of English society, including the House of Commons and the political parties. And he knew that by including American Jews in the Jewish Agency, which was established in 1929 to replace the Zionist Organization in advising and cooperating with the Palestine government on matters concerning the Yishuv, the Zionists could soon count on the wealth and influence of the world's largest Jewish community. With such influence, the Yishuv would finally be able to take over the Wall, unless he, the Mufti, aggressively opposed them. He had already reacted firmly early in October 1928 by protesting and by printing statements. But this was not enough.

The Mufti's new strategy, which began in November, was more vigorous and long-lasting. It had three major elements: publicizing the issue among the Palestinians and in the Arab and Muslim worlds, in order to unite them on the issue; cooperating with the Palestine and British governments while challenging them to adhere to and enforce their traditional policy of the status quo; and taking actions necessary to uphold Muslim rights around the Wall. On November 1, 1928, he attempted to galvanize Muslim Arabs by convening a General Muslim Conference in Jerusalem attended by Muslims from Palestine, Syria, Lebanon, and Transjordan. The resolutions they passed appeared to embody the same points mentioned in the Mufti's letter to the Palestine government on October 8, 1928. Both the memo and resolutions took positions which Amin maintained throughout the conflict. It may be useful, therefore, to analyze briefly the basic issues.[25]

The Mufti wanted to emphasize that the Wall, or al-Buraq, was part of the Haram and holy to Muslims. The Jews had the right to visit, but not worship there. There is no doubt that the Buraq, on the Haram side, where the Prophet Muhammad left his "fabulous steed," was considered holy. The outside, where Jews came to worship, was considered important because of its proximity to the Haram, because it had been made waqf by the son of Salah al-Din (or Saladin), al-'Aziz, and because the shari'a courts and the Mufti's own house were nearby. But despite that, the Wall itself was not so holy to Arabs, nor did they treat it with the respect due holy sites. It was infinitely holier to Jews, and no exaggeration by the Mufti could obscure the overpowering fact that the outer side of the Wall was the most important religious shrine in Judaism.

The Mufti must have calculated that if he could emphasize that the Wall was holy to Muslims, the Jews might be prohibited from freely worshiping there. Their right at the Wall, he claimed, did not "go beyond a mere favor" granted by the Maghribi residents to any visitor. And they certainly could not bring appurtenances with them. The Palestinians had official documentation, dating back to 1840 and 1912, to prove their contentions. The Mufti, however, ignored the legal point that after centuries of worship the Jews had established a customary right to pray at the Wall.[26] He also ignored informal agreements between the Maghribis and the religious Jews to allow the latter to place appurtenances on the pavement.[27] He was alarmed not so much over these minor infractions as over the ultimate intentions of the Jews, as he perceived them. The Arabs, he said, having learned "by bitter experience the unlimited greedy aspirations of the Jews" in Palestine, believe that the aim of the Jews is "to take possession of the Mosque of al-Aqsa gradually on the pretense that it is the Temple, by starting with the Western Wall of this place."[28]

These charges concerning the Wall and the Haram go to the heart of Palestinian apprehensions throughout the 1920s, and finally led to the violence of 1929. It is important to examine briefly the merits of these charges and, in so doing, determine whether the Mufti was a responsible leader warning his people of impending Jewish takeover, or an inciter using the legal and religious issue to arouse the passions of Muslims and Arab nationalists. Aside from the Jewish outcry and Zionist posturing, did the Mufti have tangible proof to justify his claim that the Zionists had designs on the waqf property around the Wall?

An "Elaborate Scheme." Sufficient evidence existed of Jewish attempts to purchase the Wall and the area around it. It seems Weizmann thought the purchase of the Wall would stimulate enthusiasm for Zionism. A few months after the British entered Jerusalem, he sought, in 1918, through Ronald Storrs, district governor of Jerusalem, to purchase the Wall and vicinity.[29] The Moroccan shaykhs of the Maghribi district were interested in the offer of P£70,000. But the Palestinians learned of the deal, their leaders protested, and the scheme was dropped.[30] It was, however, revived eight years later. Colonel Frederick H. Kisch, head of the political depart-ment of the Zionist Executive, devised in 1926 what he called an "elaborate scheme" to purchase, with the help of Judge G. Frumkin, properties in front of the Wall, for which he was raising a sum of P£100,000.[31] He intended to start by purchasing partial waqf property facing the Wall. This, he wrote Weizmann, would "tend to break the Moslem sanctity of the whole property as a Moslem Waqf." It would set a precedent and out-maneuver the Supreme Muslim Council, which would be faced with a legal fact.[32] He planned to evacuate the Moroccan Muslims from the purchased property, then demolish the houses,[33] or turn them into "Jewish waqf." If this could be achieved in three years, he wrote, "the political effect would be very great."[34] By November 1926 the Jews had bought a large property fifty meters from a gate of the Haram and the Wall, and were negotiating with owners of properties in front of the Wall.[35] In late 1928 Weizmann had P£61,000 with which to purchase the Wall. Sir John Chancellor, third High Commissioner of Palestine, advised the Jews to defer action until the excitement over the dispute ended.[36]

We do not know how much the Mufti knew about Kisch's "elaborate scheme." He knew about Jewish attempts to purchase the Wall, but was probably embarrassed to admit in public that fellow Muslims in his neighborhood were selling to Jews. He did reveal, however, that the Zionists had approached him, through a prominent person, with a bribe of P£50,000 and offered another P£400,000 for the property itself.[37] The figures were probably inflated, by the Mufti or the Zionists, but the attempted bribery may be true. Colonel Kisch and H. M. Kalvarisky, head of the Arab department of the Zionist Executive, often used bribery, in exchange for which Palestinian leaders, mainly from the Mu'aridun (Opposition), performed specific tasks.[38] Amin refused the bribe, and grew more suspicious of Jewish objectives. He also knew that the Jews wanted the British to expropriate the Wall and turn it over to them. There was a hint of this in 1928 when Storrs, while trying to persuade the Muslims to sell, used the argument that they might later get nothing for it because it might be taken in a city improvement plan.[39] After an incident at the Wall in 1925 the Jews called on the British to force the Muslims to sell their properties and, failing that, to expropriate the Wall and its surrounding area and hand it over to the Jews.[40] In April 1929 Chancellor suggested to the Mufti that the Muslims sell the Maghribi district, which would be replaced by an open courtyard for Jewish worshipers and visitors. Amin responded that it may appear inhuman but the Muslims rejected surrendering any rights at the Wall which might endanger their exclusive title to the Haram.[41]

The Mufti often charged the Jews with planning eventually to take over the Haram, since it had been the site of the Temple. It is not easy to determine how Jews felt before 1928 about the restoration of the Temple. Weizmann wrote in 1918 that Jews went to the Wall to "bewail the destruction of the Temple and to pray for its restoration."[42] In the spring of 1921, Sir Alfred Mond (later Lord Melchett), minister of health in the British cabinet and the financer of large Jewish projects in Palestine, told the Palestine Foundation Fund that a new "edifice" should be erected "where Solomon's ancient temple once stood."[43] This became well known in Palestine. So did pictures showing the Star of David over the Dome of the Rock.[44] The Jews themselves were far from unanimous in their views on the Temple: some, whose orthodox beliefs forbid them from stepping on the holy of holies, talked about restoration of the Temple in the spirit or in the afterlife; others used the symbolic pictures for advertising or to raise funds; still others actually meant to take over the Haram. The Palestinians did not notice the distinctions and believed the worst: that the Jews had designs on the Haram, just as they did on all Palestine.

Whether the Mufti also believed the worst is difficult to ascertain. In any case, he had little proof beyond a few statements about the restoration of the Temple, and some pictures with the Star of David over the Haram. But, as we have seen, he had ample proof concerning Jewish intentions for the Wall; the September 1928 incident only confirmed his conviction. This is why he had convened the Muslim Conference in November of 1928. He wanted the conference work to be sustained, and to that end he helped create a Society for the Defense of al-Masjid al-Aqsa and the Muslim Holy Places. The society's job was to publicize the conflict, which it did with zeal and even exaggeration. It published "appeals" and "manifestos" in the pro-Mufti weekly *al-Jami'a al-'Arabiyya* in late 1928 and early 1929, and its members, some of them militant, traveled around the country to spread the word about the Zionist threat. Once established, the society apparently functioned on its own, and not under the direction of the Mufti.[45] He had direct control, however, over construction work on or near the Wall. Repairs within the Haram had been under way since 1922 and now included the erection of a four-foot wall on the Wall itself, to screen from public gaze Muslim women in their dwellings inside the Haram. It is not clear if the Mufti, like the shammas a few weeks before, was using the screening of women to protect women from the gaze of men, or to enforce his community's right at the Wall.

The Mufti also decided to place a *mu'adhdhin* (caller to prayer) on top of a house, which was later turned into a *zawiyya* (small mosque and hospice). The melodic calling, five times a day, was to inspire Muslims to stop their activity and pray. But Orthodox Jews who were trying to meditate, chant, or pray at the Wall found the call disturbing and irritating. They found a recently revived Sufi ceremony (*dhukr*) equally disturbing. The ceremony, held in a garden near the Wall, included the playing of cymbals and gongs, and the shouting of "Allahu Akbar." The Mufti said that the cacophonous Sufi ceremony was part of the religious obligation of the Sufi Maghribi residents,[46] but his real purpose was probably to confirm Muslim rights at the Wall. For the Jews, the Arab discovery of the holiness of the area was belated and provocative. They complained to the British that the Mufti's actions were innovations and should not be permitted.

British Policy. The British, however, were constrained by their own policy. In Jerusalem and London they sought a mutual agreement between Palestinians and Jews concerning the Wall, but, failing that, they fell back on a policy of the status quo. Rule through traditional leaders and traditional practices, as long as it did not conflict with British interests, had been a basic tenet of British imperial policy in such places as Egypt. It kept the "natives" serene and happy. But what was good for Egypt was not good enough for Palestine, because in Palestine they had to satisfy the conflicting claims of two peoples.

The conflicts in 1928 seemed to immobilize the British, leaving the contending parties at odds. Part of the problem was that Palestine was in an administrative interregnum. Lord Plumer, who had replaced Sir Herbert Samuel as High Commissioner in 1925, had resigned and left the country in 1928 after three years of a rule whose peacefulness was as much due to his firm and imposing personality as it was to the decline of the fortunes of the Yishuv. The new High Commissioner, Sir John Chancellor, did not arrive until December 1928, when the two communities had already turned the September incident into a major confrontation. The British were torn between their political policy in Palestine, which favored the Zionists, and their religious policy of enforcing the status quo, which favored the Palestinians.

In the 1950s, the Mufti claimed that he fought against the British as well as the Zionists during the Wall controversy, because the British were helping the Jews.[47] The evidence indicates the opposite. Almost all his statements and actions, from September 23, 1928, until September 1, 1929, indicate that he cooperated with the British during the fateful year, and opposed provoking them either by not yielding to their desires or by advocating violence. The reason is that he believed, correctly, that British policy concerning the Wall in 1928, based on the status quo, was pro-Arab.

The Mufti approved of British policy from the time the British police forcefully removed the Jewish screen on September 23, 1928, onward. The British issued a White Paper on November 19, 1928, justifying their actions and reaffirming the status quo, that is, Muslim ownership and Jewish limited right of access.[48] Amin thanked them for their "just" and "impartial" decision.[49] The document did not deal with the specific appurtenances that could be brought to the Wall. For that the British had asked, three months earlier, the Supreme Muslim Council and the chief rabbinate to furnish documentary legal evidence of Ottoman practice. The Mufti promptly furnished the documentary evidence confirming Muslim ownership and limitations on Jews. The chief rabbinate did not respond for fear that the production of documentary evidence "might even weaken the well-known truth," as the rabbis later said.[50] The Jews apparently did not possess such evidence, but their delaying tactics must have been useful, since the government suspended the full enforcement of the status quo during the three-month delay. This annoyed the Mufti, who repeatedly insisted on the enforcement of the White Paper.[51] Sir John Chancellor assured him on May 6, 1929, that since the Jews did not furnish the evidence, it seemed likely "that the contention of the Moslems as regards the bringing of benches and appurtenances to the Wall will be established."[52] He reminded the Mufti that the Palestine government had done "their best to support your claims," which resulted in the favorable terms of the White Paper of 1928. Amin agreed and said that he "depend[ed] on the Government."[53]

Although the Mufti relied on the Palestine government, he had less confidence in the London government, which had postponed the final ruling on the matter for about three months. The delay, undoubtedly due to Zionist pressure in London on the minority government of Ramsay MacDonald (1929–1931) and on his colonial secretary, Sydney Webb (Lord Passfield),[54] further upset and annoyed him. Although he continued to demand the implementation of the White Paper and carried on with the Haram's construction work, he remained cooperative. When the Palestine government requested him to suspend the Sufi ceremony, for example, he stopped it. When they asked him to suspend renovation at the Wall until the law officers of the Crown reached a decision on the legal rights of the communities, he acceded; and although one of the officers, Sir Boyd Merriman, was thought to have Zionist sympathies, the Mufti pledged to abide by the law officers' findings. Subsequently, their report restricted Muslim activities to those which would not interfere with Jewish worshipers "during customary times of prayers," but allowed Muslim work to resume as long as it did not disturb or annoy Jewish worship.[55]

Despite these limitations, the Mufti accepted the report and the High Commissioner's restrictions. No wonder he was accused by the Arab Opposition press of trying to make himself agreeable to the Palestine government.[56] His opponents were vehement in their denunciations of him between November 1928 and August 1929. They charged that the Muslim

Conference was prompted by the British.[57] They accused him of using the Buraq campaign to fortify his position as president of the Supreme Muslim Council,[58] a weak charge, since he had already been appointed president for an additional nine years.[59] They also hinted that he had embezzled funds to build his house in Shu'fat, a Jerusalem suburb. Yet the money was a loan from George Antonius, a Christian confidant and an adviser to the Mufti.[60] If some of these accusations sounded like Zionist charges, it is because they probably were. Certain Opposition papers, like *al-Sirat al-Mustaqim*, and several Opposition leaders were on the payroll of the Zionists, through Colonel Kisch.[61] The Zionists did not invent the Arab Opposition. They capitalized on it. The enmity between the Nashashibis and the Husaynis predated the British mandate.[62] As was pointed out earlier, Raghib opposed nearly every major position by the Mufti,[63] no matter what the merits of the position might be or how high the cost to the cause of Palestinian unity and opposition to Zionism.

Political Violence. The resumption of the Arab building operations in July 1929 was interpreted by the Zionists as a violation of their rights at the Wall. There were the predictable protests by the Sixteenth Zionist Congress at Zurich, the Palestine Zionist Executive, and the chief rabbis. Rabbi Kook praised the Jewish youth who were ready "to sacrifice their lives in the cause of their Holy Place," and there were other intemperate statements.[64] But generally the moderate leaders began to calm public anxieties in late July. Telegrams between the leaders of the Palestine Zionist Executive, who were in Zurich, and their subordinates in Jerusalem show that they had become alarmed by the activities of the militant Revisionists, supporters of Vladimir Jabotinsky.[65] The moderate leaders were clearly "embarrassed" and fearful of an "accident." They appealed to Jabotinsky to control his press and his followers. But the militant press called for "insubordination and violence."[66] One paper pleaded with Jews not to stop protesting and demonstrating until the Wall was "restored to us."[67] Militant activity was stepped up. Joseph Klausner, who formed the Pro-Wailing Wall Committee, helped organize several demonstrations. On August 14, 6000 youths marched around the wall of the old city of Jerusalem. A demonstration at the Wall was planned for the next day. The moderates tried to prevent it and, when this failed, kept the authorities informed on the militants' moves.[68] The demonstration occurred nevertheless.

The demonstration of August 15, 1929, which the Shaw Commission later called the immediate cause of the violence,[69] set in motion a chain reaction. Provocative actions on that day angered the Palestinians. The Jewish youths shouted, "The Wall is ours," raised the Zionist flag, sang the Zionist anthem ("ha-Tiqvah"), and, according to rumor, beat up Muslim residents and cursed the Prophet Muhammad. The demonstration took place in the Muslim Maghribi district in front of the house of the Mufti, who watched the whole thing. The following day 2000 Muslims marched to the Wall, tore up a Torah scroll, and burned some religious documents. Although the Mufti failed to stop the demonstration, he did succeed in keeping the demonstrators within waqf property, but this Palestinian counterdemonstration increased tension to the point that when a Jewish boy accidentally kicked a ball into an Arab woman's tomato garden the following day, he was stabbed by an Arab man who had come to the rescue of the shrieking woman. An Arab youth, picked at random, was stabbed in retaliation. The funeral of the Jewish boy was turned into a large and belligerent demonstration against the British officials of the Palestine government and against the Palestinians.[70]

The Palestinians were alarmed. They had heard of the new Jewish Agency, which meant more money and power for the Yishuv. They were upset by Jewish press articles and Jewish demonstrations. These activities were exaggerated by militant Palestinians who were traveling around the country inciting villagers and spreading rumors.[71] Extremists on both sides capitalized on the dispute. It is obvious that both the moderate Zionist leaders and the Mufti did their share to increase the tension over Jewish demands for free access and Arab fears of Jewish encroachment on Muslim property. But it took Jewish and Arab militants to turn these demands and fears of late July and early August into a violent confrontation.

At noon on Friday, August 23, Amin al-Husayni hurriedly left his house in front of the Western Wall for the nearby al-Masjid al-Aqsa. He had just been told by the chief of police of Jerusalem, Major Allen Saunders, that thousands of "nervous" Muslims had gathered in the Haram al-Sharif.[72] Indeed, throngs of Palestinians had poured into the city that morning from the countryside, responding to what they believed to have been an appeal from the Mufti (and which later turned out to be a rumor supported by a forged note) to gather in Jerusalem on August 23 in defense of the Haram. The crowds that greeted Amin were not dressed for the Friday worship. They were in their work clothes and were armed with clubs, knives, swords, and a few guns. After all, they were at the Haram to defend it against Zionists who, the Palestinians had heard, intended to march to the Muslim shrine, as they had belligerently marched on the Western Wall nine days before to demand Jewish ownership, and try to take it because it had been the site of the Jewish temple.[73] The Muslims had hoped that al-Hajj Amin al-Husayni would lead them against the Jews. When the Mufti appeared in the Haram courtyard, the crowd began to chant "Sayf al-Din, al-Hajj Amin!" (The sword of religion, al-Hajj Amin). He was their Mufti,[74] and the most powerful Muslim leader in Palestine. Ever since a legal dispute had arisen over Jewish religious rights at the Wall, the Mufti had led the Palestinians in resisting Jewish nationalist demands for possession of the Wall and the surrounding area which included the Haram. Nevertheless, the Mufti instructed the Friday preacher, Sa'id al-Khatib, to give a pacifying sermon and urged the crowds to go inside the mosque to attend the service. He also sent word to the British authorities to quickly increase the number of policemen at the Haram and in the old city.[75]

Soon after the Friday prayers, the crowds gathered outside the mosque. There they listened to a few militant shaykhs. Some members of the audience got up on a platform and exhorted the crowd not to take notice of the Mufti because he was unfaithful to the Muslim cause.[76] The Mufti and some Arab and British policemen went from group to group in an attempt to disperse them, but failed. Soon the Muslims began pouring out of the Haram, one group heading toward Jaffa gate, the other toward Damascus gate. The Mufti rushed to Damascus gate, where he attempted again to disperse the crowd, which had picked up more Muslim and some Christian Arabs. But again he failed. The mob would not listen to him and marched on outside the old city to attack the nearby Jewish community of Me'ah She'arim. The other crowd attacked another Jewish community, Yemin Moshe, but there they were met by Jews armed with guns and bombs. The violence spread throughout Jerusalem.[77] The Mufti and other leaders issued an appeal to the Palestinians to arm themselves "with mercy, wisdom and patience, for verily God is with those who bear themselves in patience."[78]

But there was little mercy, wisdom, or patience in the next week. Palestinians in Hebron, upon hearing that their fellow Palestinians were being killed in Jerusalem and that the Haram was in danger, attacked the largely non-Zionist Jewish community there. They murdered 64 and would have killed more had other Palestinians not hidden their Jewish neighbors, and had a British officer not stood up to the rioters. More killing took place in Safad, where 26 Jews were murdered. Meanwhile, Jewish mobs murdered Palestinians in Jerusalem, Haifa, and Jaffa, where an imam and 6 Muslims were killed in a mosque. The British finally suppressed the riots, but not before 133 Jews and at least 116 Palestinians had been killed.[79] The usual British response to violence in one of their territories was to send out an investigating commission to ascertain why the "natives" had become "excited" and to recommend pacifying measures. The London government sent the Shaw Commission. Its report remains the most thorough and balanced study of the disturbance.

The commission determined that the Zionist demonstration of August 15 was the immediate cause of the violence, and blamed Arab and Zionist extremist groups.[80] The Mufti had contributed to the political tension but was absolved of a major share of responsibility for the violence. The commission found much evidence that he did not incite the riots: it established, for example, that the written appeal purportedly sent out for Arabs to come defend the Haram was a forgery. Moreover, the violence had taken place in several towns, like Hebron, where his influence was weak, and did not take place in many areas where he was strong. Had he called for violence, the response would have been greater and more widespread; instead, he called for nonviolence before, during, and after the outbreaks.[81]

The Mufti needed such vindication. The Zionist and Western press had placed most of the blame on him. But he was more concerned about Arab public opinion. He had become a major political leader immediately after the riots, but Palestinian public hostility to the British made his cooperation with the government difficult. The British had harshly suppressed the rebellion, killing and wounding hundreds of rioters and innocent Palestinians. Over the next few months they brought in 1300 Palestinians for trial, condemned 25 to death (though only 3 were actually hanged), and used the Collective Punishment Ordinance against suspected villages.[82]

Furthermore, the High Commissioner upon his return to Palestine hastily condemned the Palestinians for the violence, and though he later withdrew his angry comments, he did not withdraw his refusal to continue discussions about a legislative council, which the Palestine Arab Executive had proposed.[83] It was during this time that the Palestinians, for the first time, began thinking of actively opposing the British. But not the Mufti. As will be pointed out, he was seeking a political, not a military, solution.

The Mufti did contribute to the politicization of the September 24, 1928, religious incident and to the tension that followed. But he neither incited nor planned the August 1929 violence. He was constantly aware that if he, as an official of the Palestine government, challenged the British, they might exile him to political obscurity as quickly as they had granted him religious power in 1921. He was equally aware that the British were too strong for the Palestinians to challenge. Consequently, he practiced a dual policy between 1921 and 1936: cooperating with the British on the one hand while verbally opposing Zionism and seeking an Arab Palestine on the other. Such a policy worked well for him during the 1928–29 dispute: it confirmed to most British officials his compliance while it verified to most Palestinians his anti-Zionism. Already by late 1929, however, he was pressed by an emerging anti-British mood to choose between the two masters he was serving, the British and his own people.

4. The Politics of Moderation and the General Islamic Congress

THE AUGUST 1929 violence, which stemmed from years of political frustration and antagonism to Zionism, took the form of spontaneous attacks by Arabs against Jews. Many Arabs were also killed or injured by such indiscriminate force as British air power and Zionist bombings. Nevertheless, the High Commissioner condemned only the Palestinians in his uncharacteristically emotional proclamation of September 1, 1929. He also suspended discussions on a legislative council, which the Palestinians sought, and applied the hated Collective Punishment Ordinance to entire Arab villages. Moreover, 90 percent of the people arrested on charges connected with the disturbances were Palestinians.[1] These actions embittered the Palestinians, who turned militantly anti-British.

Cooperation. The Mufti emerged from the political violence as the most popular Palestinian leader. He was perceived as having thwarted Zionist attempts to acquire al-Buraq and the Haram al-Sharif. Palestinian militancy, however, confronted Amin with a political dilemma from which he could not extricate himself: how to continue cooperating with the British while opposing their Zionist policy, and how to oppose Zionism more effectively. He and the Palestine Arab Executive opposed Zionism during the 1920s with petitions, delegations, peaceful protest, and an abundant amount of nationalistic oratory. But these methods were increasingly perceived as innocuous and exposed the Mufti and the executive to criticism. With each successive setback to the Palestinians, the Opposition reminded the public of the Mufti's cooperation with the British and his ineffectively moderate methods.

Despite the new militancy and the Opposition's charges, the Mufti resisted joining the militants. In late September a Syrian militant, Shabib Wahab, approached him with an offer, according to a British police source, "to organize bands for a guerrilla campaign." The Mufti reportedly responded that he "considered this unnecessary at present."[2] He was seeking a political solution, not a military one. On another occasion he said that the Palestinians were not ready for a confrontation with the British army.[3] He may have considered that if he joined the militants, he would set himself on a collision course with the British, who could deprive him of the two offices from which he derived religious and political legitimacy, and also financial support. He therefore continued to cooperate with the British, as he indicated in two private conversations with the High Commissioner, in October.[4] "The Mufti promised to help in the maintenance of order and to cooperate with the Government. He had always held this attitude and he held it still and should continue to hold it even if Government did not listen to his representations. He regarded this as his duty not only to the Government, to God, and the people, but also to his own conscience."[5]

Amin also said that the Arabs were amicably disposed toward Great Britain both out of self-interest and because they believed in Britain's tradition of justice. They were, however, embittered by the harsh treatment they had received during and after the riots and, ultimately, by a British policy which favored the Jews. He attributed this policy to Jewish intrigue in Britain and Europe, and reminded the High Commissioner that it was Jewish intrigue with the Roman government and officials in Palestine which had brought the Lord Jesus to trial and condemnation two thousand years before. These and other comments indicate that the Mufti was intending to continue to oppose Zionism, champion the Palestinian cause, and cooperate with the British on political issues as he had done on religious and legal matters.

How cooperative was the Mufti? This is a crucial question in view of Zionist statements regarding his involvement in the planning and execution of violent activities[6] and the Mufti's own later claims that he had fought the British occupation since its inception.[7] Some of these accounts were corroborated by a few of his associates, in their books and in interviews.[8] Although, as noted, both Jews and Palestinians were misled about the Mufti's activities because of their adherence to their own myths about the man, there was a basis for these misconceptions.[9] For Amin, in his attempt to keep up with the increasingly militant mood and as a result of his own sympathies, maintained relations with the radicals, giving them vague moral support and keeping the confrontation option open. At the same time, however, he was, as the more impartial and accurate British documents confirm, a reasonable and pragmatic leader,[10] and therefore, in practice, a moderate.

The Mufti's moderation went beyond private assurances to a British civil servant. In October 1929, he and his associates on the council were involved in discussion concerning a settlement of the Palestine problem with the British Arabist and explorer Harold St. John Philby, acting in a private capacity. The draft settlement provided for the establishment of a parliament in which Arabs and Jews were to be proportionally represented, under the authority of a British High Commissioner who would safeguard Britain's Balfour obligations to the Zionists, including continued Jewish immigration to Palestine. Zionist leaders, including Weizmann, David Ben-Gurion, and Pinhas Rutenberg, rejected the plan. So did the Colonial Office. But the Mufti accepted it, and sent Jamal al-Husayni, the secretary of the council and Arab Executive, to London to discuss it along with the Western Wall problem.[11]

This was the Mufti's first diplomatic initiative since the August events had made him the most powerful Palestinian leader. It is thus significant that Jamal's starting position in the negotiations on December 19, 1929, with the colonial secretary, Passfield, was conciliatory. He suggested granting Palestine "some form of representative government," including an elected legislature based on proportional representation. He objected to British representatives in the legislature but accepted "some form of veto to be exercised by the High Commissioner."[12] Passfield rejected these proposals because they would reduce British authority and, no doubt, because both the British and the Zionists could contemplate no democratic institution based on proportional representation until Jews were in the majority. Otherwise, a Palestinian-dominated government would curtail the growth of the Yishuv, to which the British were committed. Despite the negative response in London, the negotiations encouraged the Mufti and the executive to seek more talks with the Colonial Office.[13]

In a meeting of the executive on January 9, 1930, the Mufti was elected to head a delegation to resume negotiations in London. His election was an official confirmation of a public recognition of his political leadership. He had, however, displaced the respected octogenarian Musa Kazim al-Husayni, who had been president of the executive and head of the delegations in the 1920s. The usurpation was premature and therefore resented by Musa Kazim and his supporters. During a new election two weeks later, the Mufti agreed to cede leadership of the delegation to Musa Kazim. After arriving in London in late March, the delegation, which consisted of Musa Kazim, the Mufti, Raghib al-Nashashibi, and 'Awni 'Abd al-Hadi, offered a moderate proposal similar to that which the Mufti's representative Jamal had submitted: a democratically elected legislature proportionally representing Arabs and Jews, under a British High Commissioner who could veto legislation that he considered inconsistent with the mandatory obligation. Once again the British rejected the moderate Palestinian proposal for the same reasons as before. The British did not want to restrict their authority in Palestine, and they knew that the Zionists would not accept a democratically elected legislature, where they would have 18 percent representation and therefore be dominated by the Palestinians.[14]

The Palestinian delegation raised two other points: restriction of Jewish immigration and of land sales to Jews. These issues had already been championed by the High Commissioner in a letter to the Colonial Office on January 17, 1930. They were later reiterated in the Shaw Commission Report in March and the Hope-Simpson Commission Report on August 22, and finally incorporated in the Passfield White Paper on October 20, 1930.

Setbacks. When Amin al-Husayni returned to Palestine in June, he was faced with several emotional issues. The first concerned the legal proceedings against thirteen hundred mostly Arab defendants for their part in the August 1929 uprising. Twenty-five Arabs and two Jews had been sentenced to death for murder. After appeal to the Supreme Court, seventeen death sentences were upheld; all but one of them were Arabs. The Palestinians reacted with strikes, demonstrations, and petitions. The Mufti, the executive, and other leaders appealed to the High Commissioner. They also solicited the help of friends in Arab and Muslim countries, who agreed to intervene. The High Commissioner commuted the death sentences of all but three, whose executions were set for June 17. Once again the Mufti and other leaders requested help from Syrians, Iraqis, and Sa'udis but to no avail. The hanging of three Arabs incensed the Palestinian community. The three were convicted murderers, but what focused Palestinian attention was that no Jews were hanged even though dozens of Arabs had been murdered and injured as well. Moreover, the judges were all British and the attorney general, Norman Bentwich, was an avowed Zionist. That was enough to turn the hanged men into political heroes worthy of a general strike and a commemorative celebration.[15]

The second issue, involving Britain's attempt to reach a final settlement of the Western Wall dispute before a Wailing Wall Commission sent by the League of Nations imposed one, was potentially more volatile. The Mufti, despite legal advantages and British backing, was reluctant to reach an agreement with the Jews unless Muslim ownership was recognized. He was willing to allow Jews to visit the Wall, but not as a matter of right. This had been his position during the 1928–29 controversy, and he did not budge from it for fear that if he were to admit any legal right to the Jews, it might later be interpreted to the disadvantage of the Muslim community. The Jews, on the other hand, were reluctant to admit Muslim ownership because, no doubt, many wanted eventually to possess the Wall, despite their public denials. The Mufti claimed that the Wall was also holy to Muslims. Yet no claims by him could obscure the fact that the Wall was much more important to Jews.

The High Commissioner Chancellor warned the Mufti that either a settlement would be reached which would be partly formulated by the Arabs and therefore favorable to them, or the international commission would impose a settlement which would almost certainly be "favorable" to the Jews and "repugnant" to the Arabs. Amin replied that he would settle for the latter rather than acquiesce in a settlement, however favorable to the Arabs, which was in any way contrary to his "convictions." To the High Commissioner's suggestion that the Mufti's participation in a settlement would show him to be a statesman, he replied that he was "not a statesman but a man of religion."[16] This comment bode ill for the future, for it showed that the Mufti's suspicion and antagonism toward the Zionists made him incapable of pragmatism where they were concerned—something he was able to do with his British and Arab opponents—even when compromise would have benefited the Palestinians. Subsequently, the settlement regarding the Wall, while confirming Muslim ownership, granted Jews free access and greater use of appurtenances.

The third setback concerned British policy in Palestine, which had recently seemed to tilt toward the Arabs with the Shaw and Hope-Simpson reports and especially with the Passfield White Paper. This document, which proposed a legislative council and restricted land sales and immigration—measures that would retard the development of the Yishuv—was greeted with consternation in Zionist circles. Using all the political and diplomatic means at their disposal, the Zionists thus exerted pressure on the weak minority government of Ramsay MacDonald to get it to rescind the White Paper.

When the British government began to waver, the Mufti sent Jamal to London once again to hold discussions with the Colonial Office. He wanted Jamal to do three things in London: influence the British to maintain the Passfield policy, encourage the Indian Muslims to speak on behalf of the Palestinians at the Round Table Conference in London, and, presumably, reach an agreement with the Colonial Office which would allow the Mufti to retain his hold on the shari'a courts and waqf funds. In return, the Mufti would agree to a limited legislative council.[17]

Al-Hajj Amin's effort in London was again unsuccessful. Jamal was an intelligent and persuasive representative, but he was no match for the Zionists, who were represented in every level of British society and politics. On February 13, 1931, MacDonald published a letter to Weizmann, which, despite the disingenuous British claim that it was a mere clarification of policy, was in fact an abrogation of the White Paper. It was called the "Black Letter" by the Arabs. No document, except the Balfour Declaration, was so unfavorably received by the Mufti and the Palestinians. Amin had based his policy of cooperation with the British on the belief that they were just and fair. During 1928–29 his cooperation had resulted in favorable British decisions for the Arabs. Yet now both the legal battle over the Western Wall and the political battle over Palestine were in jeopardy for one reason, as he perceived it: Zionist diplomacy. That is, world Jewry, particularly in London and Geneva, was reversing all the gains made in Palestine by the Palestinians. The Palestinians were diplomatically weak and needed the help of fellow Arabs and Muslims.

Looking Beyond Britain for Support. Seeking Muslim and Arab support against the Zionists was not a new idea. Amin al-Husayni's father, Tahir, who had been Mufti of Jerusalem until 1908, had briefly succeeded in influencing the Ottoman rulers of Palestine to restrict Jewish immigration and land sales.[18] When Amin attended Dar al-Da'wa wa al-Irshad in Cairo in 1913, he learned from Rashid Rida, a founder of Pan-Islamism, that Muslims should unite in order to resist the Western incursion into Muslim lands.[19] Between 1918 and 1921, Amin favored a unity between Palestine and Syria, largely to foil Zionist plans in Palestine. Later, he appealed to Husayn, King of Hijaz.

Shortly after he became president of the Supreme Muslim Council in January 1922, when his efforts would be more likely to bear fruit, the Mufti began leading or sending delegations to Arab and Muslim countries. He sent a delegation to Mecca in 1923, led a mission to several countries in 1923–24, and went to Mecca himself in 1926. He held a celebration in Jerusalem in August 1928 after the completion of the first stage of repairs at the Haram. The purpose of these activities was to make fellow Arabs and Muslims aware of the perceived threat to Muslim holy places, and to enlist their political and financial support for the Palestinian cause.[20]

Political support for the Mufti and the Palestinians in the 1920s, however, was meager. Arab and Muslim rulers and dignitaries had their own problems and were wary of getting entangled in the Palestine problem and straining their relations with Britain, from whom most were trying to gain concessions. Besides, there seemed to be no immediate threat to Palestine. But in September 1928 the Wailing (Western) Wall controversy erupted. The Mufti's warnings about Zionist designs on Muslim holy places seemed to be justified in the light of Revisionist and other Zionist statements and demonstrations challenging Muslim ownership of the Wall. Amin's first major response, as we have seen, was to call for a General Muslim Conference to be held in Jerusalem on November 1, 1928. The conference, with delegates from Syria, Lebanon, and Transjordan, organized a committee which appealed to Arabs over the next few months, to resist Zionist demands.[21]

With the August 1929 violence, Muslim and Arab solidarity with the Palestinians increased. Amin called on Muslims to contribute to a Central Relief Committee, which he established to aid arrested and injured Arabs and the families of those who had died in the violence. The Muslims contributed about P£13,000 in less than a year.[22] At about the same time he had asked them to manifest their solidarity with the Palestinians by striking and holding a Palestine Day on May 16, 1930. Several Muslim countries did. He had also invited representatives from Muslim countries to testify before the League of Nation's Wailing Wall Commission, and Muslims from several countries were present at the October 1930 hearings, during which they emphasized the universal importance of the Haram to Islam.[23] The Mufti therefore succeeded in drawing Muslims into the Western Wall and Palestine problems and in renewing personal ties.

The most useful of these ties was with the Indian Muslims. In 1924 and 1926 during the hajj, the Mufti had met Muhammad and Shawkat 'Ali, leaders of the caliphate movement, which sought to restore the office of the caliph. Muhammad 'Ali visited Palestine in 1928 to propose a Pan-Islamic association, and again in 1930 to testify before the Wailing Wall Commission.[24] In late October the Mufti went to Cairo to meet the delegates of the Indian Round Table Conference en route to London to discuss Indian reforms with the Colonial Office. The Mufti urged the delegates to raise the question of the Wailing Wall with the British.[25] Two months later he sent Jamal to London in part to work closely with the Indian delegation,[26] but within three weeks (January 4, 1931) Muhammad 'Ali died. Muhammad 'Ali had had a deep attachment to the Haram in Jerusalem, so Shawkat 'Ali and Jamal returned his body for burial near al-Aqsa. The interment may have been encouraged by the Mufti: it reemphasized his point that the Haram belonged to all Muslims and was in keeping with his aim of turning the Haram into a Muslim pantheon to strengthen the attachment of Muslims to their holy sanctuary.[27] A few months later, in June, he urged that Husayn ibn 'Ali, the former King of Hijaz who as the sharif of Mecca had led the 1916 Arab Revolt, be buried next to Muhammad 'Ali. And in 1934 Musa Kazim al-Husayni, too, was buried there.

The Mufti's association with the Indians was based on mutual self-interest. He needed their political and financial support, while they sought support in the Arab world for their idea of restoring the caliphate and fighting imperialism. They found the Mufti receptive to both ideas.

The General Islamic Congress. But the culmination of the Mufti's efforts to rally Muslim and Arab support came with the Islamic Congress in December 1931. The idea of holding an Islamic conference in Jerusalem, one of the holiest cities of Islam, was shrewd and ambitious. The conference would focus Arab and Muslim attention on the Palestine problem and enlist support for the Palestinians' struggle against the Zionists. As its organizer and president, the Mufti would enhance his prestige in Palestine, and would make himself a leader in the Arab and Muslim worlds.[28]

While there had long been talk among Amin and the Muslims of holding a Pan-Islamic meeting, nothing specific was formulated until after the MacDonald letter of February 13, 1931.[29]

A few days after the letter was published, the Mufti and Shawkat discussed the idea of a Palestine-centered world movement which British intelligence described as Pan-Arab, Pan-Islamic, and anti-Zionist. The ultimate aim was a Muslim federation which would attain independence from the Western powers. A Muslim university in Jerusalem would be set up through world Muslim financial support and become a nucleus of the movement. Shawkat 'Ali tentatively formed a committee to prepare for the congress to discuss such plans.[30]

He and the Mufti considered Egyptian participation crucial to the success of the congress. Shortly after the publication of the MacDonald letter Shawkat tried to interest Mustafa Nahhas Pasha, the head of the Wafd party in Egypt, in the scheme. The Mufti himself went to Egypt on March 17 to enlist support. He reportedly told Muslims that the "Black Letter" brought Muslims and Christians in Palestine closer together against the British and Jews, that the revitalization of the Arab movement might change things in the Middle East, and that the Islamic conference would discuss Islamic federation which would end Western domination of Muslim countries.[31]

The objectives were kept general, probably to assure broad Muslim and Arab public support for the questions of Palestine and Pan-Islamization. More impetus was given to these questions in June, when the International (Wailing Wall) Commission issued its report, which recommended that Jews be given more rights at the Western Wall. The recommendation, which was implemented by the British in an Order-in-Council, united the majority of the Palestine Arab Executive and the Supreme Muslim Council behind the Mufti, whom they authorized to send invitations for the congress. After a few weeks and several postponements, the congress was set for December.

The Mufti sent out, in October 1931, invitations to rulers of Arab and Muslim countries, and to religious and political organizations and individuals, to attend the General Islamic Congress, Mu'tamar Islami 'Amm, in Jerusalem. The Mufti was obviously aware that the British would not allow a meeting to be held in Palestine that would discuss Islamic federation and independence and opposition to British law concerning the Wall. The announced purpose of the congress was thus general: to "investigate the actual situation of Islam and measures to be taken in defense of its interests."[32] The real aim, as the Mufti later confirmed in his *Haqa'iq 'an Qadiyyat Filastin*, was to investigate the Zionist danger to Palestine and to its Muslim holy places,[33] and to consolidate Muslim efforts against French and British domination.

The specific objectives of the congress, which were published in October, were all religious, though they were still vague enough to leave much to the political imagination:

1. Muslim cooperation.
2. Diffusion of Islamic culture.
3. Defense of the Muslim holy places.
4. Preservation of the tradition of Islam.
5. Establishment of a Muslim university in Jerusalem.
6. Restoration of the Hijaz Railway to Muslim ownership.[34]

The Mufti's proposed congress received enthusiastic popular support in the twenty countries to which invitations were sent. The Pan-Islamic notion of reuniting the *umma* (Muslim community) was still popular. Even more so was the prospect of Arab unity. But the rulers of these countries were suspicious of the Mufti's intentions. There was, for instance, a rumor that Amin might reopen the volatile question of the caliphate (historical ruler of the Muslim community), an office that had been abolished in March 1924 by Mustafa Kemal Atatürk after the Turkish Republic supplanted the Ottoman Empire.

There were three rivals for that position: Fu'ad, King of Egypt; 'Abd al-'Aziz ibn Sa'ud, King of the Hijaz and Nadj; and 'Abd al-Majid, who had been the last caliph. The Mufti did not mention this issue, and even claimed that the Zionists had spread the rumor that he was planning to discuss the caliphate to undermine the congress.[35]

In Egypt, the Mufti came under strong attack from three groups: The Egyptian modernists attacked his planned congress as reactionary and contrary to the modern development toward national states. He was also attacked by the shaykhs of al-Azhar University, who were afraid that a Muslim university in Jerusalem would undermine al-Azhar. And he was opposed by some politicians and newspapers who suspected that he wanted to establish a caliphate in Jerusalem for local purposes, such as to fight Zionism and to increase his own influence.

The Mufti found it necessary to go to Cairo again in October and November to dispel rumors, clarify aims, and enlist support. He assured the 'ulama' that the Jerusalem university would not compete with al-Azhar but with the Hebrew University, and he promised officials that the caliphate question would not be discussed.[36] Only after such assurances to Isma'il Sidqi, the prime minister, did the government decide to send a delegation, though it later decided merely to allow private groups to attend, including leaders of the Wafd and Liberal parties, and al-Azhar representatives.[37]

The Turks were even more critical than the Egyptians, mainly because they were anxious that rumors of the revival of the caliph 'Abd al-Majid and of the Ottoman regime would stir the "reactionary" element in Turkey.[38] The foreign affairs minister, Tevfik Rustu, declared in Parliament, "We are opposed to any internal or external policy which makes use of religion as a political instrument." He was speaking of the Mufti, whom he privately called "irresponsible."[39] There is no doubt that in his attempt to unite the Arabs, Muslims, and Palestinians, the Mufti used religion in the service of Palestinian nationalism. He admitted as much in Cairo in November when he declared to *al-Balagh* newspaper that he hoped the congress would maintain Muslim interest in and gather support for Arab Palestine as world Jewry had done for the Jews in Palestine.[40]

The Sa'udis were also suspicious of the Mufti. Ibn Sa'ud was hesitant to send a delegation to a congress that might discuss a caliph in Jerusalem where he had little influence. The Sa'udi foreign minister warned the British that the congress would be anti-Sa'udi and anti-British and sought advice about attending. Upon receiving an inconclusive reply, the Sa'udi government sent a delegation which arrived in Jerusalem after the congress was over.[41]

Indeed, many of the invited rulers could not decide if their interests would be better served by sending a delegation or not. If they did send a delegation, they could be used by the Mufti and thus put in conflict with Britain. If they abstained, they would antagonize their Muslim constituents. To get themselves out of this dilemma, many turned to Britain for a cue.[42]

The British were, however, in a similar predicament. If they canceled the congress, they would appear anti-Islamic. If they allowed it to take place, the congress could embarrass them and others, particularly the French, Dutch, and Italians, who might be denounced for occupying Muslim lands. Italy, which then controlled Libya, was particularly worried that if the Mufti criticized Italy's actions in Tripoli, as he had done in the past, such criticism in the congress might lead to a boycott of Italian goods in the Muslim world, and to a revolt in Tripoli. The Italians warned the British of the unfavorable consequences for Italian-British relations in the event of such repercussions from the congress.[43]

The Foreign Office was thus deluged by European, Muslim, and Arab inquiries and warnings. The office felt "much anxiety" about the "international repercussion" which the congress might cause, and consulted the Colonial Office and India Office about what to do. One proposal was to ask the Mufti to cancel it, but they decided they could not trust the "sly" and "untrustworthy" Mufti, as they called him, to cooperate. Another suggestion was to hold the Mufti responsible for any political questions raised on penalty of being found unfit for office as president of the Supreme Muslim Council or "any other threat that may be thought effective." The High Commissioner in Jerusalem opposed this suggestion, since the Communists would gain the most from a reduction of his power.[44] Finally the British decided to acquiesce to the congress but to give it no official blessing, keep the ex-caliph out of Palestine, and caution the Mufti.[45]

The High Commissioner invited the Mufti to see him in November. Amin was quite cooperative and promised that no political discussions on Tripoli, the caliphate, or al-Buraq would take place. In a second meeting he even agreed to change any reference in the declared statement about the congress which might harm relations between Muslims and non-Muslims.[46] Through political compromise and maneuver, the Mufti thus pacified or gained the confidence of Muslims, Arabs, and British; and neutralized Zionist, Turkish, and Palestinian opposition. He used the same skills to make the divergent Muslims speak in one voice at the congress. The Mufti opened the Islamic Congress on December 6, 1931 (27 Rajas

1350 A.H.), which that year was the Laylat al-Mi'ra, the holiday commemorating the Prophet's nocturnal journey to Heaven. Some twenty countries were represented by about 145 delegates, including some major intellectual and political figures of the Muslim and Arab worlds. The Mufti's mentor, Rashid Rida, was present, as were Muhammad Iqbal, the poet-philosopher of India; 'Abd al-Rahman 'Azzam, later secretary general of the Arab League (1945–52); Shukri al-Quwwatli, who would twice be president of Syria (1943–1949, 1955–1958); Riyad al-Sulh, who would twice be the Lebanese prime minister (1943–1945 and 1951–1956), and Ziya al-Din Tabataba'i, the exiled Iranian political leader.[47]

The Mufti drew upon the various institutions and organs under his control. He used the band of the Muslim Orphanage at the opening ceremony in the Aqsa mosque; the school facilities of Rawdat al-Ma'arif for meetings; the newspaper *al-Jami'a al-'Arabiyya* to publish articles on the proceedings, the participants, and their countries; and the funds of the Supreme Muslim Council (SMC) to pay the expenses of some of the guests, among them Rida.[48]

The Mufti's influence on the congress, which lasted from December 6–17, is indicated by the language and content of the pro-Palestinian resolutions that it passed. The congress condemned Jewish immigration and land purchases, Zionist designs on Muslim holy places, and the decisions of the International (Wailing Wall) Commission. It recommended the boycott of Zionist goods (the sale of which was, in any case, negligible in Muslim countries), the establishment of a fund to purchase and develop Palestinian lands, and the founding of a Muslim university in Jerusalem. And it affirmed solidarity with the Christian Arab Palestinians.[49]

Even some of the Pan-Islamic resolutions bear the Mufti's imprint. An association was established, under the leadership of Rida, to combat the spread of atheism and Christian missionary activity. Missionaries, mainly Protestant fundamentalists, often attacked Islam (although most were ignorant of that religion, its culture, and the Arabic language), attempted to convert Muslims to Christianity, and supported Jewish claims to Palestine, all of which were resented by the Mufti. The congress attacked Communist Russia for its anti-Muslim policies in predominantly Muslim regions of the USSR. It resolved to recover the Hijaz railway, which had been built with Muslims' money and for Muslim pilgrims, but which had been "usurped" by France and Britain during the war.

France was also attacked for its policy in Morocco, as was Italy for its actions in Libya. British sensitivity over the Italian issue made them evict the anti-Italian 'Azzam. The Mufti had promised the British not to allow political issues to be introduced, but since the delegates kept the terminology vague and since he identified with the issues, he allowed them to be discussed. He permitted amorphous attacks on colonialism and the mandate system, but prevented a speaker from attacking Zionism because he was too specific.[50]

Most of Amin's aims for the congress were realized. He increased Muslim and Arab support for the Palestinians, strengthened his ties with fellow Muslims and Arabs, and enhanced his prestige in Palestine and in the Islamic world. The congress elected him, before it adjourned, to the presidency of an Executive Committee of twenty-five Muslims, who were to carry out religious and political activities. The new position allowed him to maintain his ties and increase his popularity. He sent out protests in the name of the Muslim world concerning the Wailing Wall decision, persecution of Muslims in Communist Russia, and harsh Italian actions in Tripoli.[51] In 1934 he and the Executive Committee, which included the two Syrian politicians Shakib Arsalan and Nur al-Din Atasi, began a mediation effort to end a war between Sa'udi Arabia and Yemen. After two months the mediation helped conclude a peace treaty between Ibn Sa'ud and Imam Yahya.[52]

Not all of the aims of the Mufti, however, were achieved. Although he pledged SMC waqf revenues and the Palace Hotel, recently completed by the SMC, for the Muslim university, the Mufti was never able to build it. He and Muhammad 'Ali 'Alluba traveled to Iraq and India between May and September 1933 to collect funds for the university, and for the land fund, but they found that Muslims' contributions did not match their enthusiasm. Amin later claimed that the Indians, particularly the Nizam of Heydarabad, had been willing to contribute but were discouraged by the British.[53] It is more likely that contributions were scarce because of the economic depression which swept the Muslim world in the early 1930s. Disappointed, the Mufti gave up on establishing a university and rented the Palace Hotel to the Palestine government in 1934. However, using Council money he launched a vigorous land purchasing drive which severely limited Jewish land purchases.[54]

By the time the Mufti became the political leader of the Palestinians in late 1929, his people had become frustrated, more militant, and anti-British. He sensed the new mood, tried to warn the British, and undertook diplomatic initiatives to find a solution to the Palestine problem. When that failed, and after several setbacks, he tried to rally Arab and Muslim support on behalf of the Palestinians by holding an Islamic congress. The meeting was an immediate success for him and his people, but the gains, while substantial in terms of moral support, were small in terms of material and political help because his coreligionists were too poor, too weak and politically divided and dominated. It seemed to the Palestinians that if the Yishuv continued to grow, they would inevitably find themselves dominated in their own homeland. They did not focus on the reason for Jewish immigration in the early 1930s, namely Nazi persecution, but on its effect on Arab economic and political power in Palestine. The increase in Jewish immigration—4075 in 1931, 9553 in 1932, 30,327 in 1933, 42,359 in 1934 and 61,854 in 1935—highlighted the bankruptcy of such moderate methods as petitions, delegations, and demonstrations. The new militant mood caused the demise of the Arab Executive, even before its respected leader, Musa Kazim al-Husayni, died in 1934. A new generation of leaders, the Istiqlalists from the left and the Qassamites from the right, challenged the Mufti's methods, particularly his cooperation with the British. Time was running out on the moderate leadership of Amin al-Husayni.

5. The Arab Revolt: The Challenge

A FEW days before the General Islamic Congress ended on December 17, 1931, Pan-Arabists held a meeting in Jerusalem, whose outcome proved to be more enduring than the ephemeral achievements of the congress. The meeting was attended by fifty Pan-Arabists, mainly Palestinians and Syrians who had been supporters of King Faysal of Syria (1920). The group, which included followers of the Mufti, formulated an Arab Covenant which stressed anti-imperialism, and Arab independence and unity.[1] The Mufti supported this pledge, and was active in promoting an Arab congress to be held in Baghdad. This congress was not held, however, because Sa'udi-Hashimi rivalry split the ranks of the planners and because Faysal, now King of Iraq (1921–1933), did not want to antagonize the British, who were about to grant Iraq "independence," by hosting an Arab nationalist congress. Moreover, the Mufti withdrew his support and supporters from the scheme when it became apparent that the Palestinian Pan-Arab members were coalescing into a new party called Istiqlal (Independence),[2] which was officially

founded on August 4, 1932. While several parties were formed during the next few years, none so successfully challenged the Mufti, on personal and political grounds, as did the Istiqlal.

Al-Istiqlal. The Mufti viewed any strong, independent minded individuals with leadership qualities and pretensions as personal challengers to himself, irrespective of their nationalism or ideology. His supporters later argued that the Istiqlalists threatened to diffuse the leadership and increase disunity.[3] That may be true, but the fact remains that the Mufti, like many Arab leaders, was authoritarian and could not tolerate competition. This in part explains why during the 1930s he surrounded himself with yesmen like Ishaq Darwish, Abu al-Sa'ud, Munif al-Husayni, Haydar al-Husayni, and Emile al-Ghuri who lacked strong personalities. They were uncritical and loyal to a fault.

The leaders of the Istiqlal were, by contrast, independent, intelligent and articulate men who appealed to the emerging militant mood. Men such as Akram Zu'aytir, 'Awni 'Abd al-Hadi, 'Izzat Darwaza, and Ahmad al-Shuqayri advocated active opposition not only to the Zionists but also to the British mandate, which they demanded should be dismantled and replaced with a parliamentary Arab rule in Palestine.[4] They opposed the moderate methods of the Arab Executive and the Mufti as ineffective, and criticized the Husayni-Nashashibi rivalry as weakening the Palestinian cause. In 1932 and early 1933 they were perceived by a frustrated public as the alternative to the moderates, and began to encroach upon the Mufti's constituency.[5]

Amin initially did not respond and probably would have tried to ride out the challenge, had the new party not set itself on a collision course with him by sharply criticizing his cooperation and collaboration with the British. The earlier Opposition had often used this attack effectively because it struck a sensitive nerve in the Mufti and his supporters. The Opposition, however, had not had a charismatic or respected leader, had been suspected of opportunism or worse, and therefore had never had a wide following except in the mid-1920s. They had been an irritant and an embarrassment to the Mufti, but not a political threat. The Istiqlalists, on the other hand, were attracting his supporters and appeared to be the wave of the future. They could not be ignored.[6]

So the Mufti fought back. He dismissed his key rival, 'Awni 'Abd al-Hadi, the general secretary of Istiqlal, from his job as lawyer for the Supreme Muslim Council. He then allowed his supporters to reveal that 'Abd al-Hadi had provided legal assistance to Jews purchasing Arab lands during the 1920s. A campaign was unleashed against other Istiqlalists as well. The Istiqlalists had had the sentimental support of many Palestinians, but they had little else. They had no political machinery, no grass-roots organization, and no press support with which to fight the Mufti. Amin controlled the shari'a courts, the awqaf, and other institutions, and for all his caution remained a charismatic religious and political leader. The Istiqlal party was already beset by internal rivalry and financial difficulties, and by late 1933 the Mufti's assault had crippled it.[7]

Al-Qassam. The Mufti was able to overcome the Istiqlal challenge, but not the radical spirit which sustained it. This sentiment found expression in a secret religious organization led by 'Izz al-Din al-Qassam, a deeply religious shaykh and a man of integrity, social concern, and eloquence. He was also a dedicated revolutionary. It will be recalled that back in the mid-1920s he had demanded that waqf money be spent on arms rather than mosque repairs. This had caused the Mufti to deny him employment as an itinerant preacher for the Supreme Muslim Council. But al-Qassam founded a mosque in which to preach his revolution, and he practiced what he preached. He not only preached a jihad (holy war) against the twin infidels, the Jew and the Briton, but also began buying arms and recruiting workers and peasants in northern Palestine, his power base.[8] In 1933, he sent a follower to the Mufti requesting him to start a revolt in the south, while he, al-Qassam, started one in the north. The Mufti reportedly refused, affirming again that he was seeking a political, not military, solution.[9]

By 1935 al-Qassam was unalterably convinced that the methods of the Palestinian leader were ineffective. Jewish immigration had reached an alarming rate, and it seemed only a matter of time before the Zionists would establish a Jewish nation in Palestine. Al-Qassam refused to wait any longer. But before he could announce a revolt, he and a dozen followers were surprised by a British police detachment. Instead of escaping from or surrendering to the British troops, al-Qassam resolved to fight to the end, which came on November 19, 1935.[10]

The news of al-Qassam's death sent a wave of grief and rage over Palestine. He became a symbol of martyrdom and self-sacrifice, embodying for the people the selflessness conspicuously absent among their leaders.

His death also helped to illuminate in stark relief the futile tactics of the politicians, which is probably why they did not attend the funeral. But neither Amin nor leaders of the parties could escape his shadow. Indeed, al-Qassam achieved more in death than he did during fifteen years of preaching. He offered his people, hitherto largely peaceful and hospitable, a radical alternative—revolution. Throughout Palestine, radical youth groups formed to take up the mantle of al-Qassam, to fight Zionism and the British mandate.[11] A British intelligence report in December 1935 predicted that the party leaders "will find themselves forced to adopt an extremist policy" in order "to restore their prestige and prevent the leadership of the nationalist movement from passing out of their hands"; they would have "to satisfy public opinion and try a new course of action, as all their previous efforts in protest, demonstrations, public meetings, etc. had failed to attain their object."[12]

Violence and Strike. The catalyst which finally forced the Mufti's hand came on April 15, 1936. Armed Arabs, presumably members of Ikhwan al-Qassam (the Brothers of Qassam), stopped a bus and robbed its Jewish and Arab occupants, telling the Arabs that their money would be used to fight for the cause. They then murdered one Jew and seriously injured two others. The next night the Hagana, the militia of the Jewish community, retaliated by murdering two Arab farmers. During the funeral of a second Jew, who had died of his wounds, a group of Jews beat several Arabs. Two days later (April 19) Palestinians from Jaffa, believing that fellow Arabs had been killed in Tel Aviv, attacked the adjacent neighborhoods in Tel Aviv, killing nine Jews. The government proclaimed a state of emergency.[13]

Some writers have concluded that the Mufti inspired the events in April. Joseph Schechtman, for example, wrote that he incited the Jaffa Arabs to violence.[14] Emile al-Ghuri suggested that the Mufti secretly inspired and led Palestinian affairs in April.[15] No source is supplied for these conclusions and both authors had axes to grind: Schechtman was a Revisionist Zionist who sought to implicate the Mufti in the violence; and al-Ghuri was a Christian Palestinian who tried to show that the Mufti, his hero, was responsible for the Palestinians' greatest revolt against the British.

The Mufti's secret as well as public actions indicate that during the crucial days between April 15 and 25 he had not yet discontinued his dual policy of nonviolent opposition to the Zionists and political cooperation with the British. Together with Palestine Arab party leaders, he had been discussing with Arthur Wauchope, the fourth High Commissioner, the possibility of sending a delegation to London. Amin wanted the delegation to counteract Jewish propaganda in Britain and to press for the establishment of a legislative council.[16] The discussions were interrupted by the violence of April 15–19. According to Zionist intelligence, the Mufti visited Jaffa on the afternoon of April 18 but had neither advised nor hinted that the Arabs should retaliate. Arab reprisals on April 19 were largely led by his opponent Fakhri al-Nashashibi. When rumors spread in Jerusalem the same day about the murder of an Arab in the Jewish quarter, the Supreme Muslim Council quickly investigated and denied the rumor.[17] The Mufti told Wauchope the same evening that, barring an accident, no more rioting would occur.[18] When on the following day Beersheba leaders telephoned him to ask what action they should take, he said that he had not decided on a definite policy and that they should do what seemed best for them.[19] The next day (April 21) he promised the High Commissioner to do his best "to prevent continuance of disorder."[20]

Anticipating a disturbance at the Haram al-Sharif after the Friday prayer on April 24, the Mufti assured the High Commissioner that the sermon would be moderate. Before the sermon, one of his aides urged villagers to ignore the young radicals and to refrain from disturbances and return to their villages after the sermon. The Mufti attended the sevices, and the sermon by Sa'id al-Khatib was indeed nonpolitical. When it was over, men came to him asking him to make a speech. He declined and walked toward his office, while his assistants told the angry men who were following him that they would be foolish to demonstrate because the police had orders to shoot demonstrators.[21]

The Mufti had as little to do with the violence as he did with the general strike that was declared on April 19, 1936. The decision to strike was taken without his consultation. The committees that reached the decision, first in Nablus, Jaffa, and Haifa, then, during the following five days, throughout Palestine, were composed of Istiqlalists, Ikhwan al-Qassam, Young Men's Muslim Associations, and other zealous nationalists. The Nablus committee was led by Akram Zu'aytir and the Haifa committee by Rashid al-Hajj Ibrahim, both Istiqlalists who had little use for the Mufti's moderation.[22] Yet the Istiqlalists wanted to widen support for the strike. The committees met with the Mufti and leaders of the parties to seek their support. The Mufti's party, the Palestine Arab party headed by Jamal al-

Husayni, was the first to support the strike but Amin remained aloof, reluctant to lead or join them.[23] The fact is that he was still serving two masters, the British and the Palestinians, and was now being forced to choose. Although the violence was between Arabs and Jews, the general strike was directed against both the Jews and the British. Anti-British feeling was present in all the manifestos and letters of protest. Arabs attacked British policy and declared that the strike would continue until the Arab national demands were met.[24] The Mufti was no doubt aware that assuming the leadership of such an anti-British movement could set him on a political collision course with the British, who would need as little legal justification to dismiss him from his offices as they had needed to appoint him.

Fortuitous events and the public consensus were making it difficult for the Mufti to stay aloof. The public mood, reflected in public meetings and enunciated in the press, was overwhelmingly for the strike and for his assuming the leadership. If he refused to join, he stood to lose public confidence and forfeit his leadership to the young radicals. Ultimately, the people's expectations and his deep commitment to the national cause forced him to make one of the most serious decisions of his life. But he made the decision grudgingly and by stages. After several days of discussions with Istiqlalists and young radicals, the Mufti accepted, on April 25, 1936 an Istiqlalist request that he lead a united movement. He did so only after they promised to meet his conditions,[25] one of which was apparently that there be national unity, presumably under his leadership. The Istiqlalists therefore convinced the reluctant Raghib al-Nashashibi to become a member of a committee they sought to form. It was thus that what was subsequently to be called the Arab Higher Committee (al-Lajna al-'Arabiyya al-'Ulya) was established with the Mufti at its head.

The Arab Higher Committee. The formation of the committee was the first attempt at national Palestinian unity since the demise of the Palestine Arab Executive in 1934. Besides Amin al-Husayni as president, it consisted of the heads of the six parties: Jamal al-Husayni (Palestine Arab party), Raghib al-Nashashibi (National Defense party), Husayn al-Khalidi (Reform party), 'Abd al-Latif Salah (National Bloc), and Ya'qub al-Ghusayn (Youth Congress). The Christian community was represented by Alfred Rock, a Greek Catholic supporter of the Mufti, and Ya'qub Farraj, a Greek Orthodox member of the Opposition. Two members of the Istiqlal, 'Awni

'Abd al-Hadi and Ahmad Hilmi 'Abd al-Baqi, were elected general secretary and treasurer, respectively.[26] Thus the committee represented the Husaynis and the Nashashibis, Muslims and Christians, moderates and radicals. They were forced together by a public that was tired of family feuds, policy divisions, and moderate tactics.

The committee was the child of the spontaneous revolt. During the first few months, it did not lead the revolt so much as be led by it. Actual leadership was more in the hands of semi-independent national committees, controlled by young radicals,[27] with which the Arab Higher Committee often consulted before making public statements or policy decisions. The Mufti and the committee were, therefore, relegated to a position of moral national authority. Yet, because that authority was derived from the collective wish of the public, and because of the unity of purpose among the various groups, the committee was more than a symbol of a united front. It sometimes imposed its will throughout the country.

In its first manifesto to the "Arab Nation," the committee called for national unity and urged that the general strike continue "until the British government makes a fundamental change in its present policy in Palestine in a manner which will be manifested by the stoppage of Jewish immigration."[28] It declared its determination to achieve three major demands: a complete halt to Jewish immigration, prohibition of the transfer of Arab lands to Jews, and the establishment of a national government responsible to a representative council.[29]

The Mufti sent the manifesto on April 26 to Wauchope accompanied by a long letter in which he explained Palestinian national frustration.[30] The following are the salient points:

1. "The Jews have always declared their intention to make Palestine a land of Israel . . . for all the Jews of the world."
2. Their efforts in increasing immigration and land purchase have one object in view, namely, the establishment of a Jewish state in Palestine.
3. The British government has always ignored Arab rights, Arab national existence, and Arab demands; instead it administers Palestine under direct colonial rule and facilitates Jewish immigration and the usurpation of Arab lands.
4. The British government trespassed on Arab rights when it issued the Balfour Declaration, "which affects a country which is not its own and which is included within the pledges given to the late King Husayn";

and the declaration stipulates that "nothing will be done to prejudice the rights of the Arabs in the country."

5. The 1930 White Paper admitted there was no surplus of land for Jewish immigrants, yet the government helped to increase Jewish immigration more than ever before.

6. The government's failure to remove the dangers to the Arabs resulted and still results in regrettable riots.

7. "The Arabs are of the strong belief that the continuation of the present policy will lead them to immediate annihilation. They find themselves compelled, moved by their struggle for existence, to defend their country and national rights." The Mufti closed the letter by indicating that he was confident that the High Commissioner "appreciates the critical position of the present crisis and [I] trust that you will endeavour to effect a fundamental change" in British policy.[31]

The significance of the Mufti's letter was the public forum in which he chose to enunciate anti-Zionist and anti-British points, which indicated that he was identifying with the strike. Much had happened to bring Amin to this point. He had little to show for his petitions, negotiations, and co-operation with the British. While Syria and Egypt were being granted self-government, in Palestine a legislative council was denied. Continued land purchases by Jews had resulted in the dislocation of Arab villagers. Jewish immigration had increased, reaching the alarming rate of 61,854 in 1935. Zionist hegemony—through diplomacy, money, landholdings, and immigration—seemed inevitable to most Palestinians. They supported the strike, hoping it would force the British to change their policies, and expected the Mufti to lead them. The political realities and the public pressure on the Mufti forced him to become more radical. It was the beginning of the end of his cooperation with the British and, consequently, of British confidence in him.

Jaffa port, crippled by the Arab strike, and the Jewish schedule of immigrants was announced.[3]

These measures, which served as reminders of British partiality to the Zionists, antagonized the Palestinians still further. By late May, civil disobedience and political violence had grown into a full-fledged armed insurrection. The detailed story of the Arab Revolt, which lasted until 1939, has often been told, but the Mufti's role in it is still shrouded with misconceptions and contradictions.

Far from being the instigator of the revolt and its leading spirit during the first few months, as some of his Palestinian supporters and Zionist critics would have us believe, the Mufti tried to limit the general strike and to keep it from becoming a violent revolt. Although he had bowed to public pressure and accepted the presidency of the Arab Higher Committee, he did not wholeheartedly adopt the tenets of the revolt. The revolt had a force of its own, which he could not control and which, in fact, forced him into positions he was hesitant to adopt. That is why during the first few months he vacillated, not knowing which course to take. That he was a loyal nationalist is clearly indicated in his speeches, interviews, and actions. But he also showed restraint toward the British and opposition to violence.

The High Commissioner apparently was aware of the dilemma in which the Mufti and others in the committee had placed themselves. He wrote the colonial secretary: "It is important that the position of the Arab leaders be understood. A demand was pressed upon them from all Arab quarters in Palestine that the strike should continue until immigration had been stopped and this they foolishly endorsed in the excitement of the first few days of disorder. . . . [They] are at present powerless to stop the strike unless immigration is suspended as the feeling of Arabs is now so strong."[4]

The first major problem the Mufti faced as president of the Arab Higher Committee was a demand by Hasan Sidqi al-Dajani, the secretary of the National Defense party, that the Arab officials of the Palestine government join the strike.[5] This was a curious suggestion, since al-Dajani was not only a member of the supposedly moderate Opposition, but also a known Zionist collaborator.[6] British intelligence attributed this demand to an attempt by the Nashashibis and their followers to embarrass the Mufti and the mayor of Jerusalem, al-Khalidi, both government officials,[7] by confronting them with the difficult choice of either striking and risking dismissal from their powerful positions, or refusing to strike and becoming discredited among their constituents. The Mufti obviously did not like the proposal, and the committee, which discussed it, was unable to reach an agreement. The issue would not go away because 'Awni 'Abd al-Hadi, too, was urging officials to strike. Amin reportedly complained to Wauchope, whereupon 'Abd al-Hadi was arrested and detained.[8]

The second problem the Mufti faced was a demand for nonpayment of taxes. Aware of the consequence of such an illegal act, he informed the High Commissioner on the evening of May 4, 1936, that the committee might support illegal actions, such as the nonpayment of taxes. Wauchope immediately summoned the committee to meet him the next morning, when he cautioned them against associating themselves with the move or similar actions.[9] The committee disavowed violence, but refused the High Commissioner's suggestions of ending the strike and of sending a delegation to London.[10] The same evening, the police detained Hasan Sidqi al-Dajani for publishing a manifesto urging people to stop paying taxes and calling on officials to strike.

The Mufti's ability to resist activist pressures was declining. The radical committees requested a general meeting on May 8, 1936, where Amin delivered an emotional speech attacking Zionism and calling on the Arab and Muslim worlds to support the Palestinians. His criticism of Britain was mild. But when Raghib al-Nashashibi supported a proposal to stop paying taxes to the government, the proposal passed. Concluded a British police report: "Certain of the leaders particularly the Mufti and Jamal al-Husseini were against the proposal and only supported it because it was clear that opposition was useless."[11]

A week later Wauchope suggested to the Arab Higher Committee that if they would end the strike, he would appoint a Royal Commission. During a meeting at the home of 'Awni 'Abd al-Hadi, the Mufti's men, Ahmad Hilmi and Alfred Rock, recommended that the proposal be accepted not because they were unaware that previous commissions (Palin, Haycraft, Shaw, Simpson, French) produced no long term benefits, but because the revolt's cost to the Arab economy was high, and its benefits to the Yishuv enviable. Zionist intelligence, which frequently received reports from Arab informers on these meetings, stated that the moderate Husayn Fakhri al-Khalidi pointed out that the youth would not accept the proposal, and that its acceptance would turn the masses against the Arab Higher Committee. 'Abd al-Hadi was also against acceptance, saying, in essence, that because of the public's mood and solidarity, this was the last opportunity to force the British to change their policy. It was that view that prevailed.[12]

The committee then met with the High Commissioner to give their answer. The transcript of the interview indicates that the Mufti took a conciliatory position,[13] stating that all the members of the committee wished for peace and urged as much in their travels around the country. When Wauchope suggested that the committee issue a direct appeal against lawlessness, the Mufti replied that they needed "to find a formula which would not make them appear weak in the eyes of the people."[14] The High Commissioner then suggested that the appeal could be issued the same day the appointment of the Royal Commission was announced, and the Mufti found this "the proper course." But Raghib al-Nashashibi stated that the appointment of the commission "without the stoppage of immigration would create a dangerous situation." 'Abd al-Hadi likewise rejected the proposal on the grounds that past commissions had gained the Arabs nothing; this new commission was the "affair of the British," while the first concern of the Palestinians was stopping immigration.

The next day, May 15, 1936, al-Liwa', a pro-Mufti newspaper, issued an appeal calling upon the public to avoid violence and to use peaceful means, such as the committee decision to stop paying taxes, to attain the national goals. Furthermore, the president of the Mufti's party, Jamal al-Husayni, soon left for London with three other leaders to negotiate with the Colonial Office a way of ending the stalemate.[15]

The Mufti's moderation did not go unnoticed in the Palestine government. The High Commissioner pointed out to his advisory council that the members of the committee "have publicly dissociated themselves from violent methods."[16] He wrote the Colonial Office on May 23 that the Mufti had used his influence in keeping the Friday sermons calm, and that he and members of the committee had a moderating influence on extreme leaders.[17] The same day, the Palestine police arrested sixty-one Palestinian leaders, including Fakhri al-Nashashibi. The Mufti and the committee were not included.[18]

The arrests and detentions of Opposition figures did not, however, serve the Mufti's interests. Raghib al-Nashashibi and some Istiqlalists spread rumors that the Mufti had had prior knowledge of the arrests and that he had promised the High Commissioner on May 21 to end the strike. Opposition papers escalated their attacks on him, and the public mood began to turn against him. During a meeting of the Arab Higher Committee the majority of members voted for a proposal of no confidence introduced by the Jerusalem national committee concerning the Mufti and the mayor.

But 'Abd al-Hadi, brought to the meeting by Jamal al-Husayni, pointed out that the vote would harm the revolt and asked that it be withdrawn. The advice was heeded, but criticism of the Mufti continued, particularly from the Nablus and Gaza national committees.[19]

While Amin's position with his fellow Palestinians was becoming increasingly untenable, his relations with the British were becoming strained. Even though they appreciated his moderating influence, he had accepted the presidency of the Arab Higher Committee and had agreed to the nonpayment of taxes. This caused the High Commissioner to draw up contingency plans, approved by the Colonial Office, for deporting the Mufti and the committee should it become necessary.[20]

Britain's changing attitude did not escape Amin's notice. The Mufti had become aware of this because on May 20 the colonial secretary hinted in the House of Commons that the British would consider "special action" against the Mufti, who received his salary from government funds. The Mufti sent a tart letter to the colonial secretary stating that his salary was partly from waqf funds and partly from the treasury, which in turn received funds from revenues of shari'a courts. He further noted that one of his duties was to "defend the rights of Moslems."[21] Then, on June 17, the colonial secretary issued a statement during the parliamentary debates asserting that the Supreme Muslim Council "has ordered no strike and Shari'a Courts and Waqf Administration are open and working."[22] The statement had been made on the advice of Wauchope, who had predicted that it would have an excellent effect on the civil service, but it only increased the strain in Palestine. Two days later, on June 19, the colonial secretary compounded the error by stating that the Supreme Muslim Council had "decided not to take part in the strike."[23] In fact, the Mufti had not even called a meeting of the council, perhaps to prevent it from deciding to strike. The colonial secretary's statement received wide publicity in the Palestine press, causing embarrassment to the Mufti and putting pressure on him to fall in line.[24] The statement highlighted his paradoxical position as president of the Arab Higher Committee, which supported the strike, and of the Supreme Muslim Council, which only partially supported it as of June 11.

The Mufti was obviously angered by the statement. The next day he sent the colonial secretary a strongly nationalistic memorandum in which he stated that the Supreme Muslim Council identified with all the demands and lawful actions of the Palestinian people and that British policy must

change fundamentally. He seemed to justify the council's political involvement on the basis that the Jews were a threat to Palestine and its Muslim
holy places, primarily the Haram al-Sharif.[25] The British, therefore, succeeded where the Opposition had failed, in pushing the Mufti to declare
support for the strike as an official of the council and in its name.

The High Commissioner, through his chief secretary, refuted Amin's
claims that the Zionist case was fundamentally a religious case and that
the Muslim holy places were in danger. The chief secretary went on:
"Remembering your correct attitude up to the present in reprobating acts
of violence, he [Wauchope] would remind you of the responsibility which
rests upon you as the Head of the Moslem Community in Palestine to
declare publicly and emphatically that you are on the side of law and
order."[26] The Mufti replied a few days later: "I am still of the same
attitude . . . in that I am actuated by keen and distinct desire to follow
lawful means in asserting the nation's rights."[27]

As the revolt became more widespread and violent, the British took
harsher actions. Unable to subdue Jaffa, they destroyed a large portion of
the old city, leaving many Palestinians homeless. In other towns, they
blew up the houses of Palestinians suspected of harboring rebels, damaged
mosques during armed clashes, and imposed fines on villages supporting
the rebellion. Such methods, together with the deaths of hundreds of Arabs
during armed conflicts with the British or Zionist forces, increased Palestinian bitterness. During the Mufti's travels around the country, he was
visibly moved by the death and destruction, particularly to the Palestinian
peasants. He had always praised British fairness and justice, but now he
began to point out the "cruelty of the English."[28]

During the summer of 1936, the Mufti accepted the use of political
violence to change British policy and gave moral and monetary support to
the rebels. He instructed preachers to use the religious theme of the Jewish
threat to Arab Palestine and Muslim holy places,[29] and provided some
guidance to the military commanders, but he did not assume direct control
of the rebellion. Military recruiting, organization, and operations were left
to local and regional leaders.

The High Commissioner realized the change in the Mufti's attitude in
late August and attributed it to his fear of being "criticized loudly by his
many opponents as a traitor to the Arabs and a tool of the English."[30] A
few weeks later Wauchope wrote: "There are many factors that weigh
with that astute mind but his chief fear is to be left alone in the open,

liable to be accused by friend and foe of treachery to the Arab cause."[31] According to the High Commissioner, the Mufti feared more than criticism from the young radicals: he borrowed a bulletproof jacket to protect himself from them.[32]

The High Commissioner also attributed the change in Amin's attitude to the influence of George Antonius, a Christian adviser to the Mufti, who was later to gain fame as the author of *The Arab Awakening*. Wauchope described Antonius as "evil" and "extremist."[33] Both terms were often used by the British and Zionists to mean a Palestinian nationalist opposed to British rule and Zionism. In any case, it is doubtful that Antonius had that much influence on the Mufti.

Despite his radicalization, the Mufti did not give up on a political solution and called for the intervention of Arab rulers, notably Nuri al-Sa'id of Iraq and Ibn al-Sa'ud of Sa'udi Arabia, who tried to mediate. He did not want the help of Transjordan's Amir 'Abdullah, because of the latter's involvement with the British, the Nashashibis and, at times, the Zionists; but 'Abdullah undertook a mediation on his own in May. Shortly beforehand, 'Abdullah had received a suggestion from Moshe Shertok of the Jewish Agency that the Jews would support 'Abdullah as head of the Palestinians if the Amir recognized the Zionist interest in solving the Palestine problem. When 'Abdullah subsequently met with the Arab Higher Committee, he suggested that they end the strike and send a delegation to London. The committee refused to compromise as long as the British and Zionists refused to consider suspending immigration.[34]

If the British and Zionists sought to divide the committee by encouraging 'Abdullah's intervention, then their efforts succeeded. The split between the old enemies widened, with Raghib al-Nashashibi now taking a moderate stance, and Amin al-Husayni reflecting the radicalization among Palestinians.[35]

By mid-October, however, the public began to tire of the revolt. The strike was costly to the Palestinians in economic terms, and 1000 Palestinians (together with 80 Jews and 37 British) had died in the armed clashes. Furthermore, the British threatened to institute harsh martial law measures, and by September their troops had been reinforced to reach 20,000, against about 2000 Palestinians. The Arab Higher Committee therefore sought a way to end the rebellion through another Arab mediation. After consultations with the committee, the Arab rulers sent them an appeal to end the general strike and the rebellion, because "we rely on the good intentions of our friend Great Britain, who has declared that she will do justice."[36] The committee accepted.

The immediate intention of Britain was to conduct an inquiry and a Royal Commission, the Peel Commission, was appointed for that purpose. When the colonial secretary announced that there would be no suspension of Jewish immigration during the inquiry, the Arab Higher Committee declared it would not cooperate. On the eve of the commission's return to London, however, the committee bowed to the pressures of Arab rulers and agreed to give evidence. The final Palestinian statement, dated January 6, 1937, stressed yet again the McMahon pledge, the invalidity of the Balfour Declaration, and the fact that the Palestinians had never acquiesced to a British mandate, which was contrary to the League of Nations' principle of self-determination. The committee demanded that the mandate be removed and that Palestine be allowed to have an independent government.[37] It was the first time that the Mufti, as head of the committee, had formally asked for the end of British rule.

Despite this demand the Mufti and the committee were conciliatory. Amin told the High Commissioner in February 1937 that he hoped friendly relations with the British would be established.[38] He advocated moderation and asked his subordinates in the Supreme Muslim Council to do the same.[39] But this was short-lived. The Arab economic situation had deteriorated. The landless Arabs now numbered a quarter of the rural population, and Arab unemployment increased because, as the Arabs saw it, the government favored Jewish workers, to whom it paid twice the wages it paid the Arabs for the same output.[40]

Tensions were increased in May by a hunger strike by 180 political internees in Galilee, and by rumors in June that the Peel Commission was going to recommend partition. The partition scheme was anathema to the Mufti. It would split Palestine into three parts: the British would keep a strategic and religious region, including Bethlehem and Jerusalem; the Jews would establish a state in Galilee, which would include some of the best land in Palestine and which would affect its Arab residents; the Arabs would establish a state united with Transjordan under 'Abdullah.

The main reason the Mufti opposed partition relates to his Pan-Arabism. During World War I, he had aided the British war effort because Britain promised to free the Arab world from the Ottomans. He had worked for the unity of Syria and Palestine under Faysal. Instead, France and Britain had split the two regions between them. Now Britain was planning a

As an Ottoman officer in 1917.

Two of the Mufti's aides:
Jamal al-Husayni (right) and Emile al-Ghuri (left),
London, 1947.

Al-Hajj Amin al-Husayni (right) and King Faysal of Iraq (left), Jaffa Harbor, 1925 (W. Khalidi, Before Their Diaspora).

The Arab Higher Committee, formed April 1936. Front row, left to right: Raghib al-Nashashibi, al-Hajj Amin al-Husayni, Ahmad Hilmi, 'Abd al-Latif Salah, and Alfred Roch. Second Row, left to right: Jamal al-Husayni, Dr. Husayn al-Khalidi, Ya'qub al-Ghusayn, and Fu'ad Saba (W. Khalidi, Before Their Diaspora*).*

The Mufti (far right, front row) standing with Musa Kazim al-Husayni (center) and Raghib al-Nashashibi (left) as members of the Palestinian delegation, London, April 1930 (W. Khalidi, Before Their Diaspora*).*

The Mufti with King Husayn of Jordan, Amman, 1967.

Left

(Top) In Lebanon in 1949.

(Bottom) With Jamal 'Abd al-Nasir, President of Egypt (right) and Shukri al-Quwatli, President of Syria, Cairo, 1958.

In Beirut, June 1974, weeks before the Mufti's death.

further division of Palestine among themselves, the Zionists, and 'Abdullah, whose Arab nationalism Amin found suspect.

The prospect of partition was thus the last straw for the Mufti. He became more defiant and began actively preparing for a resumption of the rebellion. He met with Syrian and Palestinian rebel leaders in Damascus. The British, like the Zionists, had their Arab informants there, and knew about his plans to "declare war on the British on the 8th July,"[41] the day after the Peel Report was scheduled to be issued. Before that time, Raghib al-Nashashibi and another supporter resigned from the Arab Higher Committee, denounced the Mufti, and, together with 'Abdullah, prepared to accept partition.[42] The Nashashibis expected to take over the political leadership of the Palestinians in a state under 'Abdullah.[43]

On July 7, 1937, the Peel Commission published its report, which was accompanied by a statement by the British government accepting in principle its recommendation on partition. The Zionists, though they did not like the partition boundaries, shrewdly accepted. Weizmann told Ormsby-Gore that he would help the British transfer the Arabs of Galilee to Transjordan.[44] The Palestinians were overwhelmingly against partition. Because of that, and because the Jewish state included the pro-Nashashibi districts of Galilee and Acre, the Opposition rejected the partition.[45]

The following day the Arab Higher Committee sent the British a long memorandum, signed by the Mufti, demanding the cessation of immigration and of land sales to Jews. It also asked for the establishment of a national democratic government, with a treaty agreement safeguarding Britain's interest in Palestine and protecting all legitimate rights of the Jews.[46] Interestingly, the Mufti did not openly reject partition, as Raghib al-Nashashibi had done. He further agreed to start negotiations, through an Arab intermediary, with the Jewish Agency.[47] But the effort was unsuccessful.

The Mufti claimed that the British tried to influence him to accept partition. A high official told him Britain was planning free elections in Palestine. According to Amin, the official had added, smiling: "We know who is the people's choice and who would get a big majority of the votes." When that approach failed, according to the Mufti, the head of military intelligence sent him a warning that the British would do anything to protect their empire, including killing him if he got in their way. "Do not be stubborn," the message added. "Think of your life and have pity on your family and relatives."[48] There is no way to confirm this account.

However, three years later, in 1940, Winston Churchill did approve the kidnapping and assassination of the Mufti.[49]

The British also considered giving Raghib al-Nashashibi a P£10,000 bribe to support partition. The High Commissioner thought Raghib could be bought but nonetheless opposed the idea,[50] probably because he considered him an insincere and unreliable ally.[51]

The High Commissioner was more concerned about moving against the Mufti. His problem, he told the Colonial Office, was that he could find "no proof of undesirable activities" by the Mufti. He wanted to wait until Amin committed "some illegal act," yet he also wanted to be rid of him soon, to prevent him from arousing the population against partition and from supporting those who favored a disturbance.[52] Wauchope quoted a letter by the Arab Higher Committee to Arab kings in which the Mufti urged them "to work for rescuing the country from Imperialism and Jewish colonization and partition." This anti-British appeal, the High Commissioner wrote, was sufficient reason to deport him, although it should not be the reason given to the public.[53]

Wauchope could not wait for proof of illegal activities and sent the police to arrest the Mufti while he was attending a committee meeting on July 17, 1937. Someone, perhaps an English friend, warned him of the impending arrest, and he escaped through a back door to the Haram al-Sharif. The British hesitated to arrest him in the Muslim sanctuary, because of the negative reactions they expected from the Arab world.[54]

The Mufti continued to issue statements against partition from the Haram and went on meeting with supporters. He also organized and financed a Pan-Arab congress (called the National Arab Congress), which met in Bludan, Syria from September 8 to 10, 1937. The congress, attended by 400 leaders of the Arab world, rejected partition and reiterated its opposition to the Balfour Declaration and the mandate, and called for the establishment of an Arab Palestinian state which would guarantee British rights to Palestine under treaty.[55]

When violence resumed in late July and August 1937, the Mufti, still ensconced in the Haram, issued an appeal, repeated in mosques throughout Palestine, calling for peace and self-restraint and condemning acts of terror, even in retaliation against Jewish terror.[56] But on September 26, the violence flared up, when Palestinian extremists murdered L. Y. Andrews, the district commissioner of Galilee. Even though the Mufti and the Arab Higher Committee published a statement condemning the murder, the

British seized the opportunity to move against the Palestinian leadership. The Arab Higher Committee and the national committees were declared illegal, and 200 leaders were arrested. Some members of the committee were deported to the Seychelles. The Mufti was stripped of his chairmanship of the waqf committee.[57] Fearing imminent arrest by Muslim troops from India, he climbed down the walls of the Haram during the night of October 14; he was driven to Jaffa and fled by boat to Lebanon.[58] He would not return to Jerusalem until a brief visit in 1966.

The rebellion escalated the following day, perhaps on instructions from the Mufti. A rebel headquarters (known as al-Lajna al-Markaziyya li-l-Jihad) was set up at Damascus, administered by 'Izzat Darwaza under the guidance of the Mufti from his house in al-Zug, north of Beirut. Although the headquarters helped with the coordination and cooperation between independent rebel leaders, the local rebel leaders were not dependent on it. Besides their military operations, they had to levy taxes and set up administrative offices and courts in the north as the civil government was expelled from most Palestinian cities and towns. The Mufti tried to give the revolt a general direction, and since his popularity in Palestine had increased, he was more effective in persuading leaders to follow his policies; but guiding the revolt from outside Palestine meant he had less knowledge of and impact on the daily decisions of the revolt.[59]

The revolt reached its climax in the summer of 1938, when major cities were in the hands of the rebels. But after the Palestinians gained control over the old city of Jerusalem, the British struck back. With two divisions, squadrons of airplanes, the police force, the Transjordanian frontier forces, and 6000 Jewish auxiliaries, British troops outnumbered the Palestinians ten to one. The rebellion's ultimate defeat was ensured. The absence of political leadership on the scene did not help, nor did the abuses in tax collection and the political assassinations and executions of collaborators and moderates that were carried out by the rebels.[60] Such excesses forced the remaining collaborators and moderates to active defiance. Fakhri al-Nashashibi, a nephew of Raghib, for example, wrote a letter on behalf of many moderates challenging the leadership of the Mufti. But support for the Nashashibis was negligible, partly because of the radical mood of the public and partly because Fakhri was a suspected collaborator.[61]

Meanwhile, the prospect of world war loomed ever larger. Britain, under a new government and mindful of the need to station troops abroad and of Arab support, dropped the partition scheme. Instead, they proposed a round-table conference of Arabs and Jews, to be held in London. The Mufti was excluded, and he grudgingly sent Jamal al-Husayni as his representative. But the London conference, in February and March 1939, was a failure. In an effort to break out of the deadlock, the British unilaterally issued a White Paper in May, which reversed its former policy: Jewish immigration was now restricted to 75,000 during the next five years, after which immigration would be subject to Arab consent. Land transfers would be restricted in a few areas, and prohibited in most. Finally if Arab and Jewish relations were good, within ten years Palestine would become independent, and enter into treaty agreements with Britain.[62] Naturally, the Zionists rejected the White Paper.

The Arab Higher Committee was divided on the White Paper, but Palestinian rebels were not. They showed their defiance by issuing a declaration in which they rejected the leadership of the Husaynis, the Nashashibis, and the Arab kings who ruled by British sufference. They refused both a truce and the White Paper, and demanded total independence in an Arab Palestine. They backed these statements with a renewal of the violence.

Had the Mufti accepted the White Paper, he probably would have been challenged by the rebels in the field. But he rejected it. He did so partly because the British refused to deal with him directly even though he was the most popular Palestinian leader, and partly because the British refused to grant amnesty to the rebels, whose cooperation he needed. Moreover, the faltering revolt had made him bitter and uncompromising. The terms of the document were the most advantageous concessions that Britain had ever made. The Mufti's rejection clearly indicated that he was putting personal considerations and his idealism above practical politics.

The implementation of the terms of the White Paper was not conditional on Palestinian or Zionist acceptance. Although both rejected the policy, it was put into effect. The provisions concerning immigration and land transfer were implemented. But the establishment of a Palestine government was postponed by Winston Churchill, who was pro-Zionist and against the White Paper. The document was further undermined when the extent of the Nazi genocide against the Jewish people became known, causing world sympathy for the Zionist cause.

The Mufti's rejection of the White Paper ultimately did not affect its implementation. But the decision indicates the degree of his transformation during the Arab Revolt. When violence broke out in April 1936, he resisted joining the young radicals, believing he could maintain his dual policy of cooperation with the British and nonviolent resistance to Zionism. But the general strike and public pressure drew him in. He tried to contain the slide into violence, but the revolt had a force of its own. Political violence, British suppression, destruction, and a rising death toll forced him to choose sides. He became the moral leader of the revolt, and, after the announcement of the partition scheme and his exile, he became as uncompromising toward the British as he had been toward the Zionists.

The final crushing of the Arab rebellion only confirmed the Mufti in this path. The defeat took a high toll on the Arab economy, social fabric, and military and political structures. A conservative British estimate put the Palestinian death toll at over 3074. About 110 were hanged, and 6000 were under detention in 1939 alone—out of a population of 960,000.[63]

Above and beyond the national dimensions of the calamity, the Mufti suffered a personal loss of many relatives and friends, and the French High Commissioner of the Levant, Gabriel Puaux, reported that he was very depressed and contemplating suicide.[64] In any event, he had become a bitter man, a rebel in search of another anti-British revolt. He found one brewing in Iraq, and was determined to help it achieve its ends. The British were equally determined to stop him—if necessary by killing him.[65]

7. Iraq's Quest for Independence, 1939–1941

 GERMAN ADVANCES in Europe provided Iraqi Pan-Arab nationalists with an opportunity to challenge British discretionary power in Iraq, theoretically independent since 1932, and to press for a change in Britain's Palestine policy, over which there was considerable Iraqi resentment. The arrival of the Mufti of Jerusalem, Amin al-Husayni, in Baghdad in October 1939 strengthened the Pan-Arab challenge to British control and threatened the loss of British oil supplies and military bases in Iraq, Egypt, and Palestine.

Pinhas Rutenberg, chairman of the National Council of the Jewish community of Palestine, visited the British Foreign Office in London on May 23, 1940, to offer a "remedy" for the declining fortunes of the British in Iraq.[1] Rutenberg told an official, Bruce Lockhart, that the Arabs were awake and anti-European, and that the only one capable of leading them was the Mufti of Jerusalem. He criticized the British for allowing the Mufti to escape from Jerusalem in 1937 and from Beirut in 1939, and for allowing him to reside in Baghdad, where he became "the force" in Iraqi politics. The Mufti's movement, he warned, would spread like wildfire and cause much bloodshed if the Allies suffered a disaster in France. "There are times in history," Rutenberg continued, "when one must be sacrificed in order to save hundreds of thousands of lives. There are easy means of getting rid of the Mufti. They should be used—and used swiftly."[2]

The officials of the Foreign Office's Eastern Department agreed with Rutenberg's analysis of the rapid deterioration of the British position in the Arab world, and the Mufti's influence in it. But they considered his assassination proposal impractical. "Even if we were in the habit of indulging in political assassination," wrote an official, "the elimination of the Mufti would not make up for the intense outburst of feeling which his murder would surely provoke."[3] To which another replied: "Accidents will happen sometimes and they do not produce the same feeling as murder. But if Mr. Rutenberg believes what he says, he could quite well realize his ambition."[4]

The British official believed that Rutenberg was capable of assassination because a British intelligence report about Rutenberg's earlier life in Russia alleged that while he had been a member of the Social Revolutionary Committee, he had been ordered to kill an agent provocateur in January 1905. The report stated that he "killed Father Gapon in his own hands in a public lavatory."[5] Rutenberg became the chief of police under the revolutionary leader Aleksandr Kerensky before moving to Palestine when the Bolsheviks came to power. It was there that he obtained in 1921 a controversial concession from the British to establish the Palestine Electric Company, and where he used his wealth and prestige to work, through the Palestinian Opposition, against the Palestinian national movement led by Amin al-Husayni.[6]

The Foreign Office finally decided against Rutenberg's remedy. The head of the Eastern Department, Lacy Baggaley, wrote: "He [Rutenberg] is mistaken in thinking that the disappearance of the Mufti would make any difference. The Mufti is merely the man thrown up by the moment. If he had not been on the scene, someone else would have played his part."[7]

From Jerusalem to Baghdad. Al-Hajj Amin went to Iraq to resume his struggle against the British. As we have seen, he had not always been overtly anti-British, and indeed, from his appointment by the British as Mufti in 1921 until 1936, he had pursued a dual policy of coooperating with the British while uniting Palestinians against Zionism. To his mind, it was the Zionists who were the real threat to Palestinian national goals.

The British were too strong to evict, but could perhaps be induced through petitions, delegations, conferences, and demonstrations—and with the help of the Arab and Muslim worlds—to alter their pro-Zionist policy. In any case, they would eventually leave, as they now appeared to be leaving Egypt, Iraq, and Transjordan. For these reasons and, perhaps, for fear of losing his positions as Mufti and president of the Supreme Muslim Council, he rejected revolutionary armed methods.[8]

The Mufti had succeeded in uniting Palestinians behind the national goal of self-determination, even while being criticized by the Istiqlal party, the Opposition, and young nationalists for failing to reverse the British policy that allowed the Yishuv to grow. His 1929 proposal for an elected legislature based on proportional representation was not even considered by the British (even though it gave the High Commissioner veto power over legislation) because the Zionists opposed it. Jewish land purchases had continued, and Jewish immigration reached an all-time high in 1935 fueling Palestinian fears of domination by an eventual Jewish majority. When violence flared on April 15–19, 1936, and a general strike began to spread, the Mufti found it difficult to resist public demands that he assume the leadership of the strike and, later, of the revolt against further Jewish immigration and land acquisition, and for the establishment of a national government.[9]

The collapse of the three-year Arab rebellion, which the Mufti had led from his exile in Lebanon, left him a frustrated and bitter man. He was eager to resume the armed struggle in Palestine, but the rebels were overwhelmed and the population was exhausted. Furthermore, although he had enjoyed a relatively free political asylum in French-mandated Lebanon and had established a personal relationship with the French High Commissioner Puaux, the gathering clouds of war increased French-British cooperation and political restrictions on him. When France and Britain declared war on Germany on September 3, 1939, the Mufti was asked to announce his support for the Allies and was placed under virtual house arrest.[10]

He sent a letter to Puaux expressing his gratitude for the good treatment he had received during the previous two years and explaining why he had to leave: to spare the French worry over his presence and to seek to recover his personal liberty.[11] He bribed the French chief of police in Syria, Columbani, £500 to allow him to escape. Apparently the French knew that Columbani had been bribed by the Mufti at least once before, but they could not fire him. According to an intelligence report, Columbani was awarded his job after he had murdered a French politician, Stravinsky, "to save the French Government embarrassing revelations."[12] Disguised as a heavily veiled woman, the Mufti escaped to Baghdad on October 13, 1939, two years to the day after he had escaped from the British in Palestine.[13]

British Reaction. The Mufti was regarded by the Iraqi public as the leading Arab nationalist and by some as the spiritual heir of King Faysal, the leader of the Sharifian forces during the Arab Revolt of 1916 and the founder of modern Iraq. Consequently, the politicians, including the pro-British Prime Minister Nuri al-Sa'id, entertained and honored him at official banquets, provided him with comfortable accommodations, and gave him and hundreds of Palestinian émigrés generous subsidies.[14]

The British were worried about the Mufti's presence and reception in Iraq. Their policy had been, as one official put it, to "help him to oblivion" by ignoring him.[15] Now they considered actively opposing him because otherwise, the War Office warned, the "Mufti and his circus will fully exploit the situation to our detriment."[16] The Foreign Office asked Prime Minister Nuri al-Sa'id to obtain a promise from the Mufti not to get involved in politics.[17] The Palestinian leader pledged not to interfere in Iraqi politics and asked his followers to do the same, but he did not consider the pledge to include political activities on behalf of Palestine and Arab nationalism.[18]

Nuri tried to reconcile the Mufti and the British. He had earlier tried to bridge the gap between Palestinians and British officials during the Arab Revolt (1936–39) and at the London Conference on Palestine (1939). Indeed, the Palestine problem was a major obstacle in Iraqi-British relations. If Nuri could contribute to its settlement, he could secure some credit and stem the tide of Iraqi Arab nationalist resentment against British domination in Iraq and Palestine. He advised the Mufti to declare himself for the Allies and to criticize the Germans.[19] Amin considered the suggestion, but was reluctant to support the Britain that had destroyed Palestinian villages, executed and imprisoned Palestinian fighters, and exiled their leaders.[20] Nuri also sounded out the British, but they refused to change their position on the Mufti, which was that Britain would have nothing to do with the leader of terrorism and assassinations in Palestine during the Arab Revolt.[21]

Actually, terrorism had been employed by all sides during the revolt. Palestinian guerrilla warfare included violence against British officials, Jewish civilians, and members of the Opposition, some of whom were collaborators. The British and Zionist forces, in an attempt to suppress the rebellion, indiscriminately shot and bombed civilians, used suspects as human minesweepers, executed Palestinians for minor offenses, and cooperated with the Opposition to assassinate rebels. Nonetheless, political assassination was used more frequently by the supporters of the Mufti, resulting in the deaths of innocent people as well as of collaborators and opposition members. It also led to family feuds that undermined the revolt.[22]

The Mufti's role in the violence is not always clear, primarily because he did not have direct control over military operations, which were undertaken by local leaders. Neither the British nor anyone else had sufficient proof of his involvement.[23] Yet his influence in Palestine was such that it is difficult to believe, as he and his supporters later claimed, that he did not know about, acquiesce in, or even plan at least some of the violence against his opponents.[24]

British aversion to the Mufti, however, was not based on their moral indignation, but on his rejection of British policy in Palestine. The Colonial Office wrote the Foreign Office that they would consider allowing his return to Palestine if he gave up his active opposition to the British and subscribed to the White Paper, declared himself for the Allies, and "if it were also clear that he had lost all influence for effective harm and that his return would flutter no dove-cotes."[25] Otherwise, the British wanted him neither in Palestine nor in Iraq. So their man in Iraq, Nuri, advised the Mufti to go to America to gain American sympathy. The Mufti declined.[26]

The Mufti's Role in Iraqi Politics. The Mufti spent the first few months in Iraq establishing personal relationships with the political and military elite. He initially refrained from interfering in internal politics,[27] but against a background of growing turmoil over the course to be followed with the outbreak of war, the Arab nationalists among the young politicians and the military increasingly sought his counsel. The Mufti's advice was unequivocal: obtain arms for Iraq; cooperate with the British, but limit the 1930 Anglo-Iraqi treaty (which provided for mutual military aid in time for war); avoid antagonizing the Axis; and if Russia, Japan, and Italy joined the war, rise in revolt against Britain and France. In such an event, the revolt should start in Palestine, not Syria, under the leadership of the Syrian soldier Fawzi al-Qawuqji in order to compel the British to remove all Zionist forces and recognize the independence of Palestine.[28]

Pro-British Iraqis such as Nuri, meanwhile, wanted Iraq to break relations with the Axis, declare war against them, and send two army divisions to fight with the British. Nuri was able to make Iraq break relations with Germany as Britain requested, but popular sentiment against sending troops was too strong. General Husayn Fawzi, an Iraqi friend of the Mufti, captured the public mood against Nuri's proposal by saying: "Supposing the two Iraqi divisions were to pass through Aleppo and an Aleppan were to ask an Iraqi soldier: 'O brother, where are you going?' and the Iraqi were to answer: 'To the Balkans to fight the Germans,' what do you expect from the Aleppan except to say: 'Allah, Allah, O brother, what about Syria and Palestine?' "[29]

Three trends worked to the advantage of the Mufti and other Arab nationalists. First, there was increasing friction between Iraq and Britain over British unwillingness or inability to fulfill its promise to arm Iraq, and over Iraq's reluctance to declare war against the Axis in fulfillment of its 1930 treaty obligations. Second, public expectation for full independence from Britain, which had granted Iraq formal independence in 1932, increased with the declaration of war and with each British setback. Axis propaganda beamed at the Arab world through German and Italian Arabic radio stations[30] encouraged this expectation by reminding the Arabs of British imperialism and pro-Zionist policy in Palestine, and by stressing German victories which could ultimately free the Arabs. Third, there was increasing resentment over the Palestine problem. As historian Stephen Longrigg pointed out: "No element in all Iraqi-British relations of the period 1937 to 1941 was more powerful in poisoning them than the tragically mishandled Palestine Question."[31]

The Palestine question also poisoned relations between the Mufti and Nuri. Between November 1939 and June 1940 thirty-nine Arabs were condemned to death in Palestine in secret British trials. The Mufti personally knew most of the condemned rebels or their families. He received desperate appeals to intervene, but all he could do was call upon fellow Muslims and Arabs to intercede with the British. In one such effort, he wrote an Indian friend that the British were annihilating the "best element," whose only crime had been "to defend the country."[32] In his memoirs, Rashid 'Ali al-Kilani, the Arab nationalist leader of the ill-fated anti-British coup in April 1941 and at the time chief of the Royal Diwan (palace), described a scene in which the Mufti asked Prime Minister Nuri to intercede with the British to spare the life of a rebel. When Nuri casually refused to intervene, the usually placid Mufti became very angry and later told al-Kilani that the Arab nation was threatened with ruin if people like Nuri were to direct its affairs. The rebel was executed the next day.[33]

Aside from the ideological problem, there was a personal rivalry between the two men. The Mufti had never been able to countenance the sharing of power and constituency, particularly with leaders of an independent bent of mind. This had been true in Palestine, where his entourage had been uncritical and compliant followers and where his relations with independent and articulate nationalist leaders had been stormy. It was equally true abroad: he had the same problem with al-Kilani in Germany between 1941 and 1945, and with Nasir in Egypt in the 1950s.

Nuri al-Sa'id realized that public opinion was turning against him and coalescing around the nationalists, who were being aided and abetted by the Mufti. He had not wanted Amin to come to Iraq in the first place, but once in Baghdad, he tried unsuccessfully to influence him and to reconcile him with the British. His efforts to help resolve the Palestine question had failed. By March 1940, Nuri was isolated in Parliament, unpopular with his people, many of whom saw him as a traitor who subordinated the Arab nationalist cause to Britain's. He resigned on March 31, 1940, and recommended Rashid 'Ali al-Kilani to take his place.[34]

Nuri thought that by relinquishing the premiership in favor of Rashid 'Ali, he could secure the latter's support for a pro-British foreign policy.[35] Al-Kilani, however, was reluctant to form a government, fearing that the military, which had supported Nuri, might intervene. The Mufti, cognizant of the opportunities presented by an Arab nationalist power, abandoned his promise of nonintervention and persuaded Rashid 'Ali to become prime minister. Since the latter needed the support of the "Golden Square" (a Pan-Arab, anti-colonialist group of four officers who had been an important factor in Iraqi politics since the late 1930s) the Mufti invited the colonels, with whom he had considerable influence, to his house and convinced them that Rashid 'Ali deserved their support. Al-Kilani then agreed to set up a government in which he was premier and Nuri was minister of foreign affairs.[36]

Nuri made one more attempt at conciliation over the Palestine problem. This took place during a semi-official visit to Baghdad in July 1940 by Colonel S. F. Newcombe and the Mufti's representatives, Jamal al-Husayni and Musa al-'Alami. A firm proposal was drawn up in which the Mufti accepted the White Paper of 1939 as the basis for a settlement of the Palestine problem. In return for British implementation of the White Paper, which restricted Jewish immigration into Palestine to 75,000 during five years, restricted land purchases, and pledged independence for Palestine, with an Arab majority, after ten years, the Mufti would support the British war effort and the Iraqis would supply two divisions to fight with the British forces.[37] Nuri took the proposal to General Archibald Wavell, commander of the Middle East Command, and Newcombe took it to Winston Churchill, the new prime minister. But Churchill refused to enforce what he called the "anti-Jewish policy" of the White Paper. He also accepted the Zionist request to organize a Jewish brigade in Palestine, despite warnings that arming the Jews would antagonize the Arabs and the troops could be used later against the British.[38]

Failure to extract concessions from the British on Palestine, the installation of an Iraqi government headed by the Arab nationalist al-Kilani, German air attacks on Britain, and the Italian offensive in North Africa seem to have convinced the Mufti that the time for Arab independence and unity had come. In preparation for a revolt, he sought to unite the Arab leaders who were in Iraq in the summer of 1940.

A secret Arab Committee—composed of leaders from Syria, Iraq, Palestine, and Transjordan with the Mufti as their spokesman—was established. Their goal was to achieve independence through rebellion and then to unite the liberated Arab countries into an Arab nation. The Mufti was also the leader of two other committees, with which the Arab Committee was sometimes confused: a Palestinian group of former associates of the Mufti concerned with Palestinian matters, and a Committee of Seven made up of six Iraqi leaders, including al-Kilani, and the Mufti. As the head of all three committees, Amin was in a better position to conduct negotiations with the Axis aimed at receiving material and diplomatic support for the revolt and obtaining a declaration of recognition of Arab independence and unity.[39]

Assassins and Rebels. The British knew about these negotiations, which were conducted between July 1940 and April 1941, through the Mufti's private secretary in Berlin and a German Foreign Ministry representative in Baghdad. They also knew that the Mufti and the Iraqi Arab nationalists were gaining in power over Nuri al-Sa'id and other pro-British politicians,

and were causing Iraq to resist British demands. If Iraq were to conclude
a secret agreement with the Axis, the British would suffer a major setback
in the Middle East, jeopardizing oil supplies and the overland and air routes
to India which, according to the Middle East commander in chief, would
enable the Germans to threaten India.[40] This kind of analysis led the British
to consider several kinds of actions against Iraq and the Mufti, who was
by late 1940 considered the most influential and respected man in Iraq.[41]

In October 1940 the India Office suggested to London that the Mufti be
kidnapped. The secretary of state for India, Leo Amery, wrote: "Would it
be possible for a few bold lads to kidnap the Mufti in Baghdad, run him
South by car out to a waiting aeroplane, and then to Cyprus? Nashashibis
in Palestine, Jews and indeed all the Middle Eastern world would laugh
and a real big danger might be averted."[42] The secretary of state for the
colonies replied that the suggestion "made us think," but that it was not
practical. While the Jews and the Nashashibis would be "pleased," it would
be "difficult to explain it" to Iraq, Egypt, and Arabia, where the action
would be "widely resented." Also, continued the colonial secretary, the
Mufti had his own private bodyguards, who would resist: "Perhaps the
Mufti himself would be killed, which, however desirable in itself, would
be embarrassing."[43]

The British chiefs of staff reached a different conclusion. "The Mufti's
removal," they reported, "is unlikely to have ill effects, since it is strength,
not weakness, which is admired in the Arab world." So they recommended
to the cabinet of Winston Churchill that the Mufti be killed.[44]

After a brief discussion of the chiefs of staff report in the cabinet, Churchill, according to the Foreign Office, approved the assassination of the
Mufti in early November 1940. The Foreign Office continued to doubt the
usefulness of such an action. Wrote Baxter of the Eastern Department:
"Even if the murder were successfully carried out, it would probably not
turn out to our advantage, whereas if the attempt were unsuccessful . . .
the results might be disastrous . . . it would alienate Arab opinion
throughout the Middle East."[45] For that reason the Foreign Office hoped
that they would not be the ones to "carry out" the assassination.[46] Apparently, it was left up to the Chiefs of Staff, whose position in Iraq was
deteriorating rapidly in early 1941, despite British success in forcing the
al-Kilani government to resign in January.

The showdown between the pro-British element (Nuri al-Sa'id, the regent, Amin 'Abd al-Ilah, and their supporters) and the Arab nationalists

(the Mufti, Rashid 'Ali al-Kilani, and the Golden Square) reached its climax in a coup on April 1, 1941, led by the four colonels of the Golden Square, which reinstalled al-Kilani as prime minister. The new regime promised to uphold the Anglo-Iraqi treaty of 1930, but relations with Britain continued to deteriorate. Winston Churchill informed Leo Amery, on April 8: "The situation in Iraq has turned sour."[47] The British decided to act.

While British troop reinforcements began entering the country through Basra, General Percival Wavell, head of the Middle East Command, ordered the release from a Palestine jail of David Raziel, a leader of the outlawed Zionist underground organization Irgun Zeva'i Le'ummi, and a few of his companions. They were to go to Iraq, disguise themselves as Arabs, kidnap or kill the Mufti, and destroy oil installations. The Irgunists claim that it had been their idea to "acquire" the Mufti.[48] Be that as it may, on May 18, 1941, a British plane brought the Irgun group, headed by Raziel and Ya'kov Meridor, to the besieged RAF base at Habbaniyya, Iraq. Before they could fulfill the mission, however, Raziel was killed by a German plane, which strafed his car on May 20. The mission was aborted.[49]

The German plane that killed Raziel was one of the few that saw action since fighting had begun in early May. The Iraqis had called upon the Germans to provide help as soon as Churchill began dispatching troops to Iraq in late April, thereby thwarting the nationalists' attempt to free Iraq from British tutelage. But the Germans, busy with preparations to invade the USSR, sent only one squadron, part of which supported Iraqi artillery which had surrounded Britain's Habbaniyya air base. Other Iraqi forces had surrounded the British embassy compound in Baghdad. Meanwhile Wavell had brought in British troops from India and a mobile force from Palestine which included British and Jewish troops, Amir 'Abdullah's Arab Legion, and the Transjordanian Frontier Force (Arab troops recruited by the Palestine government). In a desperate attempt, the Mufti issued a fatwa urging Arabs and Muslims to help Iraq free herself from British imperialism. The fatwa was the most anti-British statement he had ever made, pointing out how the British had promised to free the Arabs from the Ottomans but instead had divided the Arab world and imposed British rule, and committed "unheard of barbarism" in Palestine.[50] After a month of fighting and another show of force at the outskirts of Baghdad by the Arab Legion and British troops on May 29, the poorly armed and disorganized Iraqis gave up the fight.[51] After the British victory, a mob attacked the Jewish quarter in Baghdad on June 1–2. Neither the British troops nor the regent tried to stop the two-day pogrom until after 120 Iraqi Jews had been murdered.[52]

The Arab nationalist leaders fled the country on May 29, though some, including the four army colonels behind the revolt, were captured and hanged by the pro-British government of Nuri al-Sa'id. Their revolt had been a genuine attempt to achieve full Iraqi independence at what seemed to be an opportune moment. In fact, however, their revolt was premature: the Iraqi military was hardly prepared to challenge Britain's military power, and the British Empire could not afford to lose its oil supplies and military bases while it was in a desperate struggle with Germany in Europe and North Africa. Another miscalculation was Arab nationalist confidence in material German support, promised in the winter of 1940–41. Even if Germany had sent sufficient troops and the combined German and Iraqi forces had defeated the British, there is no reason to believe that Germany would have honored the promises of Arab independence or been less perfidious with the Mufti and al-Kilani than Britain had been with Sharif Husayn in World War I. Once again, the Arabs may well have fought for the privilege of exchanging imperial masters.

The Mufti and his colleagues managed to escape from Baghdad on the night of May 29 for Iran, where Riza Shah gave them political asylum. While in Tehran, the Mufti learned from the Iraqi ex-minister of defense, Salah al-Din al-Sabbagh, that Britain planned to invade Iran. He revealed the plan to the Iranian foreign minister, but the latter dismissed it. After Germany invaded Russia on June 22, the Mufti decided to move to Turkey, but he was refused both an entry and a transit visa.[53] He next considered Sa'udi Arabia, but British influence there was strong, and in any case, he thought the trip would be hazardous. Finally, he applied for a visa to Afghanistan, but while awaiting a reply, Britain and Russia invaded Iran with such speed, two days, that he could not escape from Tehran in time. Riza Shah abdicated in favor of his son Muhammad Riza, who agreed to cooperate with the British.

The new Shah's officials now tried to flush out the Mufti and his colleagues by inviting them to meet the foreign minister and promising that they would not be harmed. The Mufti, who had hidden in the Japanese legation and then moved to another refuge in a private house, refused to come out. Most of his colleagues did and were arrested. Wavell, according to the Mufti, offered a reward of £25,000 to anyone who captured the

Mufti dead or alive. He thus remained in hiding in Tehran for several weeks. The Iranian police together with the British military police almost captured him, but he managed to escape to another house.

Then on September 23, Amin, clean shaven and dressed in a suit, took a taxi through Russian-occupied territory toward Turkey. Although the Russians were forewarned by their British allies, they did not recognize him at the army checkpoints. But the Mufti realized he was being followed by a British intelligence officer whom he had known in Tehran. He and his Armenian driver created a problem between the suspected agent and some Russian soldiers, and the diversion enabled them to continue. His car was stopped by two Russians who boarded the car and sat beside him, but it turned out they only wanted a ride. With the help of a Japanese diplomat, he crossed the Turkish border. He had not been in Turkey since his days as an officer in the Ottoman army during World War I, and he would have liked to have stayed: he spoke the language, he liked the people and the country, and Palestine was not far away. But Turkey was allied with Britain, and if he were discovered, he would be turned over to the British. So he planned to proceed to Italy via Bulgaria after a short stay in Istanbul.[54]

In the meantime, the Mufti's wife, young children, and some relatives were captured by the British and put under house arrest in Iraq. They were then moved to Ahwaz in the south of the country, where they were kept for fifty-two days in the shabby local jail for common criminals—ten women and children in a small cell.

The British sources do not explain why it was necessary to imprison the Husayni women and children, particularly since they were not involved in politics. Apparently the Foreign Office considered "their potential value as hostages,"[55] but there is no evidence that they were used as such. Finally, the family was herded into a lorry, driven for seven hours over rough roads to Basra, and put on a train for the long journey to Baghdad. They were to be immediately put on another train to Jerusalem, but by then some of the children were ill. When a doctor warned the authorities of the danger of such a journey, the British allowed the group to stay for a few days before continuing to Jerusalem.[56]

The Mufti's friends and colleagues who were captured by the Shah's police in Tehran were turned over to the British. They too were taken to the Ahwaz jail for a month, before being sent to Rhodesia. The conditions

8. The Nazi Years

 NO PERIOD in the Mufti's life is more controversial and subject to distortion than the years of World War II. Zionists were so eager to prove him guilty of collaboration and war crimes that they exaggerated his connections with the Nazis. The Mufti and other Arabs, on the other hand, were so busy justifying his statements and actions in the Axis countries that they ignored the obvious and overwhelming fact that the Mufti had cooperated with the most barbaric regime in modern times.

Negotiations with Germany. In an effort to establish the early cooperation of the Mufti with the Axis, many partisan writers such as Lukasz Hirszowicz have claimed that the Nazis inspired and financed, through the Mufti, the Arab Revolt of 1936–39.[1] There is no reliable evidence for such claims.[2] The cause of the revolt, as pointed out earlier, was the fear that British policy and the Zionist program would inevitably lead to Jewish domination or the dispossession of the Palestinians. The revolt was sustained by support inside and outside of Palestine.

Similar claims are made about the Iraqi Revolt of 1941. By focusing on Arab-Nazi ideological "affinity," writers have misrepresented the central goal of Arab nationalist cooperation with the Axis: the defeat of a common enemy. The leaders of the Iraqi revolt were Arab nationalists who shared the sentiment expressed by one of the four colonels of the Golden Squares, Salah al-Din al-Sabbagh: "I do not believe in the democracy of the English nor in the Nazism of the Germans nor in the Bolshevism of the Russians. I am an Arab Muslim."[3]

Before 1940, neither the German Auswärtiges Amt (Foreign Office) nor the Mufti was prepared to begin cooperation. Germany was not ready to go beyond friendly statements and negligible financial support, because the Middle East was of only peripheral importance. In addition, its relations with the Arabs were constrained by Italy's and Britain's imperial interests in the region and by the interests of the Templars, some 1200 religious Germans who had settled in Palestine during the late Ottoman Period. Moreover, the Nazis viewed the Arabs with contempt. Arabs in Germany received the discriminatory treatment consistent with Nazi racial theories. Indeed, Adolf Hitler described them as "half apes."[4] The Mufti began his contacts with the Axis in mid-1937, but these were limited to tentative efforts to determine the basis and benefits of a diplomatic relationship.[5]

The outbreak of the war changed the strategic picture for both sides. The war against England was reinforced by Axis operations against Egypt, and Middle East oil and supply routes became important to the Wehrmacht.[6] The Axis began giving generous subsidies to the Mufti in Baghdad, and the Germans modified their racial theory of the Arabs, who were upgraded from a primitive people belonging to the lower races (though above Jews, gypsies, and blacks) to those possessing Nordic influences. The Mufti's fair hair and blue eyes convinced Hitler that the Arab leader "has more than one Aryan among his ancestors and one who may be descended from the best Roman stock."[7]

At the same time, the Mufti was becoming increasingly disenchanted with the British. The Palestine authorities continued to execute Palestinian rebels.[8] Churchill rejected the Newcombe plan in August 1940, shelved the 1939 White Paper, and accepted Zionist requests to arm Jews in Palestine.[9] These decisions coincided with the German bombardment and blockade of Britain in August.

The Mufti, who had been corresponding with the Axis and supported Iraq's negotiations with Germany in July 1940, sent his German-speaking private secretary, 'Uthman Kamal Haddad, on a secret mission in August to negotiate with the Auswärtiges Amt.[10] Haddad, under the name of Tawfiq 'Ali al-Shakir, stopped in Ankara for discussions with Franz von Papen, German ambassador to Turkey. He then proceeded to Berlin under the name of Max Müller and met Joachim von Ribbentrop, the foreign minister.[11]

The Mufti presented himself through Haddad as the leader of a secret Pan-Arab committee composed of leaders from the Arab world. At the time of the Haddad mission, he was the most popular Arab leader in Iraq, Syria, and Palestine, and his influence was spreading in the rest of the Arab world. He thus sought to convey the impression that he was in a better position than any other Arab leader to negotiate on behalf of the Arabs.[12]

Amin's negotiating position was contained in a six-point draft declaration which essentially demanded that the Axis acknowledge Arab independence and unity.[13] The Germans, in turn, asked for diplomatic and economic relations and for Iraqi resistance and Palestinian revolt against the British.[14]

The Mufti's demands were too far-reaching for the Germans, whose allies had interests in the Middle East—Spain in Morocco; Vichy France in Tunis, Algeria, Syria, and Lebanon; Italy in Libya and beyond. Indeed, the Axis powers were about to conclude a Tripartite Pact (Sept. 22, 1940) which would recognize Italy's sphere of influence in the Arab world.[15] When Haddad heard of this, he protested that the Arabs would never accept Italian hegemony. The Germans replied that Germany would not abandon its ties with the Middle East and that, in any case, the agreement with Italy was temporary.[16] Haddad returned to Baghdad to report on his talks.

On January 22, 1941, when the political confrontation between the pro-British and Arab nationalist elements in Iraq was gathering momentum, the Mufti again sent his private secretary to Berlin with a draft declaration and a letter to Hitler. Amin tried to impress upon Hitler his leading position in the Arab world, and the vital role the Arabs could play in disrupting British imperial communications and denying Britain Middle East oil.[17] The draft declaration echoed the Arab position taken in the August-October negotiations. Haddad also asked for arms to be used by Iraq to invade Palestine.[18]

The Führer replied to the Mufti on April 3, 1941, through an Auswärtiges Amt representative, E. von Weizsacker. According to Haddad and the

Mufti, he stated that Germany did not aim to seize any part of the Arab countries. On the contrary, Germany recognized the total independence of some Arab countries and hoped the rest would achieve independence, and would give military aid if the Arabs fought the English. The Germans hoped that an Arab representative would continue the discussions, which had thus far been inconclusive.[19] When the Mufti fled Tehran and reached Rome, he was ready to resume his negotiations with the Axis in Rome and in Berlin on the same basis as he had indicated through letters and through his private secretary. Now, however, he could negotiate directly with Benito Mussolini and Hitler.

Negotiations with Mussolini and Hitler. The Mufti had a meeting with Mussolini in October 1941, shortly after he arrived in Rome from Istanbul. He outlined the Arab demands: full independence for all parts of the Arab world and the rescue of Palestine from British imperialism and Zionism. He stressed that the struggle against the Jews was not of a religious nature, but for Palestinian existence and for an independent Palestine. Mussolini told the Mufti that he knew about Arab affairs, had studied the Qur'an, as well as Muslim history and religion, "unlike those" (motioning toward an aide). The Duce said he would agree to Arab demands. Concerning Palestine, he added that "if the Jews want [a state] they should establish Tel Aviv in America."[20] The Mufti was encouraged by the conversation, but he wanted Mussolini's statements in a public declaration. He also knew that the center of Axis power was not Rome, but Berlin. So within two days of his talks with the Italians, he left for Berlin to speak with Hitler.

In his 95-minute conversation with Hitler on November 28, 1941, the Mufti stressed the need for a statement to the Arabs in which Germany would disavow imperial interests in the Arab world and would support Arab independence, especially the independence and unity of Palestine, Syria, and Iraq. Such a statement would, Amin insisted, rally support for a revolt. He disputed the objection which von Ribbentrop, whom he had met with earlier that day, had raised, that an Arab revolt would occur prematurely if such a declaration were made public.[21] As head of the Pan-Arab committee, the Mufti told Hitler, he would order the revolt at a strategic moment.[22] The revolt would be preceded by appeals to the Arabs from the Mufti and by the formation of an Arab legion. The Mufti's real objective in asking for a declaration was probably to obtain Germany's public and written commitment to the independence of the Arab world, in clear and unequivocal language, so that Germany would not be able to renege on its promises as Britain had done in World War I.

Hitler pointed out, however, that such a statement would be premature. An Axis declaration anticipating a solution for Syria and Lebanon, and, by implication, French colonies in Africa, would strengthen the supporters of Charles de Gaulle, leader of the Free French, and thus require the presence of a larger part of the German army than was then needed in France. Realizing that Hitler was firmly opposed to a declaration, the Mufti asked for a secret agreement on the lines which he had suggested for the declaration. Hitler agreed.[23]

The secret agreement came in the form of identical letters from von Ribbentrop and Count Ciano to the Mufti on April 28, 1942, and to Rashid 'Ali al-Kilani, the ex-prime minister of Iraq, who was likewise in exile in Germany. Despite their agreement on Arab nationalist objectives the Mufti and al-Kilani were rivals for leadership in Berlin. By 1942, however, the Germans considered the Mufti the religious and Pan-Arab leader and al-Kilani, despite his former title, a local leader, yet one they could not ignore, since his country was expected to fall under the German sphere of influence. The key paragraph stated that Germany and Italy were ready "to grant to the Arab countries in the Near East, now suffering under British oppression, every possible aid in their fight for liberation; to recognize their sovereignty and independence; to agree to their federation if this is desired by the interested parties; as well as to the abolition of the Jewish National Homeland in Palestine."[24]

The agreement was obviously the outcome of compromises on both sides. The Mufti clearly obtained Axis commitment for aid, the abolition of the Jewish national home, and the recognition of the sovereignty and independence of Arab countries. But which Arab countries? None were specified, and no mention was made of North Africa. Nor did the agreement mention Arab unity, and "federation" was subject to the desire of "interested parties." So despite his later claims,[25] the Mufti did not obtain clear and definitive promises on all points. Besides, there was no assurance, given Hitler's perfidy, that the Axis would honor the agreement. An Egyptian journalist in Berlin asked the Mufti in 1942 how he, the Mufti, could trust the Germans and the Italians to keep their word when the British and French did not keep theirs in World War I. Amin reportedly answered that he did not trust the Axis any more than the British, and that if after conquering the Middle East the Axis decided to stay, he would fight them the way he fought the British; and, he felt, they would be easier to evict than the British.[26]

During the first two years of negotiations with the Axis, the Mufti had done very little to help Germany and Italy. Now that he had a commitment from the Axis, he had to fulfill his side of the bargain: spread propaganda, recruit Arab troops, promote sabotage, and call for revolt. After settling near Berlin (at Oybin), he began his activities in Germany about two weeks after he received the Axis commitment to the Arabs. He issued an appeal to the Arab world in his own voice from Berlin through the Bari radio station in southeastern Italy. He reportedly said on May 10, 1942, in reference to two of the members of the Golden Square who were executed in 1941 for their part in their bid for independence from Britain: "O Arabs, use and avenge your martyrs. Avenge your honor. Fight for your independence. I, Mufti of Palestine, declare this war as a holy war against the British yoke of injustice, indecency and tyranny. We fear not death, if in death there is life and liberty."[27] There were many such appeals through the radio and by means of pamphlets, which encouraged his supporters to rebel but did not cause any revolt in the Arab world.

The Mufti also began in late 1942 to help organize Arab recruits into an Arab Legion called the Deutsch-Arabische Lehrabteilung (DAL). He first suggested the idea to Mussolini in October 1941 and to Hitler in November 1941. To his mind, the DAL was a response to the Zionist recruitment in Palestine approved by Churchill in late 1940, and to the demands of Arabs living in Axis countries to free their own countries. He insisted that the recruits—Arabs living in Axis territory and Arab prisoners of war captured by the Germans in North Africa and Greece while fighting the Allies[28]— should be used only for Arab objectives, fighting under Arab command and flag, and on Palestinian, Syrian or Egyptian soil.[29] When the Wehrmacht placed the DAL under the command of Helmuth Felmy and proposed to send the unit to the eastern front, the Mufti put up strong opposition.

The Mufti's other military-related activities included helping to recruit Muslims for Yugoslavia and Albania in 1943 to fight in Croatia and Bosnia against the Communist forces of Tito and the Serbian forces of Draža Mihailović. He also supported the anti-Communist efforts of the Muslim Crimean Tartars. Finally, in 1944 and early 1945, he briefed sabotage expeditions in Palestine, Iraq, and Transjordan.[30]

The results of these efforts were an abysmal failure. The Arab Legion's activities were insignificant and those of the Muslim troops in the Balkans were a fiasco. The sabotage teams in Arab countries were either captured or killed.[31] But the failure lay less with Amin, who played little part in the actual military and strategic planning, than with Germany, which failed to adequately mobilize its diplomatic, propaganda, and military machine for a challenge to the Allies in the Middle East.

After the war, Zionist groups called on Britain to try the Mufti on charges of collaboration or treason.[32] Britain replied that since he was not a British subject he could be tried neither as a traitor nor as a collaborator. The Foreign Office asked the High Commissioner of Palestine for evidence concerning the Mufti's wrongdoing in Palestine, but the High Commissioner had none.[33]

The Zionists likewise sought the Mufti's indictment as a war criminal who had collaborated in the extermination of the Jews. To this end, the Jewish Agency for Palestine sent the British Foreign Office a number of documents on February 26, 1946, which they hoped would result in such a trial. These included letters captured in 1945 which had been written by the Mufti—mostly in unsigned draft form—in an effort to thwart Axis plans to exchange Germans residing in Palestine for Jews from German-controlled territory in 1943 and 1944. A letter of May 13, 1943 to the German foreign minister, for example, objected to the planned transfer of 4000 Jewish children and 500 adults to Palestine.[34] On June 28, 1943, he wrote the Romanian foreign minister regarding 1800 children and 200 adults leaving from Romania for Palestine.[35] He wrote a similar letter to the Hungarian foreign minister on the same day, bringing to his attention the emigration certificates of 900 Jewish children and 100 adults. In this last letter he suggested that if it were necessary to remove the Jews from Hungary, then it would be better to send them where they would be "under active supervision, for example in Poland."[36] The countries acknowledged the Mufti's letters, wrote that they would consider his request, but gave no commitment.

In a tart letter on July 25, 1944 to von Ribbentrop, the Mufti complained that some Jews had been exchanged on July 2, 1944, thus indicating that an earlier request (of June 5, 1944) had not been heeded. In protesting the exchange, he reminded von Ribbentrop of a German declaration on November 2, 1943, which promised to destroy the Jewish national home in Palestine and engage in the "battle against world Jewry" (den Kampf gegen das Weltjudentum).[37]

Zionist material sent to the British in February 1946 also included two other documents. The first was a statement by Rudolf Kasztner, a leader of the Jewish Rescue and Relief Committee in Budapest, in which he quoted Adolf Eichmann as saying in response to a request for the emigration of Hungarian Jews to Palestine: "I am a personal friend of the Grand-Mufti. We have promised him that no European Jew would enter Palestine anymore" and that he [Eichmann] "would be willing to recommend the emigration of a group of 1,681 Hungarian Jews, on condition that the group should not go to Palestine. They may get to any country but Palestine." Kasztner also quoted a colleague of Eichmann, Dieter von Wisliczeny, as saying: "According to my opinion, the Grand-Mufti who has been in Berlin since 1941 played a role in the decision of the German Government to exterminate the European Jews."[38] Another document indicates that the Mufti accepted an invitation to become an honorary member of and speak at an Anti-Jewish Congress in 1944.[39]

The Zionist documents were not taken seriously by the British. In a memo for internal consumption, a Foreign Office official wrote: "The material in this paper is very vague and would certainly not be considered as decisive evidence against the Mufti for having participated in any atrocities against the Jews."[40] Other officials wrote, also for internal use, that the Zionists were using this meager evidence for propaganda purposes, to discredit the Mufti and the Palestinians.[41] Still another official concluded that though the Mufti had committed acts hostile to the Allies he "is not responsible for acts of atrocity according to our official information." This was true, but it was also likely the British were not eager to try the Mufti, who was still popular in the Arab world at a time when they were involved in treaty negotiations with the Egyptians and in trying to solve the Palestine problem.[42]

The Mufti was never brought to trial, but the issue of his role in Nazi Germany resurfaced during the 1961 Eichmann trial in Jerusalem. At that time, a team of Israeli police under Shlomo Ben-Elkanah compiled hundreds of pages of documents concerning contacts between the Mufti and Germans between 1933 and 1944. Yet most of the evidence was not new and had been publicized in 1946 by the Jewish Agency, particularly the testimonies of Kasztner and Wisliczeny concerning the Mufti's association with Eichmann and his attempts to stop Jewish emigration to Palestine. Eichmann's own testimony confirmed that the Mufti and Eichmann were not close associates, and that Wisliczeny had mistaken Musa 'Abdullah al-Husayni for the Mufti. Moreover, although the official inquiry was considered to be the most comprehensive and incriminating evidence ever compiled against the Mufti,[43] it left unanswered such basic issues as his impact on Jewish emigration, how well he knew Eichmann, and what he knew about the Final Solution. Indeed, the thousands of captured German documents used by the many writers on the subject have produced no hard evidence of the Mufti's participation in atrocities beyond his attempts to stop the Jewish emigration to Palestine that he saw as leading to displacement or eviction of his own people.[44]

Zionist accusations have prompted Arab politicians and writers to attempt to ignore, downplay, or justify the Mufti's activities during the war. Their arguments have been, in essence, that he was driven to Germany by the British, who had tried to arrest and incarcerate him since 1937, and that while there he worked for the liberation of Palestine and Arab and Muslim countries from imperialism. He cooperated with Germany for political opportunism—the same reason Winston Churchill and Franklin D. Roosevelt cooperated with the despot Stalin. It was Churchill, after all, who said he would ally with the devil himself against Hitler.[45]

Neither Zionist accusations nor Arab justifications have enhanced our understanding of the extent of the Mufti's cooperation with the Nazis, largely because the apparent purpose for studies about his years in Germany are an extension of the Arab-Israeli propaganda war. Only a thorough and nonpartisan study, based on captured German documents, could elucidate the role of the Mufti in Germany.

9. Diplomacy and War, 1946–1948

 WITH THE collapse of Nazi Germany in 1945, the Mufti found himself, for the sixth time in his life, on the run, since he did not want to fall into the hands of the invading American or Soviet troops. On May 7, 1945, he flew from Bad Gastein in Austria, where he had been living since early 1945, to Berne, Switzerland. When the Swiss refused him asylum, he tried his luck with the French who, as he had thought, had too much at stake in the Arab world to risk mistreating him. He was placed under "residential surveillance" near Paris while the French pondered his fate.[1]

Return to the Middle East. The political climate in France and the rest of Europe was hostile to the Mufti. He was a political liability for the French; Jewish organizations were accusing him of collaboration and war crimes (a capital offense), while the Yugoslavians were about to bring charges against him for his part in organizing Muslim troops against the communists. Pressure was applied on the French and the British to turn him over to the International Military Tribunal at Nuremberg, which began its sessions on November 20, 1945. Secret correspondence between the French and the British indicates that they had two problems, one legal and the other political, which immobilized them for a year. Legally, the British did not consider the Mufti a British subject who could be charged with collaborating with the enemy, and there was no convincing evidence that he was involved in war crimes or crimes against humanity (that is, extermination, deportation, or genocide). A similar conclusion was reached by the chief research officer of the UN War Crimes commission, who advised a U.S. commission that the Mufti's actions "would probably not come within the category of war crimes."[2] Politically, action against the Mufti could cause the French and British to lose in the Arab world, where he was still very popular, a fact of which the secretary-general of the Arab League, 'Abd al-Rahman 'Azzam, reminded them in his letters urging the Mufti's release. Ibn Sa'ud also advised the British to treat the Mufti with leniency and not condemn him to death; even before receiving the legal opinion, the Foreign Office decided to respond by informing Ibn Sa'ud's son, Faysal, "for papa's ear alone" that they did not intend to enforce the "ultimate" sentence on him.[3] Meanwhile, the Arab League appealed to Yugoslavia to drop its charges, which it did.

Still, Britain was anxious about the Mufti's return to Palestine, where he would stir up trouble. Lacking legal grounds for prosecution, they sought to transfer him from France to the Seychelles, Britain's asylum for political prisoners, on the grounds that he was "a political criminal." France refused the British requests on May 22 and October 25, 1945, and the British did not force the issue.[4]

The French did not know what to do with the Mufti, but a Revisionist Zionist group in Paris did. The group reportedly consisted of soldiers of the Jewish Brigade and sympathizers of Irgun Zva'i Le'ummi, an underground military branch of the Zionist Revisionist party. It will be recalled that the Irgun, with British help, had attempted to assassinate the Mufti in Baghdad in May 1941. In May 1946 the Revisionist Zionist group in Paris wanted to kidnap the Mufti from his suburban villa and kill him. But Amin left France before a final decision was taken.[5]

The Mufti was apprehensive concerning Jewish demands on France and Britain, and wanted to return to the Middle East to have better control over Palestinian affairs. So on May 29, 1946, assisted by a perhaps intentional easing of restrictions and surveillance,[6] he escaped. According to *Le Monde*, he left a letter thanking the French for their hospitality and explaining that the Palestinians needed him. Repeating his earlier escape from Iran, he disguised himself by shaving his beard, dying his hair,

donning a suit and borrowing the name and passport of a Syrian nationalist, Ma'ruf al-Dawalibi. He left France and dropped out of sight. The
British were frantic. The High Commissioner in Palestine had just warned
of the "disastrous" consequences of the Mufti returning to the Middle
East. Intelligence soon reached the British that the Mufti was heading to
Alexandria on the SS *Devonshire* dressed as a veiled woman identifying
herself as Madame Shawwa, the French wife of Ibn Sa'ud's counselor.
Since Madame Shawwa never wore a veil outside of Saudi Arabia and since
the Mufti escaped once before dressed as a woman, the British made plans
to arrest the impostor and send him to the Seychelles. The admiralty
intercepted the ship, and the alleged Madame Shawwa was discovered to
be Madame Shawwa.[7]

The Mufti turned up on June 19 at 'Abdin Palace in Cairo. It is not clear
why he waited in Cairo for three weeks to appear in public, or what he had
been doing in the meantime besides sprout a beard and consult with his
aides and political allies. He signed the guest book and asked King Faruq
(1937–1952) for refuge—an old Arab custom requiring the host to grant
protection and hospitality, even to an enemy.[8]

Palestine. When he arrived in Cairo, the Mufti was aware that much had
happened in Palestine since his departure from the Middle East in 1941;
decisions were made during and shortly after the war in which he had little
or no role.

During the early war years, Palestine had been relatively quiet. The
British suppression of the Palestine Arab Revolt had decimated the Palestinian political and military structures. Most Palestinian leaders were in
exile or in detention camps. Thousands of Palestinian activists were in jail,
and the community was largely disarmed. Of the three major political
groups—the Nashashibis, Istiqlalists, and the Husaynis—the only faction
that had survived were the Nashashibis. But because of their open association with the British and their not so secret contacts with the Zionists,
Palestinians viewed them with suspicion. In any case, their political influence was limited to certain families of vested interest, and their elderly
leader, Raghib al-Nashashibi, suffered from inertia. They were therefore
unable to capitalize on the absence of the Husaynis to fill the political
vacuum.

A political reawakening among Palestinians began in late 1942 in reaction to external developments. Zionist leaders, who had opposed the 1939

White Paper, increasingly looked to the United States for support. They sought to activate the American Jewish community to exert pressure on Congress and the White House, and to raise funds on behalf of new objectives that had been established at the Biltmore Conference on May 11, 1942. These included: 1. opening the gates of Palestine to Jewish immigration; 2. developing "unoccupied and uncultivated" lands; and 3. establishing Palestine "as a Jewish Commonwealth." Zionist goals had escalated from the creation of a Jewish homeland in Palestine (Balfour, 1917), to a Jewish state in part of Palestine (Peel, 1937), to a Jewish Commonwealth, i.e. a state, in the whole of Palestine (Biltmore, 1942).[9]

When reports concerning the Biltmore program of 1942 and news of the magnitude of Nazi extermination of Western Jewry became public in late 1942, support for the Zionists grew around the world, particularly in the U.S. Sixty-two senators and 181 congressmen wrote President Roosevelt supporting the Zionists' right to Palestine. The Palestinians reacted with "alarm and anxiety," which manifested itself in cables sent to President Roosevelt, the Colonial Secretary, and the High Commissioner by local notables, mayors, and the Chamber of Commerce.[10]

The Istiqlal party attempted to galvanize the emerging mood, and to fill the political void. It revitalized and took control of the Arab National Fund (*Sanduq al-Umma*) which, in its attempt to reduce land purchase by Jews, had acquired Palestinian land for sale. But despite the return to Palestine of its titular head, Awni 'Abd al-Hadi, and a rapprochement with the British authorities, the Istiqlalists ran up against pro-Husayni supporters who, in response, reconstituted the Palestine Arab party. Palestinian and Arab attempts to forge a united national movement and joint representation of the Istiqlal and the Husaynis failed throughout 1944 and 1945. This impasse was particularly frustrating to the Palestinian community in the light of a series of ominous developments: the U.S. Congress passed a joint resolution endorsing the Biltmore program in January 1944; the British Labour Party recommended in May of the same year that Palestinians be "encouraged" to leave Palestine to make room for Jewish immigrants; both U.S. political parties called for unrestricted Jewish immigration in the summer; President Truman called on the British prime minister on August 31, 1945, to allow 100,000 Jews into Palestine.[11] But, leaderless and disunited, the Palestinian reaction was feeble.

Consequently, after years of Zionist diplomatic and public relations successes, an effective terrorist campaign to drive the British out of Palestine, Palestinian factional infighting, and a general inability to respond to a series of setbacks, the Palestinians were receptive to the resumption of the Mufti's leadership. He was seen as someone who had devoted his life to his people, who had been persecuted by the British after 1937 and forced to flee to the Axis countries, and who had cooperated with the Nazis only to obtain something in the event of an Axis victory.[12] Some Palestinians were uneasy about his cooperation with the Nazis, but most, now that they were in danger of domination or expulsion, saw in the Mufti a savior. He was the symbol of Palestinian struggle against Zionism, and now they needed him more than ever before. That is why the Mufti was more popular in May 1946 than he had been at the height of the Arab Revolt in 1938.

While the Palestine Arab party's revival and the return of Jamal al-Husayni in February 1946 helped reestablish organizational control for the Mufti in Palestine, after the emergence of the Arab League decisions concerning Palestine were no longer made in Jerusalem but in Cairo. In other words, neither the Mufti's popularity nor his control over Palestinian politics, through Jamal, was sufficient. Palestinian decision making had been gradually taken over by the Arab League as a result of a combination of factors: the Mufti's absence, Palestinian weakness and disunity, Arab public support for the Palestinian cause, Arab involvement in the Palestine problem, and the perceived threat that a Jewish state posed to the Arab world.

Indeed, support for the Palestinians and the need for joint Arab effort on the Palestine question was one of the primary reasons for the establishment of the Arab League. The British encouraged the venture to enhance future regional stability and maintain its own hegemony. Delegates to the preparatory committee, representing Egypt, Iraq, Syria, Saudi Arabia, Transjordan, Lebanon, and Yemen, met in Alexandria between September 25 and October 7, 1944. Palestine was represented by a moderate Palestinian leader, Musa al-'Alami. An "Alexandria Protocol" was issued which included a special resolution on Palestine stating that "Palestine constitutes an important part of the Arab world and that the rights of the Arabs cannot be touched without prejudice to peace and stability in the Arab world." The resolution also called on Britain to honor its promises in the 1939 White Paper. It stated its regret over the woes inflicted on the Jews of Europe by European dictators, but added that "there can be no greater injustice and aggression than solving the problem of the Jews by another injustice, that is, by inflicting injustice on the Palestine Arabs."[13]

Musa al-'Alami's analyses and proposals presented to the preparatory committee served as the basis for Arab League policies until the fall of 1947. 'Alami warned that the British were abandoning the 1939 White Paper policy because of British perceptions that the Arabs were irresolute. He proposed the following policies: negotiating with Britain on the basis of the 1939 White Paper; sending high-level delegations to London, Washington, and Moscow; establishing a Palestine National Fund with an annual expenditure of £1,000,000 for five years to forestall Jewish land acquisition and help agricultural development; boycotting Jewish goods from Palestine; curbing illegal Jewish immigration through Arab countries; and setting up Arab information offices.[14]

Arab League policy toward Palestine was anchored in the 1939 British White Paper, which (1) restricted Jewish immigration to 75,000 over five years, with further immigration to be subject to Palestinian consent; (2) restricted Jewish land transfer; and (3) called for the establishment of an independent state after ten years (in 1949) with an Arab-Jewish ratio of two to one. The Arab League was opposed to any arrangement, such as the partition, which violated the rights of the majority to establish a state.

The Mufti supported the league's policy of promoting a state that would inevitably be under his leadership. However, one member of the league, Amir 'Abdullah of Transjordan, was simultaneously working within and outside the league for another policy more suitable to his own political ambitions. The efforts of 'Abdullah, together with the Zionists and the British, were designed to checkmate the Mufti, as a British official put it, and keep him from seeking to establish a state in all or, later, part of Palestine. The role of 'Abdullah, therefore, is crucial to understanding the diminishing role of the Mufti within the league and ultimately within Palestine, as well as the lack of Arab unity and coordination, and ultimately, the fate of Palestine.

'Abdullah, the Zionists, and the British. During his thirty year tenure as ruler, 'Abdullah had a driving ambition to reunite Syria under his leadership. Shortly after Winston Churchill, the British colonial secretary, pledged to recognize 'Abdullah as Amir of Transjordan in 1921 (the same year that Amin al-Husayni was appointed Mufti of Jerusalem), 'Abdullah proposed

to Churchill the formation of a single Arab state out of Palestine and Transjordan. Churchill declined on the grounds that it could not be reconciled with Britain's promise to the Jews.[15]

'Abdullah accepted the Jewish national home idea early on, for a number of reasons. First, opposition to Zionism would have put him in conflict with his chief benefactor, Britain, without whose diplomatic and financial support neither Transjordan nor its Arab Legion would have been possible. Second, he sought to use the financial assets of the Zionists to benefit Transjordan, poor in resources, as well as himself. Third, he recognized the Yishuv's increasing diplomatic and military power, an attitude which he conveyed to the British commander of the Arab Legion by quoting a Turkish proverb: "If you meet a bear while crossing a shaky bridge, call to her: 'dear Auntie.' "[16]

Yet his willingness to acquiesce to the Zionist program did not mean that he gave up on his Greater Syria dream. In 1934 he proposed the unity of Transjordan and Palestine under his leadership, involving Arab recognition of the mandate and Jewish rights in Palestine. The Nashashibis accepted the proposals, but the Mufti and other Palestinian nationalists rejected them.[17] The Zionists also rejected them, although 'Abdullah felt that he had been generous to them. A year earlier, he had told the Jewish Telegraph Agency, "The Jews of the world will find me to be a new Lord Balfour, and even more than this; Balfour gave the Jews a country that was not his; I promise a country that is mine."[18]

The Arab Revolt (1936–39) provided 'Abdullah an opportunity to pursue his political goal. He accepted the 1937 Royal (Peel) Commission recommendation to partition Palestine into a Jewish state, an Arab state united with Transjordan, and enclaves of Holy Places to be placed under a new mandate.[19] Some of his Palestinian supporters were initially for it, but most Palestinians supported the Mufti in his early rejection of partition.[20]

Palestinian rejection was caused by two overriding factors. First, the Jews, after 55 years of effort, owned only 5.6 percent of the land, yet they were to get 40 percent of the most fertile land in Palestine, on which lived many Arabs who would have to be resettled in the Arab state.[21] Second, prospects for the Arab designated area were equally unattractive to the Palestinians. 'Abdullah, whom many identified as an outsider from the distant Hijaz and an enemy of Palestinian nationalists, would have annexed the rest of Palestine.

'Abdullah's aims and Palestinian attitudes remained the same a decade later when the concept was revived after World War II. This was evident in a secret meeting he had with a representative of the Jewish Agency, Eliahu Sasson, in August 1946. According to Sasson, he began by stating that "he aspired to expand the borders of Transjordan and to create a large and strong Hashimite kingdom that would enter into a treaty with Britain and Turkey and would keep the English line of defense in the East."[22] This could be done in several stages:

a. partition of Palestine and annexation of the Arab sector to Transjordan;
b. annexation of Syria to the (enlarged) Transjordan;
c. entry of the (enlarged) Transjordan into a federation with Iraq;
d. entry of the Jewish part of Palestine into federation, or alliance, with the Jordanian-Syrian-Iraqi federation;
e. Lebanon would have the choice of joining this federative block or remaining isolated.[23]

'Abdullah claimed that the British accepted the principle, not the stages, of his plan. Concerned about alienating the Arabs over partition, the British were at the time advocating a federal plan for Palestine. Consequently, 'Abdullah urged the Jewish Agency to accept the federal plan, of which the principal attractions for the Zionists, according to him, were:

1. to prevent the creation of an eighth Arab state (a Palestinian state), extremist and hostile, headed by their archenemies, the Husaynis;
2. to repair relations with Britain and win back her sympathy for Zionism by making things easier for Britain in these days of crisis.[24]

Sasson asked 'Abdullah for clarification concerning his exact position. Was the Amir for a federal plan or for partition? 'Abdullah answered that he was "temporarily setting aside his wishes for those of the English. But if we believed that we had the power to move the partition plan (i.e., creation of a Jewish state and the annexing of the Arab sector to Transjordan) through England, the United States, and the United Nations, he would be prepared to support us and fulfill any obligation falling to him. He was sure that Iraq also supported us, even if the matter caused a split in the 'Arab League.' " When Sasson asked 'Abdullah how the Amir was going to impose on the Palestinians the federal plan or partition plan together with annexation of the Arab part to Transjordan, 'Abdullah said he would present him with a plan if Sasson visited him again on August 19, the following week.[25]

'Abdullah asked Sasson to bring the first payment, £10,000, of a total of £40,000. The money was "for expenses during the [Syrian] parliamentary elections" that would lead to unification of Syria and Transjordan and to setting up a new Palestinian representative body to supplant the Arab Higher Committee, which would declare its agreement with the recommendations of the London Conference. When Sasson "pretended" that the sum was too large, 'Abdullah implied that if the Zionists wanted a state, they must invest what was required. 'Abdullah reminded Sasson that the Zionists did not have "a faithful friend" like him "in the entire Arab world."[26]

When Sasson returned to Amman on August 19, he brought with him the final answer to 'Abdullah's question as to whether the Zionists agreed to a federal or partition plan. Moshe Sharett replied through Sasson that the Zionists wanted all of Palestine or as much of it as possible, but they would "pay the price" if they found an influential Arab to compromise with them. They preferred partition with the Arab part annexed to Transjordan, but with some minor territorial adjustments in their favor. They also favored his Greater Syria scheme.[27]

Sasson also brought with him £5,000, which displeased 'Abdullah, who complained that he was not only planning rebellions in Syria but was planning the reconquest of the Hijaz to reestablish the Hashimite kingdom, for which he needed money and arms.

Nevertheless, 'Abdullah advised his Jewish "friends" to support "partition and merger" and instructed his delegation to London to support partition and establish contact with the Jewish Agency. Regarding border modifications, 'Abdullah indicated he would be flexible.[28]

The two meetings between 'Abdullah and Sasson in August 1946 represent an agreement in principle favoring partition. 'Abdullah would recognize the Jewish state, which would in turn agree to the merger of the Arab part with Transjordan. The agreement was neither explicit nor written down, but it began a period of cooperation. And as one inquiry after another took place and one plan after another failed, the 'Abdullah-Jewish Agency cooperation "developed into a political and strategic partnership," according to the historian Avi Shlaim.[29]

Indeed, the interests of 'Abdullah and the Zionists converged sufficiently in November 1947 so that they were able to reach a firm agreement over

Palestine. The agreement was confirmed on November 17, 1947, when 'Abdullah met Golda (Meyerson) Meir. He began with an assessment: "For the past thirty years you have grown in numbers and strength, and your achievements are many. It is impossible to ignore you and it is a duty to come to terms with you. . . . Now I am convinced that the British are leaving, and we shall remain, you and we, face to face. Any clash between us will be harmful to both of us."[30]

He asked what the attitude of the Zionists would be if he attempted to seize the part of Palestine allocated to the Palestinians. Golda Meir said that they would look favorably on it, especially if it were accompanied by a declaration that the seizure was to ensure order and peace until the UN could establish a government. 'Abdullah's answer was emphatic: "But I want that part for me, in order to annex it to my state, and I do not wish to create a new state which will interfere with my plans and allow the Arabs to 'ride on my back.' I want to be the rider, not the horse." Meir asked him if he would sign a written agreement along those lines to which he answered yes, and asked for a draft. No agreement was ever signed but a point of maximum understanding had been reached.[31] Now 'Abdullah needed British support.

The British had tried to interest both Arabs and Zionists in 1946 and 1947 in a number of plans (discussed later) but failed. The Foreign Office hoped that the Arabs and Jews and the UN would turn to them. "The best result from our point of view," wrote an official, "would naturally be that the Arabs and Jews should agree and should ask us to remain in Palestine for a limited transitional period to help them put the agreement into effect."[32] They were not in favor of partition for fear of antagonizing the Arabs, with some of whom they were negotiating. Should partition become a fait accompli, however, they would back 'Abdullah's claim to Palestine. As Alec Kirkbride, the British resident in Amman put it in a telegram: "Strategically and economically Transjordan has best claim to inherit residue of Palestine. . . . A Greater Transjordan would not be against our interests . . . alternative of a nonviable Palestine Arab State under the Mufti is not attractive."[33] J. E. Cable, the head of the Eastern Department of the Foreign Office, agreed early November 1947: "The only alternative (to annexation by 'Abdullah) would be a puny Arab Palestine dominated by the unreliable Mufti."[34]

Consequently, weeks before the UN partition decision, 'Abdullah, the Zionists, and the British were in agreement about Palestine. All had recognized, however, that the Palestinian nationalists, particularly the Mufti, and the other Arab states were potential impediments to achieving their goals in Palestine.

'Abdullah suggested killing the Mufti. "That man," he reportedly told Golda Meir in the November 1947 meeting, "must be removed from the scene at any price and quickly."[35] This was not a novel proposal. 'Abdullah had told Pinhas Rutenberg of the Jewish Agency in January 1939 that the Mufti must be disposed of, before he ('Abdullah) would implement a previous agreement that he had with the Zionists.[36] Rutenberg approached the Foreign Office in 1940 about assassinating the Mufti, as discussed earlier, but the British declined. "Even if we were in the habit of indulging in political assassination," wrote an official, "the elimination of the Mufti would not make up for the intense outburst of feeling which his murder would surely provoke." A few months later, however, Winston Churchill approved a proposal to assassinate the Mufti, who was then involved in the struggle for Iraqi independence from Britain. The British military sent five members of the Irgun, a Revisionist Zionist military organization, to kill or kidnap the Mufti in May 1941. But when the leader of the mission, David Raziel, was killed, the mission was aborted.[37] The Revisionist Zionists again planned to assassinate him in Paris in 1946, but failed.[38] When 'Abdullah suggested, in August 1946, and again, in November 1947, "removing" the Mufti, the Jewish Agency was not interested, presumably because the political climate was far too delicate for such a brazen act. The British also showed a similar disinclination. The Iraqi Prime Minister suggested to the British that the Mufti should be allowed to return to Palestine where he would "undoubtedly be assassinated," but the British pointed out that "we cannot avail ourselves of this attractive possibility."[39]

There was, however, another method for dealing with the Mufti, which was equally as effective. That was to neutralize the Palestinian leader politically. When the Mufti visited the Transjordanian legation in Cairo in mid-1947 to convey his "loyalty" to 'Abdullah, he was politely acknowledged but otherwise disregarded.[40] In October he requested residency in Amman, but was told that he would not be welcome.[41] A month later, he sent three "moderate" supporters to 'Abdullah to pave the way for reconciliation, but after 'Abdullah flew into a virulent diatribe against the Mufti, they dared not make any suggestions.[42] A few days later, the Mufti, who had spurned Zionist approaches, sent a message to the Jewish Agency

not automatically translate itself into influence within the league. Second, the league was a loose confederation of states, not a monolithic organization. Third, most of the member states were either dependent on Britain or constrained by it, so that defying the British often had to be measured against diplomatic and financial costs. Fourth, there were a number of rivalries, the most important of which was between Transjordan on the one hand and Syria, Lebanon, Saudi Arabia, and Egypt on the other. Syria and Lebanon considered 'Abdullah's Greater Syria scheme a threat to their independence. 'Abdullah's dream of reconquering the Hijaz and reestablishing the Hashimite kingdom there alarmed and indeed preoccupied King Abd al-'Aziz ibn Sa'ud, and the expansion of Transjordan into Greater Syria (Syria, Lebanon, Palestine) or into Saudi Arabia and its proposed unity with Hashimite Iraq threatened Egypt's leading role in the Arab world. In addition, Iraq was antagonistic to the Mufti, who participated with Rashid 'Ali al-Kilani in an unsuccessful revolt in 1929 against the British and Iraq's Hashimite house. To those individual rivalries must be added the collective Arab hostility towards 'Abdullah, who was considered subservient to the British. The Arab leaders also knew enough about his cooperation with the Zionists to make them very suspicious of his intentions to divide Palestine between the Zionists and himself. This is the context within which the Mufti-'Abdullah rivalry played itself within the Arab League.

The Mufti arrived in Egypt on May 29, the very day the first Arab summit was held in Inshas, Egypt to respond to the Anglo-American Committee recommendations. These included the immediate admission of 100,000 Jewish immigrants, the abolition of the land transfer restrictions, and the establishment in Palestine of a trusteeship under British control. If these recommendations became policy, they would in effect replace the 1939 White Paper, which had hitherto been the official basis of British policy. The summit called for stoppage of Jewish immigration, the prevention of land transfer from Arab to Jewish ownership, and the establishment of an independent state in Palestine. It warned that adoption of the recommendations would be considered "a hostile policy directed against Arab Palestine and therefore against the Arab countries themselves."[48] President Truman, mindful of congressional elections in November, supported only the recommendations regarding immigration and land restrictions and ignored the proposal of a trusteeship under British authority. British

Prime Minister Bevin was furious, but, needing U.S. financial assistance, he agreed to the establishment of a new committee. It was, therefore, U.S.-British discord rather than Arab League opposition that kept the committee's recommendation from being implemented.

The Arab leaders followed the summit with an extraordinary session of the Arab League Council in Bludan, Syria between June 8 and 12, 1946. Two days before, President Truman had reiterated his call to Britain to admit 100,000 into Palestine. The council passed a number of secret resolutions calling for economic sanctions against Britain and the United States should the Anglo-American recommendations go into effect.

The Bludan session also took measures to strengthen the Mufti, who was still in seclusion in Cairo. Two rival Palestinian groups were in existence by early June: the Arab Higher Committee controlled by the Palestine Arab party under the leadership of Jamal al-Husayni, and the Arab Higher Front led by the Istiqlal. The Arab League dissolved both, and installed the Arab Higher Committee as representative of the Palestinians, consisting of Amin al-Husayni as chairman; Jamal al-Husayni, vice chairman; Dr. Husayn Fakhri al-Khalidi (Reform party), secretary; Ahmad Hilmi 'Abd al-Baqi (Istiqlal party), member; and Emile Ghuri (Palestine Arab party), member. The committee, which was to be funded by the Arab League, was hardly representative of all Palestinians. Absent were, for example, the peasantry and the emerging middle class, but at least al-Khalidi and 'Abd al-Baqi gave the appearance of interparty representation. That lasted until January 1947 when the Mufti installed five more members, four of whom were loyalists and yes-men.[49]

The selection of the Mufti was in recognition of his enormous popularity in Palestine as well as in many Arab countries. At the same time it indicated the weakness and division of the Palestinians and the dominant role of the league not only in external but also in the internal affairs of the Palestinian community, a factor that from late 1947 frustrated the Mufti and his colleagues, particularly regarding Arab military intervention in Palestine.

Jamal al-Husayni, who represented the Palestinians at Bludan, stated the policy of the Mufti regarding the extent of Arab assistance. Jamal said that the Palestinians were aware that the Arab League consisted of seven sovereign states, each with its own political relationships, and the Palestinians did not want to embarrass any member. All they wanted was "the help from the Arab peoples with the encouragement of the Arab governments." With adequate financial assistance and materiel the Palestinians could "overcome the Jewish forces."[50]

The following month, the Anglo-American Morrison-Grady Committee issued its findings, calling for converting the mandate into a trusteeship in which Palestine would be divided into autonomous Arab and Jewish provinces, and Jerusalem and Negev districts would fall under British trusteeship. Provincial autonomy could have eventually led to partition. The committee stated that the admission of 100,000 Jewish refugees into Palestine depended on Arab and Jewish acceptance. The Zionists rejected the plan. Truman favored it, but political pressure before the elections once again made him back off, leaving the British as the only party to support it. In addition, because the British refused to allow the 100,000 into Palestine, the Hagana and the Irgun launched a terror campaign against the British in Palestine, resulting in many deaths. Britain responded by rounding up some 2700 Jews. The Irgun, under Menachem Begin, retaliated by blowing up the King David Hotel, where the British administrative offices were housed, killing 91 British, Jews, and Palestinians.

It was in this atmosphere that the London Round Table Conference opened in September 1946 to discuss the provincial autonomy plan proposed by Morrison-Grady. The Arab Higher Committee refused to attend when the British declared that the Mufti was to be excluded. The Jewish Agency also refused unless partition was the basis of the discussion. Consequently, only the Arab states and Britain met. The Arabs asked for a democratic state with an elected parliament in Palestine in which Jews would be recognized as citizens if they had acquired citizenship in Palestine before 1939 after a residency of ten years. On this basis the Jewish community would receive three seats out of ten representatives. Later the Arab Higher Committee considered the Arab League ratio too high since the committee recognized only Jews that had been in Palestine before 1919, when the ratio was six to one. With the parties further apart than ever before, Bevin suspended the conference until early 1947.[51]

The second stage of the London Conference was held in February 1947. Prime Minister Bevin held talks with Jamal al-Husayni representing the Arab Higher Committee, and informally met with Ben-Gurion. The Palestinians insisted on a unitary state and cessation of Jewish immigration, and stated that Palestinians should fight partition "with all means at their disposal." The Zionists demanded partition. Bevin then issued his proposal on February 7 calling for a five-year trusteeship leading to a Palestine state with a Jewish minority. Jewish immigration would be limited to 4000 a month for two years, after which it would depend on the country's economic absorptive capacity. Not since the 1939 White Paper did the Palestinians have as good an offer, and some of the Arab delegates thought it worthy of consideration. But the Arab Higher Committee denounced the proposal and asked for an independent Palestine state and an end to immigration. Ben-Gurion, on the other hand, wanted an unlimited Jewish immigration, which eventually would have led to a Jewish majority in Palestine.[52]

A number of factors finally forced Britain to abandon the mandate: the price of Jewish terrorism, requiring 80,000 troops in Palestine costing £40 million annually, the growing American pressure at a time of British financial need, and the seemingly irreconcilable differences between the two parties. Britain turned the problem over to the United Nations on February 26.

Meanwhile, the differences between the Mufti and the league had remained relatively minor for the year following his return. The Mufti was consulted regarding the league's policies in international forums. Both had similar, if not identical, positions regarding the need to exert pressure on Britain to maintain its 1939 White Paper policy. Both opposed Jewish immigration beyond 1944 and certainly the 100,000. They also opposed any change of restrictions in land transfer, and rejected any solution— cantons, trusteeships, and partition—that did not lead to a unitary independent state, as the White Paper envisaged.

Some disagreements did emerge. The league, for example, favored granting Palestine citizenship to Jewish residents prior to 1939, while the Palestinians chose 1919; the league was not in favor of submitting the Palestine problem to the UN, hoping to resolve the issue in a regional context and with the cooperation of Britain, while the Mufti, whose confidence in the British by now was virtually nonexistent, wanted to submit the issue to the UN.[53] Finally, the league attended international conferences in deference to Britain, with which they had treaties or because most league members belonged to the United Nations, while the Mufti refused to attend a diplomatic forum that did not adopt his frame of reference.

But when UNSCOP's majority report of August 31, 1947, called for partition and Britain declared its intention to leave Palestine a month later, serious divergences appeared between the Mufti and the league. At the same time, suspicions between 'Abdullah and other league members increased, mainly because of 'Abdullah's renewed public statements in favor of a Greater Syria under his leadership as of November 11, 1946, and, in August 1947, his call to establish a Constituent Assembly to that end. The declaration triggered brief yet bitter exchanges with Syria and Lebanon. Syria especially felt vulnerable, while Ibn Sa'ud told a Syrian envoy that he could "not sleep at night" for worry about Syria and his own kingdom. King Faruq also worried about Jordanian expansion at the expense of its ally Syria, and suggested that the Syrians expose 'Abdullah as a Zionist collaborator.[54] When UNSCOP's majority report called for partition in August 1947, suspicion of 'Abdullah's intentions increased.

Aware of Arab suspicion, 'Abdullah would "feign opposition" to partition in public to pacify the Arab leaders and masses while working strategically for partition and annexation. In confidential meetings with the British, the Zionists, and the Americans, 'Abdullah made clear his intentions: in March 1946 he advised Foreign Minister Ernest Bevin and Prime Minister Clement Attlee to dispense with consultation and enforce partition. When the United States became involved, he informed the American ambassador in June 1947 of what he had told Bevin and Attlee.[55]

The UNSCOP report was consistent with 'Abdullah's agreement with the Jewish Agency, but for one major difference. Whereas the Peel Commission's 1937 partition proposal had recommended that the Arab portion be annexed to Transjordan, the 1947 partition proposal envisaged an Arab state ruled by its inhabitants. 'Abdullah therefore had to maneuver to rectify this, aided by his membership in the Arab League (in contrast to the Palestinians), his ties with Britain, his powerful army, Arab disunity, and Palestinian weakness.

The Transjordanian prime minister condemned partition and pledged to support a Palestine Arab state at the Arab League's Political Committee meeting in Sufar, Lebanon in September 1947. The meeting was called by Salih Jabr, the Iraqi prime minister, to pass two measures: implementation of secret Bludan resolutions, and the allocation of funds for the Palestinians and other Arabs, should the United Nations recommend partition. No decision was reached regarding the first, due to Arab disunity, but it was resolved "to provide the Palestinians the most in funds, materiel, and manpower," and a Technical Committee was established. Jabr refused to allow the Mufti to participate in the meeting and sought, through a procedural maneuver, to veto the Mufti's membership, but he was over-ruled by the Political Committee.[56]

The Mufti suffered his first major setback in the league at Aley, Leba-non, where the Arab League Council held its meeting on October 7–15 to grapple with British departure and UNSCOP's partition recommendation. Again the Mufti was not invited, but to the surprise of everyone he showed up anyway. Iraqi prime minister Jabr immediately objected to the Mufti's presence but the chairman, Riad al-Sulh, prime minister of Lebanon, maintained that as a host he could not ask the Mufti to leave. The Mufti then called for the establishment of a Palestinian government under the control of the Arab Higher Committee. Since Jordan and Iraq were against the proposal, it was turned down. 'Azzam later went to Amman to per-suade 'Abdullah to change his mind, but 'Abdullah refused to consider such a government, with or without the Mufti's participation in it.[57]

At Aley the Technical Committee's key figure, General Isma'il Safwat, gave a bleak assessment of the balance of forces. Safwat, a former Iraqi chief of staff who was instrumental in setting up the Sufar meeting, warned that the Zionists possessed "political, military, and administrative institutions and organizations characterized by a very high degree of effi-ciency." The Zionists, according to Safwat, could quickly field 20,000 well-armed and well-trained troops, who would rely on 40,000 trained reserves and more recruits from Europe and the United States, and good lines of communications and well-defended settlements. In addition, they had mo-bile commando troops and an arms industry. The Palestinians had nothing remotely comparable in "manpower, organization, armaments, or ammu-nition." He warned of "very grave developments that were bound to develop to the advantage of the Zionists unless the Arab states promptly mobilized their utmost forces and efforts to counter Zionist intentions." This was the first time that the Arabs faced the issue of military prepared-ness and possible intervention by their regular forces. Safwat made specific recommendations but only a few were adopted. The council did allocate £1 million and authorized deployment of regular forces on the border with Palestine.[58]

Safwat's recommendation at Aley and the possibility of Arab direct military involvement, limited as it was, deeply alarmed the Mufti. He did not share Safwat's assessment of the bleak military condition in the Pales-tinian community. His Palestine Arab party had reorganized al-Futuwwa (a paramilitary unit active in the Arab Revolt) and, after a meeting with Muhammad Nimr al-Hawari, the leader of al-Najjada, another military group, he was able to combine both forces of several thousand under the Arab Higher Committee. Both expanded in the summer of 1946, purchased uniforms and small arms, and received training by experienced Arab officers.[59] What the Palestinians needed, he and his colleagues repeatedly argued, were money and arms to defeat the Zionist forces.

The Mufti's strong objection to the entry of Arab troops into Palestine was based on two assumptions: that 'Abdullah, given his dream of Greater Syria and British control of his army and foreign policy, would not leave Palestine if ever he entered; and that the Palestinians, using the guerrilla tactics that had been effective in 1936–39, would overpower the Zionists provided the Arabs gave arms and money and Britain remained neutral.

The interests of three powers—the Hashimites, the Zionists, and the British—converged on the eve of November 29, 1947, when the United Nations decided to partition Palestine. The Mufti along with the rest of the Arab world, immediately rejected it. The reasons for Arab opposition are summed up by the Palestinian historian Walid Khalidi:

> Partition was seen by the Palestinians as imposing unilateral and intolerable sacrifices on themselves. . . . The area of the Jewish state according to the UN plan would actually be larger than that of the proposed Palestinian state (5,500 square miles as compared with 4,500 square miles) at a time when the Jews constituted no more than 35 percent of the population and owned less than 7 percent of the land. Within the proposed Jewish state, Jewish land-ownership did not in fact exceed 600 square miles out of the total area of 5,500 square miles. Nearly all the citrus land (equally divided in ownership between Jews and Palestinians), 80 percent of the cereal land (entirely Palestinian-owned) and 40 percent of Palestinian industry would fall within the borders of the proposed Jewish state.
>
> The Palestinians failed to see why they should be made to pay for the Holocaust (the ultimate crime against humanity, committed in Europe by Europeans), and recalled that Zionism was born in the 1880s, long before the advent of the Third Reich. They failed to see why it was *not* fair for the Jews to be a minority in a unitary Palestinian state, while it *was* fair for almost half of the Palestinian population—the indigenous majority on its own ancestral soil—to be converted overnight into a minority under alien rule in the envisaged Jewish state according to partition.[60]

Hostilities between the Palestinians and the Zionists began the day after the partition vote, with the Palestinians taking the initiative. The civil war (until May 14) and the regular war after that are not within the scope of this chapter. But a brief account helps us understand the declining fortunes of the Mufti and the Palestinians.

In early December the Mufti suffered yet another setback within the league. The Technical Committee, now operating in Damascus under President Quwatli, appointed General Taha Hashimi, a former Iraqi chief of staff and former prime minister, to oversee the recruitment of three thousand Arab recruits, of whom 500 were Palestinians for the Arab Liberation Army. Furthermore, Fawzi al-Kawukji, a Lebanese officer who had fought in the Palestine Arab Revolt of 1936–39, was appointed commander of the army, and 10,000 rifles were put at his disposal. The Mufti strongly objected to these arrangements both because he was suspicious of Kawukji's loyalty and because he was losing control over the military effort. In addition, the Arab League again refused to allow him to establish a shadow government, a request he repeatedly made during the next five months.[61]

Consequently the Mufti established Jaysh al-Jihad al-Muqaddas (Holy War Army) and placed as its commander 'Abd al-Qadir al-Husayni, the son of Musa Kazim, who was at one time mayor of Jerusalem and who also served as head of the Arab Executive until his death in 1934. Because of suspicion between 'Abd al-Qadir and Kawukji, they did not coordinate their military operations with each other. In any case, 'Abd al-Qadir reported to the Mufti, while Kawukji received his recruits, aid, and instructions from the Arab League.

Despite the lack of cooperation, Jaysh al-Jihad and the army appeared to be achieving their objective by March. They had blocked the Tel Aviv-Jerusalem highway, bombed the Jerusalem Post building and Jewish Agency headquarters, and captured Hagana arms and armored vehicles. These achievements created optimism in Palestine and encouraged Arab leaders not to take tough decisions. The optimism was baseless, however, since the Palestinian irregulars and Arab volunteers were inferior to the Jewish military in numbers, organization, training, hardware, and logistics. Besides, the Hagana had not yet implemented its military plans.

The tide turned when the Hagana's military plans went into effect in early April, as the British withdrawal and Jewish mobilization reached an advanced phase, and the first shipment of Czechoslovakian arms reached the Hagana. The Palestinians suffered two major setbacks on April 9: 'Abd al-Qadir, attempting to recapture the Palestinian village of Castel from the

Hagana, was killed, and two miles away the Revisionist Irgun and Stern forces massacred up to 250 Palestinian civilians at Deir Yasin. No event except for the fall of Jerusalem in May was as demoralizing to the Mufti as the death of 'Abd al-Qadir. Furthermore, Deir Yasin alarmed the community and sped up the exodus of Palestinians. The Mufti tried to stem the tide of refugees by appealing to Arab governments to deny the refugees entry into their countries. At the same time, Kawukji's army was repulsed at Mishmar ha-Emek, southeast of Haifa.[62]

These setbacks were devastating defeats for the Mufti. His aim of quickly defeating the Jewish forces and establishing an Arab state in all of Palestine was severely undermined. He insisted after 1948 that had the Arabs supplied his forces with more arms, money, and materiel, the Palestinians could have overcome the Jewish forces. But this military analysis is not supported by the evidence regarding the total military situation in April. Indeed, by the end of the month the Palestinian and Arab volunteer forces had been decimated, Tiberias and Haifa had collapsed, and Jaffa and the Arab-populated districts west of Jerusalem were already depopulated. The use of regular Arab forces seemed inevitable. The most worrisome consequence for the Mufti was the entry of the Arab Legion.

A month earlier 'Abdullah had sent his prime minister, Tawfiq Abu-al-Huda, to see Bevin in London. Both agreed that the Arab Legion would enter Palestine after the British withdrawal and it would occupy the Arab region under the partition plan. Since a similar agreement was reached with Golda Meir in November, all three parties expected a "clean" and peaceful partition followed by annexation by 'Abdullah of the Arab part of Palestine. But the civil war caused the agreement between 'Abdullah and the Zionists to unravel by the end of April. 'Abdullah was alarmed by the mass exodus of Palestinians to Jordan, upset by the Deir Yasin massacre, moved by the desperate appeals of Palestinians under attack, and pressured by Arab public opinion and Arab leaders. Unable to send his troops to Palestine for fear of antagonizing the British, he condemned the Jews. Jewish leaders assumed, especially since contacts between both sides had ceased since November, that he was reneging on his promise, but he was not.[63]

The Palestinian collapse caused public opinion pressure on the Arab League to intervene. Yet the first meeting of the Arab chiefs of staff did not take place until April 30 and Egypt did not agree to intervene militarily until May 12. Out of desperation and despite their suspicion, they agreed to accede to 'Abdullah's demand to head the Arab armies, though instead of sending the minimum required, six divisions and six air squadrons, they sent half that amount.

However, 'Abdullah used his position as commander "to wreck the invasion plan that had been prepared by the Arab League's military experts," according to Shlaim.[64] By occupying central Palestine during the first week of fighting after May 15, he secured his basic objective. The Arab sector was controlled by him and the Iraqis. He did not trespass into Israel and took defensive positions. The only major military confrontation between the Arab Legion and the Israeli Army was over Jerusalem, which was neither within the Arab or Jewish state but in the international zone. Otherwise, both were restrained before and after the June 11 truce, and even during the ten days of fighting in July when the truce broke down. A month later 'Abdullah and the Israelis resumed their contacts and arranged for him to remain neutral while Israel attacked and defeated the Egyptian army. Both also arranged to secure the withdrawal from north central Palestine of the Iraqi army early the following year.

The All-Palestine Government. In the fall of 1948 a decision was reached that might have created a Palestine state at least in part of the area that had been allotted to the Palestinians under the partition resolution. That decision was the Political Committee of the Arab League's approval, in mid-September, of the establishment of an All-Palestine Government based in Gaza.[65]

How had this come about, given the strong objections of 'Abdullah and the British, and at a time when the Mufti's forces had been defeated in Palestine and he had been gradually marginalized within the Arab League?

The Mufti had, in fact, previously made numerous appeals to the Arab League to establish a Palestinian government so as to forestall partition and establish an Arab state in Palestine. The Mufti had pleaded with the Arab League at Aley in October 1947 and again in Cairo in December 1947 for the setting up of a shadow government under the control of the Arab Higher Committee, but the Arab League had ignored his request. In February 1948 the league again rejected his demands for a government-in-exile, the appointment of Palestinian military governors, and a loan for administrative expenses. During the ten weeks before the departure date of the British on May 14, the Mufti tried to pressure the Arab League to allow him to establish a government that would fill the political and military vacuum resulting from Britain's departure.[66]

The Arab League was not inclined collectively to support the Mufti at this stage. He had strong opponents inside the league—Iraq and Transjordan—and outside, Britain. The Hashimites in Iraq could not forget the Mufti's role in the Rashid 'Ali al-Kilani revolt in 1941 and, seeking to keep the initiative within the league, and in coordination with 'Abdullah, supported moderate Palestinians such as Musa al-'Alami.[67]

Meanwhile, the Mufti's support within the Arab League was dependent on the interests and rivalries of its members. In December 1947, for instance, the support by Egypt, Syria, and Saudi Arabia for establishment of local administration (*Idara Mahaliyya*)—an initiative the Mufti favored—was overridden by Transjordan and Iraq, as was their request for a government in February 1948. In both cases, support for the Mufti was not so great as to risk a crisis within the league or an independent action by 'Abdullah.[68] After the collapse of the Palestinians, the Mufti was marginalized within the Arab League. The committee requested on May 12, 1948, that the league allow a National Committee to take over in areas vacated by the British. The league rejected the proposal though it promised to establish a civil administration after the end of the mandate.[69]

The Arab armies entered Palestine on May 15, inaugurating the first phase of the war. By the first truce on June 11, the Israelis controlled areas beyond those allotted by the UN partition plan to the Jewish state. The land still in Arab hands was held mainly by Transjordan, with smaller sections controlled by Iraq and Egypt. Given the situation on the ground and British persuasion, Count Bernadotte, the UN mediator, recommended on June 27 that the areas assigned to the Arab state under the November 29, 1947, UN plan, should fall under 'Abdullah's control.[70]

To counter 'Abdullah and prevent him from simply annexing what remained of Arab Palestine, the Political Committee of the Arab League decided on July 8, 1948, to establish a temporary civil administration in Palestine directly responsible to the league. Dependency on the league and a temporary civil administration was not what the Mufti wanted and he therefore had reservations about the proposal. 'Abdullah, obviously, was hostile. Still, while the civil administration was not actually established, for lack of funds, it survived on paper.[71]

At the next meeting of the Political Committee of the league on September 6–16 in Alexandria, the proposal for transforming the idea of a temporary civil administration into a government for all Palestine was at the top of the agenda. Transjordan still had reservations, but it was under considerable public pressure. Suspicion of 'Abdullah, fueled by the Bernadotte proposal, had continued to grow in the Arab world, where he was accused of making a deal with the British and the Zionists and thought to be the villain behind efforts to annex Palestinian territory, especially after his overt claims that Transjordan, not the Arab Higher Committee, represented the Palestinians. At all events, Jamal al-Husayni visited Arab capitals to enlist support for the Palestine government proposal. Despite Transjordanian, Iraqi, and Egyptian reservations, the proposal was passed.[72]

The Egyptian government was not eager for the formation or wide publicity of the new government. Although the new government was convened under Egyptian auspices, it was of Palestinian creation and not a puppet government, as some historians claim.[73]

The Arab Higher Committee announced on September 22 the establishment of an All-Palestine Government in Gaza under the chairmanship of Ahmad Hilmi 'Abd al-Baqi. Ahmad Hilmi was a military governor of Jerusalem and well liked and respected among Palestinians. Besides, the Egyptian prime minister had strongly advised the Mufti against putting himself as head of a Palestine Arab state because, having sided with the Nazis, he "would never be accepted or trusted by the Western Powers."[74] Ahmad Hilmi sent telegrams to 'Azzam and members of the Arab League stating:

> I have the honor to inform you that the inhabitants of Palestine, in the exercise of their natural right to determine their own fate and in accordance with the discussions and decisions of the Political Committee [of the Arab League], have decided to declare all of Palestine, within the frontiers that were established when the British mandate ended, an independent state ruled by a government known as the Government of Palestine, based on democratic principles. I take this opportunity to express the desire of my Government to strengthen the bonds of friendship and mutual assistance between our countries.[75]

The new government set about issuing Palestinian passports and sought recognition from the international community, including sending a delegation to the United Nations. Meanwhile, 'Abdullah was repeatedly asserting that the new government had been established against the will of the

Palestinians. To counter these accusations, the All-Palestine Government decided to convene a Palestine National Council in Gaza on September 30, to which 150 representatives from the chambers of commerce, trade unions, political parties, local councils, and national committees were invited.[76]

The prime mover behind the government was, of course, the Mufti, who had been prevented from leaving Cairo by the Egyptian authorities. But with the help of the pro-Mufti Egyptian officers (Muslim Brethren and Free Officers) he secretly arrived in Gaza on September 28, 1948—the first time that he stepped on the soil of Palestine in eleven years.[77] His popularity had remained intact, especially among the refugees, and the streets of Gaza were crowded when the Mufti and Ahmad Hilmi entered the city accompanied by motorcycles and armored cars.[78]

The Palestine National Council convened on September 30, 1948. Because of difficulties of travel, between 75 and 90 attended. They quickly elected the Mufti as president of the council. A Palestine Declaration of Independence was issued on October 1, 1948, which included the following: "Based on the natural and historical right of the Palestine Arab people for freedom and independence . . . [we declare] total independence of all Palestine . . . and the establishment of an independent, democratic state whose inhabitants will exercise their liberties and rights."[79] The council passed a vote of confidence in the government, which consisted of many prominent Palestinians. Ahmad Hilmi 'Abd al-Baqi was confirmed as prime minister, Jamal al-Husayni as foreign minister, Raja'i al-Husayni as defense minister, Michael Abcarius as finance minister, and Anwar Nusayba as secretary of the cabinet. Others included 'Awni 'Abd al-Hadi, Akram Zu'aytir, Dr. Husayn al-Khalidi, Ali Hasna, Yusif Sahyun, and Amin Aqil.

The council declared that the capital of Palestine was to be Jerusalem and its flag was that of the 1916 Arab Revolt, with black, white, and green stripes and a red triangle. The government was to consist of a Higher Assembly, a Defense Assembly, and a National Council.[80]

In practice, however, the government had no independent existence. It had no territory of its own, Gaza having been entirely under Egyptian control. It had no administration, no money, no "army" beyond what remained, after the Israeli defeat of the Jaysh al-Jihad al-Muqaddas, the irregular force that had been crushingly defeated by Yishuv forces in April. The rest of the area allotted to the Palestinians was in the hands of the Mufti's mortal enemies, the Hashimites backed by Britain. The fact that the Mufti should declare a government in such circumstances attests to his unrealistic expectations in the face of the formidable forces arrayed against him.

The Arab regimes, under considerable pressure from the British not to recognize the government, equivocated but their actions were clear. Iraq, which held large portions of Palestine, could have allowed the government to extend its authority there but did not. The Egyptians were no more forthcoming. Within days of the declaration of the All-Palestine Government in Gaza, the Egyptian prime minister and defense minister ordered the Mufti back to Cairo, ostensibly because Gaza was a military zone.

The real reason, according to the Egyptian prime minister Nuqrashi, is that the Egyptian army "would not tolerate his having any military command in their region and they wished to restrict his political activity."[81] When ordered to come quietly to Cairo, the Mufti asked, "is this at the wish of the King 'Abdullah or of the British?" This was reported to Faruq who was so angered that he said he would have nothing further to do with him.[82] Eight days after his triumphant entry into Gaza, the Mufti was unceremoniously escorted out of the city by military police back to Cairo, where he was put under police surveillance. Many soldiers were placed around his residence, presumably so he could not perform yet another disappearing act.

Meanwhile, 'Abdullah was alarmed by the establishment of the government, and sought to legitimize his own leadership in Palestine by convening in Amman, on the very day (October 1) the council convened in Gaza, the First Palestinian Congress. Several thousand Palestinians came, either on their own initiative or because they were bribed or summoned by Transjordanian military governors. The congress swore allegiance to 'Abdullah, denounced the Gaza government, and declared that Transjordan and Palestine were indivisible.[83]

'Abdullah next ordered the British commander of the Arab Legion, Glubb Pasha, to dismantle Jaysh al-Jihad, which had been attacking Israeli troops and UN troops. When Arab officers were reluctant to perform the task, British officers swiftly carried it out on October 3.[84]

The British applied considerable pressure on the Arab regimes not to recognize the new government. Their representatives were instructed to use the following argument:

a. that a separate Arab State in Palestine would not be covered by any of our existing treaties with Arab states.

b. that, in view of the ex-Mufti's association with the new "Government," we should be most unlikely to enter into treaty negotiations with it, and

c. that under existing circumstances a Palestine-Arab State could not be economically viable and its absorption by Jews would sooner or later be inevitable.[85]

The Arab regimes equivocated for days despite strong public support for the new government. Meanwhile, the Israelis broke the second truce on October 15 against the Egyptian army, which retreated along the Gaza strip. The territory under the government's nominal authority was thus reduced, further diminishing its authority. Yet it was at this juncture, in mid-October, that the Arab regimes—Egypt, Iraq, Syria, Lebanon, and Saudi Arabia—finally recognized the All-Palestine Government. It was obviously an empty gesture designed to pacify the Arab masses. At the same time, Egypt forced Ahmad Hilmi and members of his cabinet to leave Gaza city, still in Egyptian hands. They were never to return. In Cairo, they were unable to perform their duties. The Arab League shunned them and refused to give them financial assistance. No wonder that the British Foreign Office, which had focused its pressure on Egypt and the Arab League, congratulated itself on November 2 for having "achieved our object . . . of reducing the Mufti's influence."[86] Within weeks, the members of the cabinet, most of whom were educated and talented professionals, took up positions in various Arab countries. The government became nothing more than a department of the Arab League.

The establishment of the government and the convening of the council were the last major political acts of the Mufti. They represented desperate acts in the face of formidable forces that wanted the territory the Palestinians had inhabited since time immemorial. From this point on, what little political power the Mufti possessed began to dissipate in proportion to the receding prospects of an independent Palestinian state and of the return of the refugees to their homes.

10. Decline of Power

 THE MUFTI was embittered by the loss of Palestine and the human tragedy it caused. About 750,000 Palestinians had become refugees. He claimed that all were driven out by the Jews. Israeli leaders and historians claimed that the refugees left because the Mufti and his colleagues had told them to leave temporarily until the Arab armies had liquidated the Jewish state. Studies indicate that the Palestinian leaders encouraged their people to stay in Palestine, and that up to half left to escape the war conditions, and the rest were forced out by Jewish terrorism and by the Israel Defense Forces to make room for Jewish immigrants and to establish a secure and largely Jewish state.[1]

The Mufti sought to galvanize Palestinian and Arab support against 'Abdullah's retention of the Arab region of Palestine. He encouraged the Palestinians there not to vote in the April 11, 1950, general elections on both banks of the Jordan.[2] Out of realism and some intimidation the Palestinians participated in the elections for a new parliament, which convened on April 24, and voted for "complete unity" under 'Abdullah.

In the meantime, led by Egypt, the Arab League opposed the annexation and 'Abdullah's ongoing peace negotiations with Israel. Arab League support for the Mufti was briefly revived with an attempt to influence the vote in Jordan on April 11. Three All-Palestine Government officials were invited to attend the Arab League Council meeting in Cairo held between March 25 and April 13. The council reaffirmed that the April 12, 1948, resolution, which had provided for the entry of Arab forces into Palestine for the purpose of saving it, was a temporary measure (i.e., not an occupation or annexation) and following its liberation, it should be returned to its owners.

But despite the resolution and almost total isolation in the Arab world, 'Abdullah went ahead with the elections and union resolution in parliament, and resumed his negotiations with Israel. Domestic opposition against a separate peace with Israel was intense. 'Abdullah finally settled for a compromise with the Arab League. He agreed to suspend separate negotiations with Israel in return for the league's tacit consent to his annexation and union, provided that the arrangement be accepted as a temporary measure.[3] Nevertheless, only Britain and Pakistan recognized the union.

'Abdullah spent the next year a lonely, dejected, and hated man. He was assassinated on July 20, 1951, at the Friday prayer at al-Aqsa mosque in the Old City of Jerusalem, where he was accompanied by his grandson Husayn. British and American diplomats had urged him not to go to Jerusalem because of rumors of plots to assassinate him, but he apparently had a meeting with Moshe Sasson and Reuven Shiloah on July 21, and he wanted to prove that he was in charge on the West Bank.[4]

All eyes turned to the Mufti as the chief suspect of the assassination, though no direct evidence was revealed linking him to the killing. However, a number of factors must be taken into consideration. The young Palestinian assassin Mustafa 'Asha may have been a member of Jaysh al-Jihad. He was immediately shot together with twenty others during the indiscriminate firing by 'Abdullah's bodyguards. Out of ten suspects, four were acquitted of whom two, Dawud and Tawfiq al-Husayni were relatives of the Mufti. Of the six that were sentenced to death, 'Abid 'Ubah and his brother Zakariyya hired the assassin, and a third provided the gun and the place, his café, where the assassination plans were made. All three were allegedly active in the Arab Revolt. A fourth, Musa al-Husayni, was a relative of the Mufti. Musa had befriended a fifth suspect, 'Abdullah al-Tall, who was in 1949 military governor of Jerusalem but parted with King 'Abdullah because of the latter's negotiations with the Zionists. Musa al-Husayni was accused of carrying money and instructions from al-Tall and another Jordanian, Musa Ahmad Ayyubi, both of whom were in Cairo, to Jerusalem.[5]

Unfortunately, much of the evidence on the assassination is either missing or weak. The assassin was immediately killed. His accomplices were given a trial, presided by inexperienced and biased judges, that lasted only days, and that was followed within a week of the death sentences with the hanging of the four Palestinians. When the trail reaches Cairo, it does not yield any secrets. Furthermore, Kirkbride, who provides most of the information about the plotters, is anti-Palestinian. The Mufti, as usual, denied complicity and even claimed that he was on good personal terms with 'Abdullah.[6]

The lack of evidence has allowed a number of conspiratorial theories to surface. Egypt, Saudi Arabia, Syria, Britain, and the United States have all been implicated. Yet the most plausible explanation is that the Mufti ordered or acquiesced in the assassination of 'Abdullah. The Mufti had the motive: 'Abdullah was a collaborator who partitioned Palestine with the Zionists; the means: the Arab Higher Committee possessed funds necessary for the task; and the ability: 'Abdullah was an easy target for members of al-Jaysh al-Jihad when he came to pray in the Haram al-Sharif. The deed was an act of revenge and perhaps an attempt to cause political disruption that would lead to a separate state on the West Bank under the Mufti's control.[7]

Just as Palestinian refugees began losing hope of ever returning to Palestine, a new leader in Egypt, Jamal 'Abd al-Nasir, promised them the liberation of Palestine. Palestinian allegiance shifted from the Mufti and his Arab Higher Committee to Nasir, a shift that antagonized the Mufti not only because of personal jealousy but also because of his political differences with Nasir. The Mufti was alarmed by Nasir's turning to Russia for arms, his socialist programs, and his union with the socialist Ba'thist regime of Syria. Worse, he learned of secret discussions in which Nasir reportedly agreed to accept the state of Israel as a fact of life in the Middle East in return for concessions by Israel. Nasir, on the other hand, found it difficult to accept the Mufti's independent actions, such as launching guerrilla attacks from Gaza against Israel in the mid-1950s, and resented the Mufti's support for Nasir's enemies: the Muslim Brothers, Saudi Arabia, and, in 1958, Iraq.[8] Tension between the Mufti and the

Egyptian regime increased to such an extent in 1959 that the Mufti found it necessary to move to Beirut where, his aide claimed, Nasir tried to have him assassinated.[9]

The Mufti refused to renounce the leadership of the Palestinian movement, either to Nasir or to a fellow Palestinian. He vehemently denounced Ahmad al-Shuqayri, because Shuqayri was appointed by the Arab League as the chairman of the Palestine Liberation Organization (PLO) in 1964, and the Mufti feared the loss of Palestinian independent decision making and action.[10] He campaigned against the organization's First Conference in Jerusalem in 1964 and urged Palestinians not to attend.[11] But neither his advice nor his threats were of much consequence by 1964. Far more significant was the opposition of an independent Palestinian organization, Fath, headed by an engineer named Yasir 'Arafat. Fath denounced the PLO as a tool of the Arab governments and boycotted the Jerusalem conference that established the Palestine National Council and adopted the Palestine National Charter. Within a few years 'Arafat would wrest control of the PLO from Shuqayri.

The emergence of Yasir 'Arafat, leader of al-Fath, as chairman of the PLO in 1969 eventually reconciled the Mufti to the inevitable transition of leadership. 'Arafat had worked for the Mufti in the mid-1950s while he was an engineering student at Cairo University. Amin preferred him to George Habash, whose Marxist ideology was anathema to the religious Mufti. Although he was worried about revolutionary ideology among Palestinians, the Mufti supported guerrilla (fida'iyyun) warfare for the liberation of Palestine.[12]

Amin al-Husayni was allowed in early 1967 by King Husayn to briefly visit Jerusalem for the first time in thirty years. He spent the last years of his life in Lebanon as an Islamic religious leader, especially of the World Islamic Conference, and as head of the Arab Higher Committee, which published Filastin, a monthly magazine. His days were occupied reading Arabic literature, especially poetry, and Arabic and Western papers, and listening to such Arab singers as Umm Kalthum and to the news on the BBC. He received thousands of guests who came to reminisce, and young Palestinian men and women who came to pay their respects and to receive the advice of an old warrior.[13] The new generation of Palestinians viewed him with ambivalence. Many rejected his traditionalism and use of religion in politics, his tight and exclusive control of the Palestinian movement, and his uncompromising attitude. Yet they admired his dedication and efforts on behalf of the Palestinian cause.

The Mufti died on July 4, 1974, at the American Hospital of the American University of Beirut. His last wish was to be buried in Jerusalem, his birthplace, in a Muslim cemetery outside Herod's gate overlooking his favorite spot, al-Haram al-Sharif.[14] The Israeli authorities refused to allow his body to be returned to Jerusalem. A memorial service was organized, in part by his relatives Amina al-Husayni and her husband Muhammad Naqib al-Husayni, a former physician of the Mufti, but the Israeli authorities prevented it by revoking, shortly before the service was to be held, the license of the theater in which it was to have taken place.[15]

Israel's refusal to allow the Mufti's body to be buried in Jerusalem was seen by the Palestinians as one more indication of the Zionist denial of Palestinian national existence. It could also denote Israel's anxiety concerning what the Mufti symbolized—dedicated Palestinian resistance to the Jewish presence in Palestine. Zionist and Palestinian mutual rejection, which began around the time of the Mufti's birth in 1895, has outlived him, and the bloody struggle for Palestine goes on.

11. An Overview and Assessment

 IN HIS post-1948 writings, Muhammad Amin al-Husayni portrayed himself as one who vigorously opposed both British rule and the Jewish national home. His Arab contemporaries were also eager to prove that al-Hajj Amin led thawras (revolts) in the 1920s and 1930s but was frustrated by British and Zionist conspiracies.[1] Zionist biographers of al-Husayni, on the other hand, have described him as a Muslim fanatic whose extremism and intransigence were largely responsible for the nakba (disaster) that befell the Palestinians in 1948. Ironically, Arab and Zionist authors converge on two issues: al-Husayni's political preeminence throughout the mandate and his pivotal role in the political violence against the British and the Zionists.[2]

There are a number of flaws in these interpretations. First, accounts on both sides are so partisan and polemical that the historical al-Husayni and the movement he led are scarcely discernible. That al-Husayni's political career has not received balanced and impartial treatment is, of course, not remarkable in view of the passion his name has always inspired. Some Arab biographers have lauded him and his cause, seeking to absolve him of any responsibility for the 1948 nakba, while Jewish nationalists vilify him and discredit his movement.[3]

The second flaw is the biographers' meager use of oral and unpublished primary sources. The Arab biographers, notably Zuhayr Mardini, are satisfied with interviewing al-Husayni and quarrying his memoirs; the Zionist biographers, especially Maurice Pearlman and Joseph B. Schechtman, rely on the Western press and lack an elementary familiarity with al-Husayni, Arab Palestinian society and politics, Islam, and Arabic.

The third problem is the ahistorical assumption by most authors that the Mufti's behavior and actions were static throughout his political career. In particular, biographers and historians assume the Mufti's militancy after 1936 guided his policies during the earlier years as well.

But an examination of British, Zionist, and Palestinian sources reveals a different portrait. Far from being static, al-Husayni's career went through two distinct phases: the Palestine phase, between 1917 and 1936, when he was a cautious, pragmatic, traditional leader who cooperated with British officials while opposing Zionism; and the exile phase, after 1936, characterized by bitterness, inflexibility, and political alliances of dubious value.

The Palestine Years. The fundamental explanation of the Mufti's cooperation with the British until 1936 can be traced to his formative years. Indeed, the Mufti's role in the politics of Palestine is incomprehensible unless we understand the politics of the notable or patrician class from which he emerged. The Husaynis were the most prominent of the urban notable families who dominated the politics of Palestine as the ruling elite of the local Ottoman administration.[4] Their traditional influence, based on centuries of religious office-holding, tax collection, and landholding, gave them a power base both in the countryside and within such cities as Jerusalem, Jaffa, and Nablus—local power bases through which the Ottomans were able to exercise their imperial authority.

Generally, the Husaynis and other notables were the defenders of the political status quo and worked with the local and imperial government to guarantee or enforce stability in those cities or regions in which they exercised influence. Some of them represented their society's interests and demands within official Ottoman institutions in Istanbul. On occasion, they led protests against the government over local issues, but never a movement aimed at the overthrow of Ottoman rule in Palestine. They were, in essence, partners with their fellow Muslims in the imperial government.

The Husaynis epitomized this partnership with the ruling power, first with the Ottomans, then with the British. Their relations with the British began, significantly enough, with the capture of Jerusalem by British forces in 1917; it was Salim al-Husayni, mayor of Jerusalem, who handed the key of the city to General Allenby on December 9, 1917. Cooperation with the British Military Administration (1917–1920) continued under Amin's half brother, Kamil al-Husayni, who had succeeded his father in the powerful position of Mufti of Jerusalem.

Amin al-Husayni continued this policy of cooperation. Shortly after returning from Turkey, where he had served in the Ottoman army, he helped a British officer recruit two thousand Arabs for the last stages of the war effort against the Ottomans, believing that once Palestine was liberated it would become part of an Arab state. He then became a clerk in the office of the British district governor of Jerusalem. It was because of this kind of cooperation, and his family name, that Sir Herbert Samuel, a prominent British Zionist and the first High Commissioner of Palestine, considered Amin in April 1921 for the office of Mufti, to replace his recently deceased half brother, Kamil.[5] Norman Bentwich, another British Zionist and the first attorney general of Palestine, writes of a meeting between Samuel and Amin al-Husayni in which the latter declared "his earnest desire to cooperate with the government, and his belief in the good intention of the government towards the Arabs. He gave assurances that the influence of his family and himself would be devoted to maintaining tranquility in Jerusalem."[6]

Amin was duly appointed Mufti and, in January 1922, president of the Supreme Muslim Council set up to manage Muslim affairs. This gave him control over Muslim courts, schools, religious endowments (awqaf), mosques, and an annual revenue of £50,000. No one was better placed to know whether al-Hajj Amin kept his promise than Bentwich, who felt that the Mufti kept the peace throughout the 1920s, and Samuel, who considered him "a moderate man."[7]

It is true that Amin was already an avid nationalist and in August 1922 joined in opposing the formation of a Legislative Council proposed by Samuel. Palestinian leaders like Amin feared that acceptance of the council was tantamount to acceptance of the British mandate, incorporating Britain's support for the establishment of the Jewish national home, which had been approved in July by the League of Nations. In addition, they did not find the council's composition or its powers fair. The council reserved 43 percent (ten out of twenty-three) of the membership to the Palestinians even though they constituted 89 percent of the population, and it was forbidden to discuss political matters. When the council was rejected by the Palestinian leaders, Samuel proposed an Advisory Council with a similar composition and mandate. It too was rejected.

The Mufti's opposition was not as significant in 1922 and 1923 as many authors assume. The political affairs of the Palestinian community were managed by the Palestine Arab Executive under the leadership of the former mayor of Jerusalem (1918–1920), Musa Kazim al-Husayni. Al-Hajj Amin was too new to his jobs and too busy with religious matters during the 1920s.

It was not until 1929 that the Mufti became the preeminent political leader of the Palestinians. His rise coincided with the decline of the executive and with the perception that he had stood up to the Zionists during the Western (Wailing) Wall controversy. The role of the Mufti in the Western Wall dispute has been exaggerated. Arab historians, such as 'Izzat Darwaza, argue that the Mufti used the dispute to reactive the national movement.[8] Israeli scholars, such as Yehoshua Porath, claim that the Mufti and his associates exploited what "seemed to them a Jewish provocation, in order to intensify the struggle against the Jews," and that "his agitation . . . resulted in the disturbances of August 1929," which took the lives of 133 Jews and 116 Palestinians.[9] This thesis fits nicely both with the general Arab view, which holds that al-Hajj Amin aggressively resisted Zionism, and with the Zionist view that the Mufti was responsible for most of the violence in Palestine. The thesis is particularly attractive because Amin was the prime beneficiary of the violence.

There is no solid evidence to indicate that the Mufti was involved in organizing the outbreaks of August 23. That morning he delivered a pacifying speech at the Haram al-Sharif (Islam's third holiest shrine) to a crowd that had heard a rumor that Jews were going to attack the Haram. He asked the Friday speaker to instruct the people to remain calm, and after the sermon urged people to return to their villages. Reacting to the speech, some members of the audience accused him of being unfaithful. In an effort to forestall trouble, he sent word to the British police to increase quickly the number of units at the Haram, and when the crowds came out of the Damascus gate, he tried to disperse them. Finally, when the violence spread that afternoon, he issued an appeal for Arabs to be patient.[10]

The Mufti's actions on August 23 are not the only evidence that he did not organize the riots. The Shaw Commission, which investigated the violence, reached the following conclusions:

1. The immediate cause of the violence was the Revisionist Zionist demonstration of August 15, 1929.
2. The violence was spontaneous, not organized by anyone.
3. The violence took place in several towns, like Hebron, where the influence of the Mufti was weak, and did not take place in many towns where his influence was strong.
4. A written appeal that the Mufti allegedly sent out for Arabs to come and defend the Haram was a forgery, probably written by a non-Arab.[11]

From 1929 to 1936, the Mufti cooperated with the British while at the same time attempting to change British policy. He reassured John Chancellor, the third High Commissioner, in October 1929 that he considered himself as "one who was, in a sense, an officer of the State." Chancellor reported that the Mufti promised to maintain order and to cooperate because he considered it his duty to do so.[12] The Mufti told Chancellor that the Arabs were amicably disposed toward Great Britain both out of self-interest and because they believed in Britain's tradition of justice. When a militant (Shakib Wahhab) approached the Mufti with an offer "to organize bands for a guerrilla campaign," Amin rejected the offer, stating that he was seeking a political solution instead.[13]

The extent of the Mufti's moderation during this period was indicated by his willingness to negotiate and accept compromise solutions. He was involved in indirect negotiations with St. John Philby in September and October 1929, from which emerged a draft settlement providing for the establishment of a Parliament in which Jews and Arabs would be proportionally represented and Palestine would remain under the authority of a British High Commissioner who would safeguard Zionist interests, including immigration. While the Mufti accepted the draft proposal, the Zionist leaders (except for Judah Magnes, chancellor of Hebrew University), including Chaim Weizmann, David Ben-Gurion, and Pinhas Rutenberg, rejected the plan because it would have confined their position as Jews to a minority in Palestine.[14]

It was the Mufti, too, who dispatched the secretary of the Supreme Muslim Council and the Palestine Arab Executive, Jamal al-Husayni, to

London in December 1929 to meet with the colonial secretary. Jamal's starting position was that Palestine have "some form of representative government," an elected legislature based on proportional representation and over whose legislation the High Commissioner would have a veto power. The colonial secretary rejected the proposal: the Zionists were opposed to a legislature in which they would be a minority and through which the Palestinians could curtail the growth of the Yishuv. The British objected because they feared British authority in Palestine would be reduced. A few months later Jamal again went to London with a Palestine Arab Executive delegation, which offered a similar proposal. Once again it was rejected by the British, for similar reasons.[15]

In the Passfield White Paper in October 1930, the British did meet Palestinian demands on immigration and land purchase, but this was the result of the Shaw and Simpson commissions' recommendations rather than the Mufti's efforts. However, Zionist pressure on the minority government of Ramsay MacDonald forced the government to withdraw these concessions in the MacDonald letter of January 13, 1931. Partly in response to the letter, the Mufti convened a General Islamic Congress in December 1931 to unite the Arabs and Muslims against the Zionists, and to make Britain aware that her interests lay in the Muslim and Arab worlds rather than with the Zionists. But the effect of the congress on the British was negligible.[16]

Indeed, efforts by the Mufti and his colleagues were largely unsuccessful. A general strike and demonstration against Jewish immigration, held by the executive in October 1933 while the Mufti was out of the country, resulted in twenty-five deaths. Political parties were formed, private and public protests were held, but they were ineffective in halting immigration. In fact, Jewish immigration increased from 4075 in 1931 to 61,854 in 1935. The fourth British High Commissioner, Arthur Wauchope, took notice of the Mufti's difficulties in January 1934: "I am confident that the Mufti likes me, respects me and is anxious to help me . . . but he fears that criticism of his many opponents that he is too British may weaken his influence in the country. The fact, however, that his influence is on the side of moderation is of definite value."[17]

The political situation worsened in 1935. A British intelligence report predicted that the Palestinian political leaders "will find themselves forced to adopt an extremist policy" in order "to restore their prestige and prevent the leadership of the nationalist movement from passing out of their hands" and "to satisfy public opinion and try a new course of action, as all their previous efforts in protest, demonstrations, public meetings etc. had failed to attain their object."[18]

In light of the deteriorating situation, one can ask why the Mufti continued to maintain his dual policy of cooperation with the British and nonviolent opposition to the Zionists during two decades when the threat to Palestinian national existence, except for 1926–28, was becoming more ominous. A number of fundamental reasons can be suggested.

First, the Husaynis, as discussed above, belonged to that patrician class in whom defense of the political status quo and cooperation with the imperial power to guarantee stability were deeply ingrained. Amin al-Husayni's statements to British officials and his actions indicate a constant awareness of his status as an official appointed by the Palestine government. Should he challenge British discretionary power, he would lose the posts of Mufti of Jerusalem and president of the Supreme Muslim Council.

Second, like others of his generation and despite his nationalist views, the Mufti admired what he perceived as British fairness and sense of justice—personal qualities of British officials such as Herbert Samuel and Arthur Wauchope, with whom he met frequently. He repeatedly affirmed his allegiance to the British rulers on the basic of these personal qualities, even while he was aware that British officials, regardless of their personal preferences, were the instruments of what he considered an unjust policy.

Third, he believed that the British were too strong for the Palestinians to oppose successfully and that, in any case, their presence in Palestine would be transitory, as it appeared to be in Egypt, Iraq, and Transjordan.

Finally, he thought that Britain's pro-Zionist Balfour policy would change when the British realized that their interests lay with the Muslim and Arab countries and not with the Zionists. He further believed that the Palestinians, with the help of fellow Muslims and Arabs, might influence the British through petitions, delegations to London, protests, and demonstrations. He opposed political violence or preparation for revolutionary resistance. On the contrary, he surreptitiously assisted the British authorities in defusing violent outbreaks. In short, he affirmed, by word and deed, a preference for nonviolent methods.

The Exile Years. Ever since 1921, the Mufti had managed to pacify his two masters: the British with loyalty pledges and cooperation, and the Palestinians with religious and political rhetoric. But in April 1936 he was forced by events, by the militant public anti-British mood (growing since the summer of 1929), to choose between them. When violence flared on April 15–19, 1936, and a general strike began to spread, the public urged him to assume the leadership of the strike against Jewish immigration and land purchase and for the establishment of a national government. He resisted for ten crucial days.[19] But the Mufti's propensity for inertia and timidity gave way to political action. He had remained on the sidelines with nothing to show but a record of failure, he would have been overtaken by events and by more militant leaders. By accepting the leadership of the newly organized Arab Higher Committee, which comprised all five political parties, he became the leader of the general strike. This decision was the beginning of the end of his policy of cooperation. It was also the beginning of the end of British confidence in him.

Several events over the next few years served to radicalize him further. In 1937 the British submitted a plan to partition Palestine. The Mufti, as most Palestinians, rejected partition and continued to lead the revolt. The British decided to strip him of his offices and arrest him for his part in the violence.

The Mufti escaped to Lebanon and continued to lead the revolt from Beirut and Damascus. By the summer of 1938, many cities, including Jerusalem, had been taken by the rebels. But it was only a matter of time before Britain, whose forces outnumbered the Palestinians ten to one, crushed the revolt. The Palestinians paid a high price for the 1936–39 revolt in terms of their economy, social fabric, and military and political structure. Out of a population of 960,000, the British conservatively estimated that 3074 Palestinians were killed. In addition 110 were hanged, and 6000 were incarcerated in 1939 alone. Considering the magnitude of the national calamity, and the personal loss of many of the Mufti's friends and relatives, it is no wonder that he was very depressed and considered suicide in 1939, according to a report by the French High Commissioner of the Levant, Gabriel Puaux.[20]

The Mufti grew bitter and uncompromising in matters vital to the future of his people. He rejected the 1939 White Paper, even though its terms—restricting Jewish immigration to 75,000 during five years, limiting land sales, and planning for an independent Palestine with an Arab majority of two to one in ten years—were obviously favorable to the Palestinians. Instead, he wrote thanking Puaux for his hospitality in Lebanon. He bribed the French chief of police of Syria and Lebanon, where, as the result of British pressure on the French, he was under close observation, and escaped to Iraq in October 1939. There he sought to encourage a Pan-Arab challenge to British control over Iraq and, ultimately, over Palestine.

The prospect of a revolt in Iraq alarmed three parties with vital interests in Palestine: the Zionists, the Hashimites, and the British. Pinhas Rutenberg, a Zionist representative who a year earlier had been counseled by Amir 'Abdullah to eliminate the Mufti, traveled to London to urge the British to assassinate the Palestinian leader.[21] Since the Foreign Office was not in the habit of carrying out assassinations, it found the proposal unattractive and, in any case, impractical. Yet five months later the Mufti became such a grave threat to British interests that Winston Churchill approved his assassination.[22] Members of the Irgun, a Revisionist Zionist underground movement, were flown to Iraq to carry out the assassination with the help of the British army, but failed to kill the Mufti. He escaped to Iran, and the Rashid 'Ali revolt he had helped to start was put down by the British and Hashimite forces.

The Mufti then fled to the Axis countries, first to Italy, then to Germany. He claimed that he had nowhere else to go because the British had a price on his head. He cooperated with the Nazis, believing that they would help the Arabs expel the British once Germany defeated Britain in the Middle East. There is no reason to believe, however, that the Germans, despite written commitments, would have been less perfidious with the Arabs than the British had been in World War I. That is, the Mufti may have been helping with the war effort for the privilege of exchanging imperial masters.

Despite attempts by partisan officials and writers to prove otherwise, there is no evidence that the Mufti participated in the Final Solution. Besides, the Nazis hardly needed the Mufti's inspiration or help to commit their barbaric crimes against the Jewish people.[23] Meanwhile, it is possible that the Mufti, given his penchant for ferreting out information and his contacts with Heinrich Himmler, head of the Gestapo, did know about the extermination camps. What is certain is that the Arab claim that the Mufti was not anti-Jewish but only anti-Zionist is false: his statements in Nazi Germany about Jewish greed, power, and plots indicate that he had crossed the line. His association with the Nazis tainted his career and to some extent his cause, and limited his freedom of action during the critical period between 1946 and 1948.[24]

The Mufti returned to the Arab world in 1946 with the aim of continuing the struggle against the Zionists and establishing a Palestine state. But he totally misjudged the balance of forces between the Arabs and the Zionists; when the United Nations General Assembly passed the partition resolution on November 29, 1947, the Mufti organized a general strike and political violence. There is no question that this opposition was detrimental to his people's cause.

Assessment. Though astute, charismatic, incorruptible, and ascetic in his dedication to his people, the Mufti's policies during both phases of his career were a failure and unwittingly contributed to the dispossession of the Palestinians. During the first period, even though he understood the ominous threat of Zionism to Palestinian national existence, the Mufti cooperated with the British mandatory government of Palestine and rejected methods of national self-defense at a time when such methods may have helped his cause. He opposed the Balfour policy, but through such ineffective methods as petitions, delegations and strikes. He succeeded in uniting Muslim and Christian Palestinians and helped awaken the national spirit, but did not mobilize the Palestinian masses for action. Notwithstanding Palestinian and Zionist claims to the contrary, he did not lead a single act of political violence between 1920 and 1936.

The four cases of political violence in 1920, 1921, 1929, and 1933 were not revolts, as he and Palestinian writers claimed. They were localized spontaneous riots that resulted in no sustained policy changes by the British, for whom they were inconsequential. On the other side, the Zionists had organized a quasi government together with a labor union, an educational system, national press, and, most importantly, a military force. The Zionists increased their land holdings from 650,000 dunams in 1919 to 1,410,000 dunams in 1936, while their population grew from about 50,000 in 1917 to 384,000 in 1936. They sought to become the majority in order to establish a state, and wrote and said so repeatedly. Most Zionist leaders, including Chaim Weizmann and later David Ben-Gurion, were anti-Arab and considered the Palestinians treacherous, blackmailers, fanatic, and inferior.[25] They planned, in numerous secret meetings, to expel the "natives" or otherwise dominate them. Little of these plans could have been known at the time but the Mufti and a number of Palestinians predicted some form of expulsion and domination. Nevertheless, he was mostly passive or used only ineffectual methods. In short, despite the growth of the Yishuv, he did not galvanize his people to defend themselves against what should have appeared to be inevitable expulsion or domination. It is true that the odds were against the Palestinians, but a massive revolt in 1929 combined with Palestinian compromise proposals concerning the Legislative Council (that is, self-government under British rule) might possibly have resulted in a change in British policy that would have constrained the growth of the Yishuv. It was perhaps the last opportunity for the Palestinians to alter dramatically their political future in Palestine.

It was not until 1936 that the Mufti participated in a revolt, and only after he was forced to choose between his British employers and his people. By then it was too late. The Jewish community was far too powerful. Conversely, the British had lost their discretionary power in Palestine and had become umpires adjudicating between the two communities. Moreover, they could not easily retreat from their mandate promises to the Jews. The most they could offer the Palestinians was the 1937 Peel partition plan, which was rejected by the Mufti.

A perception has emerged in Israel and among its supporters that the Palestinians—represented in this period chiefly by the Mufti—"never miss an opportunity to miss an opportunity." The Palestinian reaction is that this amounts to "blaming the victims." Both of these statements are simplistic and largely false, having more to do with the war of words than with history. A few examples will suffice. No one would pretend that the Balfour Declaration represented an opportunity for the Palestinians despite its promises to safeguard the religious and civil life of the "non-Jewish population." Had the Palestinians accepted the declaration, it is probable that a Jewish state would have been established well before 1948. Samuel's 1922 Legislative Council proposal is more debatable. The Palestinians assumed that accepting the proposal was tantamount to accepting the mandate and therefore the Balfour policy, as well as a minority political representation in the council of 43 percent at a time when the Palestinians constituted 89 percent of the population. More significant, Churchill instructed Samuel not to allow the council to discuss constitutional issues. In other words, the council could have discussed tariffs, but not Jewish immigration. Though it could have expanded its authority, the body was hardly a model of representative self-government and not a compelling proposal at the time.

Nor was the Peel partition proposal in 1937 a viable opportunity to Palestinians. Under this proposal, the Jews, who owned 5.6 percent of the land, would receive 40 percent of the most fertile region, from which most Palestinians would be expelled; the British would get the third holiest city of Islam, Jerusalem; and Transjordan's Amir 'Abdulla would be given the rest. In other words, the Palestinians were being asked to give their blessing to the dismemberment of Palestine among three outside parties: the Zionists from Eastern Europe, the British, and 'Abdulla from the Hijaz. That was an opportunity the Mufti and most Palestinians willingly missed.

The first real opportunity came in 1939, in the form of the 1939 White Paper policy. It severely retricted Jewish immigration and land transfer, and promised an independent Palestine state in ten years on the basis of an Arab majority of a 2 to 1 ratio. It came close to what the Mufti and other leaders had been asking for. To have rejected such a policy was short-sighted and irresponsible at a time when the Palestinian community was, as a result of British suppression of the Arab Revolt, depleted of leadership, institutional structures, arms, and even the will to fight on, and when the Zionist side was growing in strength.

The Mufti came back to the Middle East in 1946 to find that the struggle for Palestine was jeopardized by 'Abdulla's ambition and by rivalry and disunity within the Arab League, which now took responsibility for Palestine. Zionist military, diplomatic, and financial strength had been considerably increased. Yet the Mufti, who was consulted by the Arab League, rejected almost every offer to send Palestinians to testify in front of commissions or to meet with the British and the Zionists. He rejected all proposals—those calling for trusteeship, cantonization and partition—that did not offer Palestinians an Arab Palestine. The Palestinians' legal and moral case was a just one: they had occupied Palestine for at least 1300 years, and Palestinians were in the majority and owned most of the land. But justice seldom exists this side of heaven and certainly not in the real world of power politics. The Mufti misjudged the balance of forces and was unrealistic in not adjusting his demands to the realities on the ground. Indeed, the demands he made between 1946 and 1948 were almost identical to the position he maintained a quarter of a century before.

The 1947 partition resolution was the last opportunity for the Mufti. The resolution was less attractive than the Peel partition in terms of territory. The Jews were to get 55 percent of Palestine, when they owned only 7 percent. Most Palestinians and Arabs viewed it as a great injustice and hardly a fair compromise. Yet, because the resolution held out the prospect of an independent Palestinian state in part of Palestine, it represented the only hope of trying to keep 'Abdulla and the Zionists from, between them, taking over the whole of the country.

The 1939 and 1947 rejections were missed opportunities not merely from the perspective of hindsight but even from the facts as they appeared at the time. But this does not mean that the outcomes would have been different than they were.

Is it likely, for example, that had the Mufti accepted the 1939 White Paper, things would have turned out differently in the long run? It is improbable, because the cumulative effect of American support for the Biltmore program and pressure on the British, Britain's financial needs, Palestinian diplomatic and military weakness, international sympathy for Holocaust survivors. and the impact of Jewish terrorism would have combined to undermine the White Paper policy irrespective of Palestinian support for that policy.

Would the Palestinians have established a state in the area alloted to them by the UN had the Mufti and the Arab countries accepted the 1947 UN partition resolutions? Probably not, because such an outcome assumes that the Zionists would have ignored their agreement with 'Abdulla and allowed a Palestinian state ruled by their archenemy, the Mufti; that 'Abdulla would have abandoned both his ambition of Greater Syria and his agreement with the Zionists to partition Palestine; that both would magnanimously resist the urge, in the absence of UN forces, to fill in the political vacuum that existed in the Arab sector; and that Britain would have turned over the Arab region to the Mufti and the Arab Higher Committee.

One or two immediate causes rarely explain why major events occur. To understand the cause of an event, an historian must assemble all the causes, separate the immediate from the ultimate, and present them in order of priority. To state that either the 1939 or 1947 rejections by the Mufti caused the Palestinian tragedy is effective as propaganda but fails as an historical explanation.

At the same time, both decisions may have contributed to the disaster of 1948. This being the case, the Mufti and the Palestinians must accept some responsibility for these miscalculations, because the possibility existed that Arab compromise might have resulted in a Palestinian state in 45 percent of Palestine.

In short, the Mufti's cooperation during the first two decades of British rule and his rejectionism during the last decade unwittingly contributed to the ultimate defeat of the Palestinians. Some other leader, armed with a modern education, knowledge of world affairs, sense of strategy and timing, and above all realism, might have taken better advantage of opportunities.

Yet the overriding factors that frustrated Palestinian nationalism have less to do with the policies and actions of a single leader than with the balance of forces. The long-term causes of Palestinian dispossession were the Zionist program at Basel in 1897 and the Balfour policy of 1917. It was British policy, backed by British military might and by international (i.e., European) support for the British mandate and for Zionist colonization, that was primarily responsible for providing the Yishuv time to grow, through immigration and land purchases, and time to establish quasi-governmental and military institutions. The Palestinians were a weak, underdeveloped agrarian society and never a match for the British army nor, after 1939, for the Zionist forces. Their power to influence the destiny of Palestine was secondary to that of the three other parties with strategic and territorial interests in Palestine: the British, the Zionists, and, to a lesser extent, the Hashimites.

Notes

PREFACE

1. Compare, for example, Schechtman, *The Mufti and the Fuehrer*, pp. 15–17 and Pearlman, *Mufti of Jerusalem*, pp. 10–11.
2. The Mufti's memoirs, covering 1937 to 1948, have appeared in *Akhbar al-Yawm*, *Filastin* (the official publication of the Arab Higher Committee and, therefore, the most authentic); and *Akhir Sa'a*.
3. Porath, "Al-Hajj Amin"; Khadduri, *Arab Contemporaries*.
4. Taggar, "Mufti of Jerusalem"; Ben-Elkanah, " 'Aliyat"; Jbara, *Palestinian Leader*.

1. THE MAKING OF A PALESTINIAN NATIONALIST: THE FORMATIVE YEARS

1. Porath, "Political Organization," p. 1.
2. *Ibid.*, p. 2.
3. Hourani, "Ottoman Reform," p. 45.
4. *Ibid.*, p. 46.
5. *Ibid.*, p. 47–48.
6. *Ibid.*, p. 48.
7. *Ibid.*, p. 49.
8. *Ibid.*
9. *Ibid.*, p. 52.
10. *Ibid.*
11. *Ibid.*, p. 60.

12. *Ibid.*, p. 67.
13. *Ibid.*, p. 64.
14. Muslih, "Urban Notables, Ottomanism, Arabism," p. 76.
15. Khoury, *Urban Notables and Arab Nationalism*, p. 67; see also Dawn, *From Ottomanism*, and Khalidi, *British Policy*.
16. Khoury, *Urban Notables and Arab Nationalism*, p. 74.
17. *Ibid.*, p. 84.
18. Muslih, "Urban Notables, Ottomanism, Arabism," p. 218.
19. *Ibid.*, p. 225.
20. *Ibid.*, p. 220.
21. See Hertzberg, *The Zionist Idea*.
22. The exact date of his birth is uncertain. I could find no documentary evidence for the date 1893, used by biographers Pearlman, Schechtman, and Porath; nor for the date Amin later used, 1897, which has been accepted by such writers as Khadduri. The most reliable dates are 1896, which Amin used on visa applications between 1921 and 1923; and 1895, which he used in passport and visa applications between 1926 and 1934. The change in 1926 may have been made to correct a mistake in computing the *hijra* (emigration of the Prophet Muhammad and his followers from Mecca to Medina in A.D. 622) date of his birth (1313). Yet when the change was made in 1926, he first wrote 1897 then wrote a 5 over the 7, further adding to the confusion; see Israel State Archives (ISA) 65, 01820.
23. Khaddduri, *Arab Contemporaries*, p. 69, n. 3; Khadduri's genealogy, supplied by the Mufti, is consistent with a copy of the family tree of the Husaynis, given to me on December 26, 1978, in Jerusalem by Dr. Muhammad al-Naqib al-Husayni (a relative and a physician of Amin al-Husayni); for family genealogy, see al-Jabarti, *'Aja'ib*, 1:374–75.
24. Khadduri, *Arab Contemporaries*, p. 69, n. 4; Jbara, *Palestinian Leader*, pp. 6–8; Porath, *The Emergence*, pp. 184–85.
25. Interview, Haydar al-Husayni (aide to the Mufti).
26. *Ibid.*
27. Mandel, *The Arabs and Zionism*, pp. 19–21; Foreign Office (FO) 371/3398/92393, Ronald Storrs to Sir Mark Christopher Sykes, May 24, 1918; FO 371/3395/11053/86912, Sir Gilbert Clayton to O. Gore, April 19, 1918; FO 371/3385/747/198575, Storrs Report, November 8, 1918.
28. Porath, *The Emergence*, p. 187.
29. Bentwich and Bentwich, *Mandate Memories*, p. 189.
30. Interview, Zaynab al-Husayni (daughter of Amin al-Husayni). Central Zionist Archives (CZA) S25/10499, biography of Amin al-Husayni; interview, Haydar al-Husayni.
31. Al-'Awdat, *Min A'lam*, p. 109.
32. Interview, Zaynab al-Husayni; interview, Munif al-Husayni (a close associate of the Mufti).
33. Hourani, *Arabic Thought*, pp. 222–44; Haim, *Arab Nationalism*, pp. 19–25; interview, Haydar al-Husayni.

34. Interview, Kamil al-Dajani.
35. *Ibid.*
36. *Ibid.*
37. Interview, Zaynab al-Husayni.
38. CZA S25/10499, biography of Amin al-Husayni.
39. Nuwayhid, "Sayyidi al-Fa'iz," pp. 118–20.
40. Interview, Ghalib Sa'id al-Nashashibi.
41. Al-Husayni, unpublished diaries; CZA S25/10499, biography of Amin al-Husayni.
42. Al-Husayni, unpublished diaries.
43. *Ibid.*
44. *Ibid.* The essay is authored by Amin. The poems are in his handwriting and presumably authored by him.
45. FO 371/5121/E9379/85/44, Palin Report, June 1918.
46. Darwaza, "Tis'una 'Aman"; FO 371/5121/E9397/85/44, Palin Report, p. 4; Antonius, *The Arab Awakening*, pp. 229–30. See the Peel and Haycraft reports.
47. Al-Hut, "Al-Qiyadat wa Mu'assasat," p. 235.
48. FO 371/4182/2117/125609, Camp's report on the Arab Palestinian organizations, August 12, 1919.
    There are several good scholarly works on the history of the Palestinian national movement. Lesch's *Arab Politics* is concise, based on British, Arab, and Zionist sources, and objective though empathic; Porath's *The Emergence* is a thorough and very useful work based on a wide number of sources, poorly translated, and attempts to be impartial while incorporating Orientalist (Western) and moderate Zionist views of Palestinian history; Porath's *The Palestinian Arab National Movement* is better written but less thorough and impartial; Bayan al-Hut's "Al-Qiyadat wa al-Mu'assasat" extensively utilizes Arab sources (written and oral) and is a sympathetic account; Kayyali's *Palestine: A Modern History* is partisan, though based on British documents, and is much shorter; and Darwaza remains one of the best Palestinian historians, on whom many writers have relied without giving him sufficient credit.
    For a general history of the Palestine problem: see Great Britain, Peel Commission Report, which continues to be useful for the period before 1937; and Hurewitz's *Struggle*, an early attempt at writing a nonpartisan history, is still a reliable Western account of the period between 1936 and 1948. Two valuable anthologies are *From Haven to Conquest*, edited and introduced by Khalidi, and *The Transformation of Palestine*, edited by Abu-Lughod. For a Palestinian essay of the subject, see Said's *Question of Palestine*.
49. Darwaza, "Tis'una 'Aman," p. 21; Lesch, *Arab Politics*, p. 84.
50. Darwaza, "Tis'una 'Aman," p. 21; Lesch, *Arab Politics*, p. 84; interview, Su'ad al-Husayni (daughter of Amin al-Husayni); FO 371/4178/2117/41476, British intelligence report, February 15, 1919.
51. Interview, Haydar al-Husayni; al-Husayni, *Haqa'iq*, p. 120.
52. Herzl, *Diaries*, p. 378.

53. Al-Husayni, *Haqa'iq*, pp. 127–33.
54. Darwaza, "Tis'una 'Aman," p. 21; interview, Ghalib al-Nashashibi.
55. Nuwayhid, "Sayyidi al-Fa'iz," pp. 118–20.
56. Interview, Ghalib al-Nashashibi; Great Britain, Peel Commission Report, p. 177; CZA S25/10499.
57. CZA S25/10499.
58. Meinertzhagen, *Middle East Diary*, p. 26; Monroe, *Britain's Moment*, p. 65.
59. According to a Zionist source cited in Porath, *The Emergence*, p. 129, al-Nadi al-'Arabi worked with an "underground" organization called al-Kaff al-Sawda (the Black Hand) which in May 1919 changed its name to al-Fida'iyya (the Self-Sacrificer) the sought to achieve its political aims through violence. Amin is said to have been influential in this organization. There is no solid evidence to support this source, which for this period is of poor quality and, therefore, unreliable.
60. Porath, *The Emergence*, p. 96.
61. ISA 2/30, report on the Muslim-Christian demonstration of March 8, 1920; FO 371/5121/E9379/85/44 Palin Report, p. 4; CZA L/3, Zionist intelligence report for March 1920.
62. CZA L/3, 222, Zionist intelligence report, April 1, 1920.
63. FO 371/5119, interim Palin report of May 7, 1920; FO 371/5121/E9379/85/44, and FO 371/4121/E120/6.31, Palin report of July 1, 1920, p. 7; *Times* (London), April 19, 1920.
64. Interview, 'Arif al-'Arif; FO 371/5119.E5237, L. J. Bols Report, April 9, 1920; CZA Z/4, 2800/II Zionist intelligence report, April 13, 1920; Great Britain, Peel Commission Report, p. 177; interview, Haydar al-Husayni; FO 371/5117/E3158/85/44, Bols Report, April 14, 1920; FO 371/5118/E3474, General Headquarters (Cairo) to War Office (WO), April 18, 1920.
65. FO 371/511/E4076/E3507, *Times* (London), April 29, 1920, and *Ha-Aretz*, May 5, 1920, report that Amin and 'Arif received five years. Other sources state it was ten: WO 32/9617, 0171/320, 32/9619, 0176/481.
66. WO 32/9614, H. J. Creedy to Foreign Office, August 4, 1920.
67. Darwaza, "Tis'una 'Aman," p. 22; CZA Z4/2800/II, Zionist intelligence report, July 18, 1920. Darwaza claims that Amin joined a secret organization in Damascus called the Arab Palestine Society, which planned military attacks in Palestine.

2. RISE TO RELIGIOUS POWER

1. Interview, Zaynab al-Husayni; interview, 'Arif al-'Arif.
2. U.S. National Archives (NA), RG 226, OSS 9677, American intelligence report of October 30, 1943.
3. *Ibid.*
4. Interview, 'Arif al-'Arif; NA, RG 226, OSS 9677, American intelligence report of October 30, 1943.

5. Foreign Office (FO) 371/6375/E3882/35/88, political report of February 1921; Great Britain, Shaw Commission, Evidence Heard, items 13424–30.
6. Schechtman, *The Mufti and the Fuehrer*, p. 20.
7. Darwaza, "Tis'una 'Aman," p. 22.
8. Cited in Kedourie, "Sir Herbert Samuel," p. 55.
9. FO 371/5139, Samuel to Earl Curzon, April 2, 1920.
10. FO 371/2120/E7798/85/44, Samuel to Earl Curzon, July 2, 1920; Central Zionist Archives (CZA) S25/10499.
11. *Palestine Weekly*, July 9, 1920.
12. CZA Z4/5770/3/1; interview, 'Arif al-'Arif; Israel State Archives (ISA), CS 106/1, in Kedourie, "Sir Herbert Samuel," p. 61.
13. Interview, Ishaq Musa al-Husayni.
14. Porath, "Al-hajj Amin," pp. 125–26.
15. *Ibid.*, pp. 127–28; CZA Z/4 2800 II, Zionist intelligence report, June 18, 1920.
16. Scholars are not in agreement about who chose the Mufti, the *mutasarrif* (governor) or the Shaykh al-Islam; see the works of Kedourie and Porath cited in notes 8 and 14.
17. Darwaza, *Hawl*, pp. 46–47.
18. ISA, CS 245, March 22, 1921.
19. ISA, CA 245; *Morning Post*, April 20, 1921, in War Office (WO) 106/208/28; CO 733/3/24596, political report of April 1921.
20. Darwaza, "Tis'una 'Aman," p. 23.
21. ISA, CS 245, CID report to CS, January 24, 1921.
22. FO 371/6375/E3882/35/85, political report of February 1920.
23. Interview, Haydar al-Husayni; Bentwich and Bentwich, *Mandate Memories*, p. 191.
24. See ISA, CA 245, for the 'Awri letter (March 21, 1920) and for the numerous petitions.
25. Al-Hut, "Al-Qiyadat wa al-Mu'assasat," p. 235.
26. Bentwich and Bentwich, *Mandate Memories*, p. 191.
27. CO 733/3/CO 24596, May 9, 1920; CZA S/25/3008, Zionist intelligence report; ISA, CS 245, May 3, 1921—the file contains petitions on behalf of Amin and accounts of the election.
28. CZA S/25/3008; CO 733/3/CO 24596, May 9, 1920; ISA, CA, April 20, 1920.
29. Kedourie, "Sir Herbert Samuel," p. 64–66.
30. ISA, CS 245, Samuel to CS, April 11, 1921; Bentwich and Bentwich, *Mandate Memories*, pp. 191–92.
31. Al-Husayni, Haqa'iq, p. 29.
32. Kayyali, *Palestine: A Modern History*, p. 94.
33. ISA, CS 245, Quigley to ACS (P), May 12, 1921.
34. Interview, Ghalib al-Nashashibi; CZA 4/5770/3/1; Bentwich and Bentwich, *Mandate Memories*, p. 191.
35. Great Britain, Peel Commission Report, p. 117.
36. CO 733/6/CO47685, Political Report for August 1921, by W. H. Deedes, September 8, 1921; Porath, *The Emergence*, p. 196.

37. CO 733/6/51930, Herbert Samuel to Winston Churchill, October 8, 1921.
38. Cited in Porath, *The Emergence*, pp. 200–1.
39. For the terms of the council's regulations, see CO 733/8/CO1345, Deedes dispatch, December 29, 1921.
40. CO 733/45/CO26756, report on the work of the Supreme Muslim Council, 1922–23.
41. Porath, *The Emergence*, pp. 205–6; Jbara, *Palestinian Leader*, p. 64.
42. Yasin, *Al-thawra*, p. 23.
43. Porath, *The Emergence*, p. 213.
44. Bentwich and Bentwich, *Mandate Memories*, pp. 191–92; Elath, "Conversations," p. 44.

3. POLITICAL STRUGGLE OVER THE WESTERN WALL, 1928–1929

1. A number of the dead were not counted because their relatives, fearing collective punishment measures, did not report casualties. For a thorough and balanced treatment of the 1928–29 conflict, see Great Britain, Shaw Commission Report; Great Britain, Shaw Commission, Evidence Heard; and International Commission.
2. Sykes, *Crossroads*, pp. 99–100.
3. International Commission, pp. 15–16.
4. *Qur'an*, Sura 17.
5. Palestine Liberation Organization (PLO), Research Center, "Wathi'qat al-Dizdaz wa Qadiyyat al-Buraq," a pamphlet containing reproductions of the Ottoman documents, n.d.
6. Great Britain, Shaw Commission, Evidence Heard, items 1261–77, 1291–96.
7. Wolfgang Von Weisl, a Revisionist journalist who talked with the shammas, in *The New Palestine*, September 13, 1929, cited in Great Britain, Shaw Commission, Evidence Heard, pp. 228–29.
8. Colonial Office (CO) 733/160/57540/I, Harry Luke to L. Amery (Colonial Secretary), October 13, 1928; ESCO, *Palestine: A Study of Jewish, Arab, and British Policies*, 2:599.
9. Darwaza, *Hawl*, 2:61–62.
10. Porath, *The Emergence*, p. 266.
11. Great Britain, White Paper of 1928.
12. Kisch, *Palestine Diary*, p. 245.
13. *Times* (London), September 28, 1928.
14. *Davar*, September 25, 1928, in CO 733/160/57540/I, translated extracts from the Hebrew press dispatched by Harry Luke to L. Amery on October 13, 1928.
15. *Do'ar ha-Yom*, September 28, 1928, in CO 733/160/57540/I.
16. CO 733/160/57540/I, Luke to Amery, October 13, 1928.
17. Porath, "Al-Hajj (Muhammad) Amin," p. 164.
18. CO 733/160/57540/II, the Mufti's letters of October 4 and 8, 1928; Great Britain, Shaw Commission Report, pp. 31–32.

19. *Al-Jami'a al-'Arabiyya*, October 29, 1928, reprinted in Kayyali, *Watha'iq al-Muqawama*, pp. 116–18.
20. CO 733/160/57540/II, Va'ad Le'ummi letter of October 10, 1928.
21. *Ibid.*
22. CO 733/160/57540/I, Officer Administering the Government (OAG) to Colonial Secretary, October 16, 1928; League of Nations, Permanent Mandates Commission, *Minutes of the Fourteenth Session*, held at Geneva from October 28 to November 13, 1928.
23. CO 733/160/57540/I, Harry Luke (OAG) to Amery, October 13, 1928.
24. *The New Palestine*, November 9, 1928, and November 16, 1928, cited in Great Britain, Shaw Commission, Evidence Heard, pp. 227–28.
25. *Al-Jami'a al-'Arabiyya*, November 1, 1928, reprinted in Kayyali, *Watha'iq al-Muqawama*, pp. 119–26; the translated resolutions are in CO 733/160/57540/III and in Great Britain, Shaw Commission, Evidence Heard, exhibit 45 (i), pp. 1051–52; and the memorandum is in Great Britain, Shaw Commission Report, pp. 31–32.
26. Great Britain, White Paper of 1928.
27. Great Britain, Shaw Commission, Evidence Heard, items 1262–77, 1291–96.
28. Great Britain, Shaw Commission Report, p. 31.
29. CO 733/98, W. Ormsby-Gore to Brigadier General Clayton, May 2, 1918, encloses Weizmann letter of May 1, 1918.
30. CO 733/98, Muslim dignitaries to Storrs, May 2, 1918.
31. Central Zionist Archives (CZA) S25/748, Colonel Frederick H. Kisch to Natan Straus, June 2, 1926.
32. *Ibid.*, Kisch to Chaim Weizmann, November 3, 1926.
33. *Ibid.*, June 2, 1926.
34. *Ibid.*, November 3, 1926.
35. CZA S25/2, Kisch to Straus, November 4, 1926, M. Bercoff to Ironby, January 28, 1927.
36. CO 733/163/67013/I, Shuckburgh to Chancellor, January 1, 1929, Chancellor to Shuckburgh, January 12, 1929.
37. Al-Ghuri, *Filastin*, p. 114; Great Britain, Shaw Commission, Evidence Heard, p. 529.
38. For the exploits of Zionist bribers and Palestinians bribed, see Porath, *The Emergence*, ch. 8.
39. Co 733/98, Ronald Storrs to OETA, September 24, 1918.
40. *Davar*, October 2, 1925, in U.S. National Archives (NA) 404/15; see also a similar demand in CO 733/132/44051, reference to district officer's letter #2271.
41. CO 733/163/67013/I, Chancellor to Amery, April 20, 1929.
42. CO 733/98, Weizmann to Ormsby-Gore, May 1, 1918.
43. CO 733/2; CO 733/4, minute #4248, July 1, 1921; Great Britain, Shaw Commission, Evidence Heard, Hansard reference for April 5, 1921, p. 919.
44. Israel State Archives (ISA), AE 102, 'Izzat Darwaza to AE, August 2, 1922; ISA, AE 1541, Sab al-'Aysh to AE, September 16, 1922.

45. Great Britain, Shaw Commission, Evidence Heard, items 13,211–19, 14,699.
46. *Ibid.*, items 10,863, 10,901–13, 14,868, 16,347–49.
47. Al-Husayni, *Haqa'iq*, p. 10.
48. Great Britain, White Paper of 1928.
49. Great Britain, Shaw Commission Report, p. 34.
50. *Ibid.*, p. 35.
51. Kayyali, *Watha'iq al-Muqawama*, p. 138; CO 733/163/67013/I, High Commissioner (HC) to Colonial Secretary (SSC [Secretary of State for the Colonies]), May 6 and May 10, 1928.
52. CO 733/163/67013/I, HC to SSC, May 10, 1929.
53. *Ibid.*
54. Porath, *The Emergence*, pp. 268–99.
55. CO 733/164/67015, law officers' report, February 16, 1929.
56. *Al-Sirat al-Mustaqim*, August 8, 1929, in CZA Z4/5793.
57. *Ibid.*, November 28, 1928.
58. *Ibid.*
59. Great Britain, Shaw Commission Report, p. 71.
60. Great Britain, Shaw Commission, Evidence Heard, p. 580.
61. Porath, *The Emergence*, ch. 5.
62. Interview, Ghalib al-Nashashibi.
63. Interview, Dr. George Farah.
64. Great Britain, Shaw Commission, Evidence Heard, pp. 1102–3.
65. NA 59/8/353/84/867, 404 Wailing Wall/310, Zionist telegrams, November 7, 1930.
66. *Ibid.*, cable of August 5, 1929.
67. *Palestine Weekly*, August 9, 1929; *Do'ar ha-Yom*, August 12, 1929, in Great Britain, Shaw Commission, Evidence Heard, items 370713, 37817.
68. Great Britain, Shaw Commission Report, pp. 51–52.
69. *Ibid.*, p. 155.
70. *Ibid.*, p. 56.
71. *Ibid.*, pp. 61–62.
72. Great Britain, Shaw Commission, Evidence Heard, p. 881.
73. Great Britain, Shaw Commission Report, pp. 61–62.
74. Amin was appointed in 1921 by the British as Mufti of Jerusalem, but was popularly known as the Grand Mufti or the Mufti of Palestine.
75. ISA 65/02804, witness account, August 23, 1929.
76. NA 59/8/353/84/867n, 404 Wailing Wall/280, Palestine police records.
77. *Ibid.*
78. Great Britain, Shaw Commission Report, p. 78.
79. NA 59/8/353/84/867n, 404 Wailing Wall/279 and 280, Archdale Diary and Palestine police records.
80. *Ibid.*, pp. 155–57.
81. *Ibid.*, p. 77.
82. CO 733/175/67411/II, John Chancellor to Lord Passfield, September 20, 1929; Al-Hut, *Watha'iq al-Haraka*, pp. 323–32.

83. CO 733/155/57316, G. S. Symes (Chief Secretary) to Lord Plumer, April 1, 1928.

4. THE POLITICS OF MODERATION AND THE GENERAL ISLAMIC CONGRESS

1. Great Britain, *Report . . . on the Administration of Palestine and Transjordan,* 1929, p. 7.
2. Colonial Office (CO) 733/175/67411/III/583, Cabinet Paper 343, police summary for week ending September 21, 1929, September 28, 1929.
3. CO 733/175/67411/II/2, Chancellor to Passfield, October 5, 1929.
4. CO 733/163/67013/II, Chancellor to Passfield, enclosure 2, October 12, 1929.
5. CO 733/175/67411/II/2, Chancellor to Passfield, October 5, 1929.
6. Kisch, *Palestine Diary,* pp. 393, 433.
7. Al-Husayni, *Haqa'iq,* p. 38.
8. See, for example, al-Ghuri, *Filastin,* pp. 54, 77, 84.
9. See Ben-Elkanah, " 'Aliyat."
10. See Taggar's dissertation, "The Mufti of Jerusalem," which utilizes the British documents on the Mufti between 1930 and 1937.
11. For the text of the draft settlement, see Darwaza, *Hawl,* 3:64–67; for British and Zionist reactions, see CO 733/175/67411/III/A, Chancellor to Shuckburgh, November 8, 1929; for Jamal's visit to London, see CO 733/178/67500.
12. Darwaza, *Hawl,* 3:70–71; CO 733/178/67500.
13. *Ibid.*
14. Israel State Archives (ISA), AE 3797, minutes of AE session, January 21, 1930; CO 733/187/77105, HC to SSC; for the account of the discussions, CO 733/191/77253.
15. Porath, *The Palestinian Arab National Movement,* 2:4–5.
16. CO 733/197/77013/III, notes of an interview of the High Commissioner with the Mufti, October 5, 1930.
17. CO 733/183/77050/D/24, Chancellor to Williams, October 24, 1930.
18. Mandel, *The Arabs,* pp. 19–21.
19. Interview, Zaynab al-Husayni; Hourani, *Arabic Thought,* pp. 222–44.
20. See chapter 2 for details. See also Porath, *The Emergence,* pp. 264–65.
21. Great Britain, Shaw Commission, Evidence Heard, p. 881.
22. Al-Husayni, *Haqa'iq,* p. 172.
23. Lesch, *Arab Politics,* p. 139.
24. *Ibid.*
25. CO 733/175/77013/5.
26. CO 733/178/67500.
27. Gibb, "Islamic Congress," p. 100; *Oriente Moderno,* February 1931, pp. 84–86.
28. Foreign Office (FO) 371/15282/E5696/1205/65, summary of Egyptian press, November 1931.
29. Al-Husayni, *Haqa'iq,* p. 138; CO 733/204/87156/1.
30. FO 371/15282/65, February 18, 1931; CO 733/204/87156/6.

31. FO 371/15326/E1713/17/31, March 18, 1931.
32. *Oriente Moderno*, October 1931, p. 527; Gibb, "Islamic Congress"; U.S. National Archives (NA) 867N 404—Wailing Wall/323, Paul Knabenshue (Jerusalem) to Secretary of State, November 17, 1931.
33. Al-Husayni, *Haqa'iq*, pp. 138, 187.
34. *Ibid.*, p. 183; *Oriente Moderno*, October 1931.
35. Al-Husayni, *Haqa'iq*, p. 183.
36. FO 371/15282/E5696/1205/65, summary of Egyptian press of November 1931.
37. FO 371/15282/E5495/1205/65, *Times* (London), November 8, 1931.
38. FO 371/15282/E5725/1205/65.
39. FO 371/15282/1205/65, Rendel report on the Islamic Conference in Jerusalem, November 4, 1931.
40. FO 371/15282/E5695/1205/65, summary of Egyptian papers of November 1931.
41. FO 371/15282/E5667/1205/65, Hope Gill Jidda to FO, November 14, 1931; Gibb, "Islamic Congress," p. 103.
42. For numerous inquiries to Britain, see FO 371/15282–84.
43. FO 371/15283, Colonial Secretary to Young, November 18, 1931; FO 371/15282/E5711/1205/65; FO 371/15282/5725/1205/65, Italian Embassy to FO, November 18, 1931.
44. CO 733/193/77364, Williams memo, September 16, 1931 and December 1931.
45. FO 371/15282/E5770/1205/65, Rendel memo on meeting among FO, CO, India Office (IO) in November 1931.
46. FO 371/15283, November 21 and 25, 1931.
47. Darwaza, *Hawl*, 3:82, *al-Jami'a al-'Arabiyya*, December 13, 1931.
48. For almost daily accounts of the Congress and its participants, see the December issues of *al-Jami'a al-'Arabiyya*.
49. *Ibid.*, December 18 and 19, 1931; Darwaza, *Hawl*, 3:84.
50. *Journal du Caire*, December 18, 1931; *al-Jami'a al-'Arabiyya*, December 1, 1931; Darwaza, *Hawl*, p. 84.
51. *Oriente Moderno*, June 1931, pp. 331–32.
52. *Ibid.*, March 1934, pp. 231–32; April 1934, p. 298; May 1934, pp. 314, 340.
53. Al-Husayni, *Haqa'iq*, pp. 138–39; *Oriente Moderno*, November 1933.
54. Al-Husayni, *Haqa'iq*, pp. 11–12.

5. THE ARAB REVOLT: THE CHALLENGE

1. Darwaza, *Hawl*, pp. 86–88, 306–7.
2. Darwaza, "Tis 'una 'Aman," p. 25, *Hawl*, pp. 88–89.
3. Al-Ghuri, *Filastin*, pp. 28–39.
4. Darwaza, "Tis 'una 'Aman," p. 25.
5. Porath, *The Palestinian Arab National Movement*, 2:123–26.
6. Colonial Office (CO) 733/219/97105/2/33, High Commissioner's dispatch to CO, September 16, 1932, on criticisms of the Mufti; Central Zionist Archives (CZA) 525/4122, A. H. Cohen report of November 4, 1932, on the Istiqlal

meeting in Nablus and Ahmad al-Shuqayri speech at the meeting, cited in Porath, *The Palestinian Arab National Movement*, 2:125.

7. Darwaza, *Hawl*, 3:108–9; Porath, *The Palestinian Arab National Movement*, 2:125.
8. Yasin, *Al-Thawra*, pp. 19–21; interview of Ishaq Darwish.
9. Yasin, *Al-Thawra*, pp. 21–27.
10. *Ibid.*, pp. 21–27.
11. Al-Hut, *Watha'iq*, pp. 396–402.
12. Foreign Office (FO) 371/20018, CID Report, December 4, 1935.
13. Darwaza, *Hawl*, 3:121; Yasin, *Al-Thawra*, p. 44.
14. Schechtman, *The Mufti and the Fuehrer*, p.44.
15. Al-Ghuri, *Filastin*, pp. 57–58.
16. CO/733/307/75438/6, High Commissioner (HC) to SSC, April 1, 1936.
17. Hagana Archives (HA), 8/36, Arab Bureau, April 20, 1936, cited in Taggar, "The Mufti of Jerusalem," p. 36.
18. CO/733/297/75156/II/30, Wauchope to Parkinson, April 19, 1936.
19. HA 8/36, Arab Bureau, April 20, 1936, in Taggar, "The Mufti of Jerusalem," p. 370.
20. CO/733/307/75438/19, HC to SSC, April 21, 1936.
21. CO/733/310/75528/I/39, HC to SSC, April 24, 1936; HA File 8/36, Arab Bureau News, April 25, 1936; cited in Taggar, "The Mufti," p. 373.
22. Al-Hut, *Watha'iq*, pp. 406–17.
23. Darwaza, *Hawl*, 3:123.
24. Al-Hut, *Watha'iq*, pp. 406–15.
25. Darwaza, *Hawl*, 3:123.
26. Al-Sifri, *Filastin*, pp. 25–27; Darwaza, *Hawl*, 3:123.
27. Yasin, *Al-Thawra*, p. 45.
28. CO/733/297/75156/II/32, manifesto in Wauchope dispatch of April 27, 1936; Yasin, *Al-Thawra*, p. 45.
29. CO/733/297/75156/II/32, manifesto in Wauchope dispatch of April 27, 1936; Yasin, *Al-Thawra*, p. 45.
30. CO/733/297/75156/1/55, the Mufti to Wauchope, April 27, 1936.
31. *Ibid.*

6. THE ARAB REVOLT: THE RESPONSE

1. Colonial Office (CO) 733/297/75156/II/Appendix A, extract from Weizmann's speech, April 23, 1936; Great Britain, Peel Commission Report, pp. 96–97.
2. Lesch, *Arab Politics*, pp. 217–18.
3. Great Britain, Peel Commission Report, p. 97; Lesch, *Arab Politics*, p. 218.
4. CO 733/310/75528/1, High Commissioner (HC) to Colonial Secretary, May 16, 1936.
5. Hagana Archives (HA) 8/36, Arab Bureau, April 25, 1936, cited in Taggar, "The Mufti of Jerusalem," p. 376.
6. See Porath, *The Palestinian Arab National Movement*, 2:52, 71.

7. Foreign Office (FO) 371/20018, CID report, May 6, 1936.
8. Central Zionist Archives (CZA) S/25/3252, Arab Bureau News, June 7, 1936, and S/25, 9783, talk with Raghib al-Nashashibi, cited in Porath, *The Palestinian Arab National Movement*, 2:170.
9. CO 733/310/75528/1, Wauchope to Thomas, May 5, 1936.
10. CO 733/310/7552/1, HC to CO, May 14, 1936.
11. FO 371/20018, CID report #10/36, May 21. 1936.
12. HA 8/36, Arab Bureau, May 15, 1936, cited in Taggar, "The Mufti of Jerusalem," p. 381.
13. CO 733/311/75528/7, minutes of meeting of HC and Arab Higher Committee (AHC), May 14, 1936.
14. *Ibid.*
15. CO 733/302/75288, report on talk with Jamal, June 23, 1936.
16. CO 733/311/75528/6, May 21, 1936.
17. CO 733/310/75528, Wauchope to Parkinson, May 23, 1936.
18. CZA S/25, 3252, Arab Bureau News, May 31, 1936, cited in Porath, *The Palestinian Arab National Movement*, 2:195.
19. HA 8/38, Jewish intelligence report, May 31, 1936, in Taggar, "The Mufti of Jerusalem," p. 384.
20. CO 733/311/75528/6, HC to SSC, May 18, 1936.
21. Israel State Archives (ISA) 2, K/65/36, Mufti's letter, May 25, 1936.
22. CO 733/297/75156/3, HC to SSC, June 17, 1936.
23. Great Britain, *Commons*, 1936, fifth series, vol. 317, columns 1313–24.
24. CO 733/297/75156/3, HC to SSC, July 1, 1936.
25. Palestine Liberation Organization (PLO), Research Center (RC), B/VI/17; CO 733/310/75528/IV/604, HC to SSC (transmitting Mufti letter of June 22, 1936), June 30, 1936.
26. CO 733/310/75528/IV/604, HC to SSC (enclosing CS letter to the Mufti of June 27, 1936), June 30, 1936.
27. CO 733/310/75528/IV/702, HC to SSC (enclosing Mufti letter of July 1, 1936), July 25, 1936.
28. CZA S/25, 3247, N. Vilensky to Shertok, May 22, 1936.
29. CO 733/310/75528/IV, HC dispatch, June 30, 1936.
30. CO 733/297/75156/IV, HC dispatch, August 7, 1936.
31. *Ibid.*, September 1936.
32. CO 733/297/75156, HC to Parkinson, September 22, 1936.
33. CO 733/332/75156/2, HC to Parkinson, December 21, 1937.
34. CO 733/297/75156/IV, HC dispatch, September 8, 1936.
35. Porath, *The Palestinian Arab National Movement*, 2:207.
36. Great Britain, Peel Commission Report, p. 101.
37. Kayyali, *Palestine: A Modern History*, pp. 202–4.
38. CO 733/311/75156/7, Wauchope to W. Ormsby-Gore, February 13, 1937.
39. CO 733/311/75156/7, Wauchope to Ormsby-Gore, April 8, 1937.
40. *Ibid.*
41. CO 733/326/25023/2, MacKereth to Wauchope, July 5, 1937.

42. CO 733/332/75156/1, HC to SSC, July 19, 1937.
43. Kayyali, *Palestine: A Modern History*, p. 202.
44. CO 733/328, notes by Ormsby-Gore, July 19, 1937.
45. CO 733/351/75718/6, Wauchope to Parkinson, July 19, 1937.
46. CO 733/351/75718/6, HC to SSC, July 26, 1937.
47. CO 733/351/75718, HC to Lord Dufferin, July 30, 1937 and HC to Park, August 20, 1937.
48. Al-Husayni, "Mudhakkirat," *Akhbar al-Yawm*, August 28, 1957.
49. FO 371/24568/E2900/367/31, Foreign Office minutes, November 18, 1940.
50. CO 733/352/75718/9, HC to SSC, July 14, 1932.
51. *Ibid.*
52. *Ibid.*
53. *Ibid.*
54. CO 733/352/75718/9, Wauchope to Ormsby-Gore, including reports, August 16, 1937.
55. CO 733/352/75718/35, report on Arab congress in Bludan, September 15, 1937.
56. CO 733/341/75528/93/II, Battershill to SSC, September 11, 1937.
57. CO 733/332/75156/1, Battershill to Ormsby-Gore, October 14, 1937.
58. *Akhbar al-Yawm*, June 5, 1937.
59. Kayyali, *Palestine: A Modern History*, p. 211.
60. *Ibid.*, p. 217.
61. CO 733/386, MacMichael to MacDonald, November 19, 1938.
62. Great Britain, White Paper of 1939.
63. For a general account of the Arab Revolt, see Yasin, *Al-Thawra*; Porath, *The Palestinian Arab National Movement*, 2:chs. 7–9; Kayyali, *Palestine: A Modern History*, ch. 7; and Lesch, *Arab Politics*, pp. 221–27.
64. FO 371/23240/E7113/6/31, Harvard (Beirut) to FO, October 22, 1939. In my interview with the Mufti's daughter Su'ad and her husband Haydar al-Husayni in Beirut on November 13, 1978, both confirmed that Amin was upset, but emphatically denied that he contemplated suicide.
65. FO 371/24568/E2900/367/31, Foreign Office minute, November 18, 1940.

7. IRAQ'S QUEST FOR INDEPENDENCE, 1939–1941

1. Foreign Office (FO) 371/24568/E2083/367/31, M. Rutenberg's views on Palestine, Record of Conversation of May 23, 1940. British consideration of the possible elimination of the Mufti has also been discussed by Israeli scholar Joseph Nevo in his "ha-Hitpathut ha-Polit shel ha-Tnu'a ha-Leumit ha-'Arevit ha-Falastinit, 1939–1945" (Ph.D. dissertation, Tel Aviv University, 1977), pp. 199–200, and in his "Al-Hajj Amin and the British in World War II," *Middle Eastern Studies* (January 1984), 201:10f.
2. *Ibid.* It in unclear whether Rutenberg was acting on his own or on behalf of Zionist officials, the Arab Opposition (al-Mu'aridun) in Palestine or Amir 'Abdullah, who in January 1939 told Rutenberg that he ('Abdullah) would

implement a previous agreement of cooperation with the Zionists, but first the Mufti must be disposed of. See Colonial Office (CO) 733/309/75872/51, Sir Harold MacMichael to Malcolm MacDonald, January 4, 1939.

3. FO 371/24568/E2083/367/31, minutes on Rutenberg's views, June 6–7, 1939.
4. *Ibid.*
5. *Ibid.*
6. Rutenberg worked with Fakhri al-Nashashibi, for example. See Central Zionist Archives (CZA) S25/7644, Jewish Agency to Moshe Shertok, January 30, 1939.
7. FO 371/24568/E2083/367/31, minutes of Baggaley, June 7, 1940.
8. Yasin, *Al-Thawra,* pp. 19–22. Interview, Ishaq Darwish.
9. Darwaza, "Tis'una 'Aman," pp. 25–26; CO 733/178/67500, Jamal al-Husayni's interview with the Colonial Secretary, December 19, 1927.
10. Amin al-Husayni, "Mudhakkirat," *Akhbar al-Yawm,* October 19, 1957; FO 371/23240/E7113/6/31, Harvard (Beirut) to FO, October 22, 1939; Haddad, *Harakat,* pp. 4–5.
11. FO 371/23240/E7113/6/31, Harvard (Beirut) to FO, October 22, 1939.
12. FO 371/23241/E7229/6/31, Major D. A. L. Mackenzie (War Office) to Eyers (FO), October 27, 1939; FO 371/23241/7349/6/31, MEIC report, October 28, 1939. Wrote Eyers of the FO on November 11, 1939: "It is a pleasant thought that in a changing world, corruption in French politics maintains its usual high level."
13. Al-Husayni, "Mudhakkirat," *Akhir Sa'a,* September 20, 1972.
14. Al-Hasani, *Al-Asar,* pp. 35–36.
15. FO 371/23235/E3514/6/31, Houston Boswall (Baghdad) to FO, May 14, 1939.
16. FO 371/23241/E7229/6/31, Major D. A. L. Mackenzie to Eyers, October 27, 1939.
17. FO 371/23240/E7132/6/31, Sir B. Newton (Baghdad), October 21, 1939.
18. Haddad, *Harakat,* p. 5.
19. FO 371/23241/E7431/6/31, Newton (Baghdad) to Baggaley (FO), November 2, 1939.
20. FO 371/23240/E7132/6/31, Sir B. Newton (Baghdad), October 21, 1939; Haddad, *Harakat,* p. 5.
21. FO 371/23234/E3349/6/31, FO to Sir E. Phipps (Paris), May 17, 1939; FO 371/24568/E2080/367/31, V. Luke to V. T. Peal, June 21, 1940.
22. CO 733/368/75156/23, January 23, 1939. For details of terrorism and warfare, see CO 733/287–415, 1936–39; Kayyali, *Palestine: A Modern History,* pp. 193–220; Lesch, *Arab Politics,* pp. 122–25, 220–25; Porath, *The Palestinian Arab National Movement,* 2:233–74.
23. FO 371/23242/E7775/6/31, Downie (CO) to Baggaley (FO), September 30, 1939.
24. Kayyali, *Palestine: A Modern History,* p. 217.
25. FO 371/23242/E7775/6/31, Downie (CO) to Lacy Baggaley (FO), September 30, 1939; FO 371/24568/E2080/367/31, V. Luke to V. T. Peal, June 21, 1940.

26. Al-Sabbagh, *Fursan*, p. 114.
27. For a general analysis of Iraqi politics during this period, see Khadduri, *Independent Iraq*; al-Sabbagh, *Fursan*; al-Hasani, *Al-Asrar*.
28. Al-Sabbagh, *Fursan*, p. 111.
29. *Ibid.*, p. 115.
30. Barbour, "Broadcasting," pp. 63–65.
31. Longrigg, *Iraq*, p. 273.
32. FO 371/E2080/365/31, Mufti to Jinnah (president of Indian Muslim League), February 3, 1940.
33. Al-Kilani, unpublished memoirs, p. 151.
34. Khadduri, *Independent Iraq*.
35. *Ibid.*, p. 157.
36. *Ibid.*, pp. 159–62.
37. Hurewitz, *The Struggle*, pp. 148–50; Khadduri, *Independent Iraq*, p. 171; Furlonge, *Palestine Is My Country*, pp. 127–28.
38. Churchill, *The Second World War*, 2:148–50.
39. Al-Kilani, unpublished memoirs, p. 155; CZA S25/2968, Zionist intelligence report, July 28, 1940.
40. FO 371/24558/E2802/448/93, Middle East Commander in Chief to War Office, October 1, 1940.
41. United States, *Foreign Relations of the United States*, p. 713, Knabenshue to Secretary of State, November 11, 1940.
42. FO 371/24568/E2762/367/31, Leo Amery to Secretary of State, October 5, 1940.
43. *Ibid.*, October 10, 1940.
44. *Ibid.*
45. FO 371/24568/E2900/367/31, Foreign Office minutes, November 18, 1940.
46. *Ibid.*
47. Churchill, *The Second World War*, 3:254.
48. Yitshaq Ben-Ami, *Years of Wrath*, p. 245.
49. Ya'kov Meridor verified the details of the Raziel mission to Yitshaq Ben-Ami and, via the U.S. Herut representative, to me in New York on March 1, 1982. See *Ma'ariv*, March 25, 1961, cited in Levine, "David Raziel," pp. 309–11; Crossman and Foot, *A Palestine Munich?*, p. 20.
50. American Christian Palestine Committee (ACPC), *The Arab War Effort*, pp. 41–42.
51. Glubb, *A Soldier*, p. 311; *Oriente Moderne* 31:552–53.
52. Al-Hasani, *Al-Asrar*, pp. 224–25; ACPC, *The Arab War Effort*, pp. 41–42.
53. Al-Husayni, "Mudhakkirat," *Akhbar al-Yawm*, November 30, 1957.
54. *Ibid.*
55. FO 371/52588/E7948/3/31, FO to Bullard, December 1, 1941.
56. Al-Husayni, "Mudhakkirat," *Akhbar al-Yawm*, November 30, 1957.
57. *Ibid.*
58. *Ibid.*

8. THE NAZI YEARS

1. See Hirszowicz, *The Third Reich*, pp. 13, 26–29; Nation Associates, *The Arab Higher Committee*, p. 5; American Christian Palestine Committee (ACPC), *The Arab War Effort*, p. 6; Cooper, "Forgotten Palestinian," pp. 10–11; Schechtman, *The Mufti and the Fuehrer*, pp. 77–86.
2. See the works of Yehoshua Porath, Ann Mosely Lesch, J. C. Hurewitz, A. W. Kayyali, and Bayan al-Hut.
3. Al-Sabbagh, *Fursan*, p. 18.
4. Yisraeli, *Ha-Reich Ha-Germani V'Eretz Yisrael*, pp. 194–201; Auswärtiges Amt, *Documents on German Foreign Policy*, 10:172 (hereafter *DGFP*).
5. Amin al-Husayni, "Mudhakkirat," *Akhbar al-Yawm*, November 16, 1957.
6. U.S. National Archives (NA), RG 338, MS no. p-207, "German Exploitation of Arab Nationalist Movements in World War II," by General der Flieger Hellmuth Felmy and General der Artileries Walter Warlimont, pp. 44–46.
7. H. R. Trevor-Roper, *Hitler: Secret Conversations*, p. 512.
8. Foreign Office (FO) 371/E2080/365/31, Mufti to Jinnah, February 3, 1940.
9. Churchill, *The Second World War*, 2:148–50.
10. Al-Husayni, "Mudhakkirat," *Akhbar al-Yawm*, November 16, 1957; al-Kilani, unpublished memoirs, p. 151.
11. NA, RG 338, supplement to MS no. p-207, "Die deutsche Ausnutzung der arabischen Eingeborenenbewegung im Zweiten Weltkrieg," by Fritz Grobba, pp. 41–43; Haddad, *Harakat*, pp. 24–29.
12. Haddad, *Harakat*, pp. 27–28.
13. Haddad, *Harakat*, pp. 31–34; Auswärtiges Amt, *DGFP* 10:559–60.
14. Al-Husayni, "Mudhakkirat," *Akhbar al-Yawm*, November 16, 1957; Al-Kilani, unpublished memoirs, p. 152; Haddad, *Harakat*, pp. 2–28.
15. Auswärtiges Amt, *DGFP*, 11:204–5.
16. Haddat, *Harakat*, pp. 46–49.
17. See text of Mufti's letter to Hitler in al-Husayni, "Mudhakkirat," *Akhbar al-Yawm*, November 16, 1957; also in Auswärtiges Amt, *DGFP*, 11(680):1151–55; and in Khadduri, *Independent Iraq*, pp. 378–80.
18. Hirszowicz, *The Third Reich*, p. 109; Khadduri, *Independent Iraq*, p. 189.
19. Haddad, *Harakat*, pp. 106–8; al-Husayni, "Mudhakkirat," *Akhbar al-Yawm*, November 16, 1957.
20. Al-Husayni, "Mudhakkirat," *Akhbar al-Yawm*, December 7, 1957; Benni Morris, *Jerusalem Post International*, (April 29–May 6, 1984), no. 683.
21. FO 371/52585, memorandum of a conversation of von Ribbentrop with the Mufti, November 28, 1941.
22. FO 371/52585, memorandum of the conversation of Hitler with the Mufti, November 28, 1941. For the Mufti's optimistic version of his conversation with von Ribbentrop and Hitler, see his "Mudhakkirat," *Akhbar al-Yawm*, December 14, 1957 and December 28, 1957.
23. *Ibid.*
24. For the German and Arabic text of the secret agreement, see al-Husayni,

"Mudhakkirat," *Akhbar al-Yawm,* January 4, 1958; and for the English translation, see Khadduri, *Arab Contemporaries,* pp. 77–80.

25. Al-Husayni, "Mudhakkirat," *Akhir Sa'a,* September 27, 1972.
26. Interview, Kamal al-Din Jalal.
27. See the text in Pearlman, *Mufti of Jerusalem,* p. 46; the same text is in Schechtman, *The Mufti and the Fuehrer,* p. 126. Schechtman plagiarized the text and other portions from Pearlman's book; compare, for example, chapters 2 and 8 of Pearlman with chapters 1 and 4 of Schechtman.
28. Al-Husayni, "Mudhakkirat," *Akhbar al-Yawm,* January 25, 1958; FO 371/ 52585; De Luca, "Der Grossmufti," p. 134.
29. Al-Husayni, "Mudhakkirat," *Akhbar al-Yawm,* January 25, 1958; FO 371/ 52585; De Luca, "Der Grossmufti," p. 134.
30. Al-Husayni, "Mudhakkirat," *Akhir Sa'a,* October 18, 1972 and October 25, 1972.
31. NA, RG 226, XL5487, OSS, R and A report of December 27, 1944; NA, RG 226, L48410, OSS, R and A reports on Arab affairs in Palestine, October 14–22, 1944; NA, RG 226, XL5709, OSS, R and A report, interrogation of Khalil Rassoul, January 1, 1945.
32. *New York Times,* June 20, 1946.
33. FO 371/52586/E6116/515/31, FO minute, October 6, 1946.
34. Israel State Archives (ISA) 79/18/A3024.
35. ISA 79/12/A3017.
36. ISA 79/12/A3024.
37. Nation Associates, *The Arab Higher Committee.*
38. FO 371/52585/E1984/515/31.
39. *Ibid.*
40. *Ibid.*
41. *Ibid.*
42. FO 371/52585/E1984/515/31; also see FO 371/45421/E7689/301, September 29, 1945.
43. ISA, RG 79, box A/3061, accused Mufti, compiled by Shlomo Ben-Elkanah, February 1961; ISA 79/9/A3024.
44. For writers who used the documentary evidence, see Lukasz Hirszowicz, Nation Associates, Elias Cooper, and American Christian Palestine Committee, cited in note 1, as well as Wiesenthal, *Grossmufti.* For published German documents, see Auswärtiges Amt, *DGFP.* For unpublished microfilm material, see the holdings of the National Archives.
45. Basir, "Zalamu," *Akhir Sa'a,* January 31, 1973; al-Awdat, *Min A'lam,* p. 112.

9. DIPLOMACY AND WAR, 1946–1948

1. Foreign Office (FO) 371/52585/E1825/515/31, T. Kinley (CO) minutes, March 5, 1946; U.S. National Archives (NA), RG 226, OSS, R4A, #14167, interrogation report of Carl B. F. Rekowski, August 14, 1945.

2. FO 371/52586/E6671/515/31, Campbell to FO, July 12, 1946; NA, RG 59, box 367, 740.00116 EW/12–1346, Green H. Hackwood, legal adviser to the U.S. Commission for Investigating War Crimes, December 12, 1945.
3. Al-Husayni, "Mudhakkirat," *Akhir Sa'a,* January 24, 1973; FO 371/45420/ E3767/3032/31, Jidda to FO, May 30, 1945; FO to CO, June 4, 1945.
4. FO 371/45421/E3484/3032/31, Martin to Howe, November 3, 1945.
5. Schechtman, *The Mufti and the Fuehrer,* p. 178.
6. FO 371/52586/E6375/515/31, Campbell memo, July 1, 1946.
7. FO 371/52586/E5659/515/31, R. I. Campbell (Cairo) to FO, June 19, 1946. NA, RG 226, 135849, OSS Report.
8. FO 371/52586/E5659/515/31, R. I. Campbell (Cairo) to FO, June 19, 1946. NA, RG 226, 135849, OSS Report.
9. Hurewitz, *Struggle,* p. 158; Khalidi, *From Haven,* pp. li–liv.
10. Nevo, "The Renewal of Political Activity 1943–45," p. 62.
11. Khalidi, *Before Their Diaspora,* pp. 235–38.
12. Hurewitz, *Struggle,* p. 252.
13. Macdonald, *League of Arab States,* pp. 317–18.
14. Khalidi, "The Arab Perspective," pp. 107–8.
15. Graves, *Memoirs of King Abdullah,* p. 204. The best and most thorough treatment of this subject is Shlaim, *Collusion.* See also Wilson, *King Abdullah.*
16. Kurzman, *Genesis, 1948,* p. 913.
17. Porath, *The Palestinian Arab National Movement,* 2:73–74.
18. Cohen, *Israel,* p. 31.
19. Great Britain, Peel Commission Report. pp. 380–82.
20. Darwaza, *Hawl,* 3:162.
21. Khalidi, *From Haven,* p. xliv.
22. Caplan, *Futile Diplomacy,* 2:268.
23. *Ibid.*
24. *Ibid.,* p. 269.
25. *Ibid.*
26. *Ibid.;* Shlaim, *Politics of Partition,* p. 22.
27. *Ibid.,* p. 73.
28. *Ibid.,* pp. 74–75.
29. Shlaim, *Collusion,* p. 617.
30. Caplan, *Futile Diplomacy,* 2:277.
31. *Ibid.;* Shlaim, *Politics of Partition,* p. 96.
32. India Office, L/P and S/12/3356, FO to HM Representatives October 16, 1947.
33. Cohen, *Israel,* p. 327.
34. *Ibid.,* p. 329.
35. Caplan, *Futile Diplomacy,* 2:271.
36. CO 733/309/75872/51, Sir Harold MacMichael to Malcolm MacDonald, January 4, 1939.
37. Ben-Ami, *Years of Wrath,* p. 245; Levine, "David Raziel," pp. 309–11; Crossman and Foot, *A Palestine Munich?,* p. 20.

38. Schechtman, *The Mufti and the Fuehrer*, p. 178.
39. FO 371/61838/E664/49/31, Sir H. Stonhower Bird to FO, January 17, 1947.
40. FO 371/61834/E3999/49/31, Kirkbride to FO, May 13, 1947.
41. FO 371/61835/E9851/49/31, Kirkbride to FO, October 21, 1947.
42. FO 371/61836/E11426/49/31, Chancery at Amman to FO, November 24, 1947.
43. Kurtzman, *Genesis, 1948*, pp. 40–41.
44. FO 371/52567/E12539/4/31, 'Azzam to British Embassy in Cairo, December 17, 1946.
45. FO 371/61746/E322/2/31, CO to Ernest Bevin, January 7, 1947; FO 371/61834/E3700/49/31, Campbell to FO, May 2, 1947; FO 371/61835/E9344/49/31, Evans to FO, October 8, 1947.
46. FO 371/61835/E9696/49/31, Brig. Clayton to FO, October 8, 1947.
47. FO 371/61835/E11611/49/31, Houston-Boswall to Burrows, 27 November 1947; FO 371/61835/E4726/49/31, Beirut minute, June 17, 1947.
48. Khalidi, "The Arab Perspective," p. 110.
49. PLO, Research Center (PLO, RC), III. T. #24, Minutes of the Arab Higher Committee, June 12, 1946; *Survey of Palestine*, supplement, p. 140.
50. Khalidi, "The Arab Perspective," p. 113.
51. Caplan, *Futile Diplomacy*, 2:272–73, Hurewitz, *Struggle*, pp. 263–72; Nevo, "Arabs of Palestine 1947–48," p. 7.
52. Darwaza, *al-Qadiyya*, 2:85; Hurewitz, *Struggle*, pp. 267–72.
53. Nevo, "Arabs of Palestine, 1947–48," p. 10.
54. Khalidi, "The Arab Perspective," p. 114–16.
55. Wilson, *King Abdullah*, pp. 160–62.
56. Khalidi, "The Arab Perspective," pp. 117–18.
57. Hut, *al-Qiyadat*, p. 580.
58. Khalidi, "The Arab Perspective," pp. 118–19; Darwaza, *al-Qadiyya*, 2: 102–3.
59. Al-Husayni, *Haqa'iq*, p. 91.
60. Khalidi, *Diaspora*, pp. 305–6.
61. Khalidi, "The Arab Perspective," p. 122.
62. *Ibid.*, pp. 126–29.
63. Shlaim, *Collusion*, pp. 618–19.
64. *Ibid.*, pp. 619–20.
65. Shlaim, "All-Palestine Government," pp. 37–53.
66. *Ibid.*, p. 38.
67. Khalidi, "The Arab Perspective," p. 112.
68. Nevo, "Arabs of Palestine 1947–48," p. 28.
69. *Ibid.*
70. Shlaim, "All-Palestine Government," p. 39.
71. Nimr, *Tarikh*, 4:54–55.
72. FO 371/68382/E12098/68/65, Amman to FO, September 15, 1948; Shlaim, "All-Palestine Government," p. 40.

73. Plascov, *Palestinian Refugees*, p. 8.
74. FO 371/68641/E12502/375/31, Amman to FO, September 25, 1948; FO 371/68642/E12654/375/31, Cairo to FO, September 29, 1948.
75. Darwaza, *al-Qadiyya*, p. 211.
76. *Ibid.*, p. 213.
77. Al-Husayni, *Haqa'iq* (1957), p. 84.
78. Shlaim, "All-Palestine Government," p. 42; *NYT*, October 2, 1948; Schechtman, *Mufti*, p. 23.
79. Al-Husayni, *Haqa'iq*, p. 212.
80. Darwaza, *al-Qadiyya*, p. 213.
81. Al-Husayni, *Haqa'iq*, p. 86; FO 371/68642/E12502/375/31, Cairo to FO September 8, 1948.
82. FO 371/68642/E12976/375/31, Cairo to FO, October 8, 1948.
83. FO 371/68642, Cairo to FO, October 2, 1948; Shlaim, *Collusion* p. 299.
84. Shlaim, "All-Palestine Government," pp. 47–49.
85. FO 371/68641/E12502/375/31, FO telegram, October 9, 1948.
86. FO 141/1284/253/9/48G., minutes, November 2, 1948.

10. DECLINE OF POWER

1. See the works of Walid Khalidi, Benny Morris, and Simha Flapan.
2. PLO, RC 1/17/kh, Declaration of the Arab Higher Committee, March 23, 1950.
3. Shlaim, *Collusion*, pp. 555, 621.
4. *Ibid.*, p. 606.
5. Wilson, *King Abdullah*, p. 211; CIA, Comment on King Abdullah's Assassination, July 20, 1951.
6. Al-Husayni, *Haqa'iq*, p. 73–79; *al-Misri*, July 22, 1951.
7. U.S. National Archives (NA), 785.00/8–45, Amman to Secretary of State, August 4, 1951; NA 786.00/8–1051, Cairo to Department of State, August 10, 1951.
8. Interview Haydar al-Husayni, Beirut, 1979; NA, 674.84A/1–2055, U.S. Embassy in Amman to Department of State, Gaza Strip Quiet—Comments on Sources of Trouble, January 20, 1955; FO 371/111094/, 1062/15/54, Amman to FO, October 25, 1954. For a detailed account of the Mufti's life after 1948, see Zvi Elpeleg, *Grand Mufti*.
9. Interview, Haydar al-Husayni, Beirut, 1979.
10. PLO, RC, 2/71/dh, Mufti statement to press conference, Beirut, April 11, 1964.
11. PLO, RC, 2/71/dh/14. Mufti letter to the Arab governments, April 15, 1964.
12. Interview, Haydar al-Husayni, Beirut, 1979.
13. Interview, Zaynab al-Husayni, Beirut, 1979.
14. Interview, Amina al-Husayni, Beirut, 1979.
15. *Ibid.*

11. AN OVERVIEW AND ASSESSMENT

1. Al-Husayni, *Haqa'iq*; al-Ghuri, *Filastin*.
2. Al-Mardini, *Alf Yawm*; Waters, *Mufti Over the Middle East*; Pearlman, *Mufti of Jerusalem*; Schechtman, *The Mufti and the Fuehrer*.
3. Al-Mardini's *Alf Yawm*, for example, reads like the memoirs of an official who made all the judicious decisions. Al-Mardini tried to show that the Mufti and the Palestinians fought with tenacity and self-sacrifice; Waters (pseudonym, Maurice Pearlman) and Schechtman attempted to vilify him, discredit his movement, and blame him for the misfortune of the Palestinians.
4. Hourani, "Ottoman Reform," pp. 45–46.
5. Foreign Office (FO) 371/5121/E9397/85/44, Palin Report, p. 4.
6. Bentwich and Bentwich, *Mandate Memories*, pp. 191–92.
7. *Ibid.*; Elath, "Conversations," p. 44.
8. Darwaza, *Hawl*, 3:61–62.
9. Porath, *The Emergence*, p. 166.
10. Great Britain, Shaw Commission Report, p. 78.
11. *Ibid.*, pp. 73–78.
12. Colonial Office (CO) 733/163/67013/II, Chancellor to Passfield, enclosure 2, October 12, 1929; CO 733/175/67411/II/2, Chancellor to Passfield, October 5, 1929.
13. CO 733/175/67411/III/583, Cabinet Paper 343, police summary for week ending September 21, 1929.
14. Porath, *The Palestinian Arab National Movement*, 2:21.
15. *Ibid.*, pp. 23–26.
16. See Gibb, "The Islamic Congress."
17. CO 733/258, Wauchope to Cunliffe-Lister, January 5, 1934, cited in Kayyali, *Palestine: A Modern History*, p. 176.
18. FO 371/20018, CID report, December 4, 1935.
19. Darwaza, *Hawl*, 3:123.
20. FO 371/23240/E7113/6/31, Harvard (Beirut) to FO, October 22, 1939.
21. CO 733/309/75872/51, Sir Harold MacMichael to Malcolm MacDonald, January 4, 1939.
22. FO 371/24568/E2762/367/31, Leo Amery to Secretary of State, October 5, 1940.
23. See Klaus Gensicke, *Der Mufti von Jerusalem, Amin al-Husseini, und die Nationalsozialisten.* Frankfurt: Verlag Peter Lang, 1988, especially pp. 151–67, 207, 230–31, 296. Gensicke provides much detail but few revelations. Unfortunately, most of his conclusions are based not on documentary evidence but on innuendo and circumstantial evidence provided by partisan groups such as the Jewish Agency and Nation Associates. Nevertheless, Gensicke's data and citations can assist future scholars to write, hopefully, more dispassionate and nonpartisan accounts of the Mufti's role in Nazi Germany.
On July 22, 1991, the Simon Wiesenthal Center announced that it had uncov-

ered documents in the UN Archives indicating that the Mufti planned the extermination of Jews in the Middle East. Documents provided by the center have been published, and most of the "new" information compiled by the center is well known and inconclusive, as British and American officials had determined in 1945–46.

24. Pearlman, *Mufti of Jerusalem*, pp. 48, 59, 66; Schechtman, *The Mufti and the Fuehrer*, pp. 139, 149, 150; FO 371/68642/E12691/375/31 Cairo to FO, September 29, 1948.

25. See n. 1 in chapter 6; Ingrams, *Palestine Papers*, pp. 31–32.

BIBLIOGRAPHY

I. ARCHIVES

Central Zionist Archives (CZA), Jerusalem
  Central Office of the Zionist Organization, London (Z4)
  Political Department of the Jewish Agency, Jerusalem (S25)
Dar al-Kutub, Cairo
  Correspondence of the Egyptian Consul in Palestine
French Embassy, Cairo
Institute for Palestine Studies (IPS), Beirut
  Awraq Akram Zu'aytir
Israel State Archives (ISA), Jerusalem
  Arab Executive (AE)
  Chief Secretary of Palestine Government (CS)
  Supreme Muslim Council (SMC)
Palestine Liberation Organization (PLO) Research Center, Beirut
  Arab Higher Committee (AHC)
Public Record Office (PRO), London
  Colonial Office (CO)
  Foreign Office (FO)
  War Office (WO)
  India Office (IO)
U.S. National Archives (NA), Washington, D.C.
  Captured German documents
  Department of State
  Office of Strategic Studies (OSS)

II. UNPUBLISHED MATERIAL

Darwaza, Muhammad 'Izzat. "Tis'una 'Aman fi al-Hayat: 1888–1978." Damascus, 1978.

Al-Husayni, Muhammad Amin. Unpublished memoir, 1948–49. Cairo.

—— Unpublished diaries, 1914–37. Beirut.

Al-Hut, Bayan Nuwayhid. "Al-Qiyadat wa al-Mu'assasat al-Siyasiyya fi Filastin, 1917–1948." Unpublished Ph.D. dissertation, Lebanese University, 1977.

Jbara, Taysir Y. "Al-Hajj Muhamad Amin al-Husayni, Mufti of Jerusalem, The Palestine Years: 1921–1937." Ph.D. dissertation, New York University, 1982.

Al-Kilani, Rashid 'Ali. Unpublished memoirs, 1939–41. Berlin, 1945.

Kuperschmidt, Uri M. "The Supreme Muslim Council, 1921–1937: Islam under the British Mandate for Palestine." Ph.D. dissertation, Hebrew University, 1978.

Levine, David. "David Raziel: The Man and His Times." Ph.D. dissertation, Yeshiva University, 1969.

Muslih, Muhammad Y. "Urban Notables, Ottomanism, Arabism, and the Rise of Palestinian Nationalism, 1856–1920." Ph.D. dissertation, Columbia University, 1984.

Nevo, Joseph. "ha-Hitpathut ha-Politit shel ha-Tnua'a ha-Leumit ha-'Arevit ha-Falastinit, 1939–1945." Unpublished Ph.D. dissertation. Tel Aviv University, 1977.

Taggar, Jehuda. "The Mufti of Jerusalem and the Palestine Arab Politics, 1930–1937." Ph.D. dissertation, University of London, 1973.

III. OFFICIAL PUBLICATIONS

Germany, Auswärtiges Amt. Documents on German Foreign Policy, 1918–1945. Series D, Vol. X. Washington, D.C.: GPO, 1949–66.

Great Britain, Colonial Office, Report of His Majesty's Government to the Council of the League of Nations on the Administration of Palestine and Transjordan, 1929. No. 47. London: His Majesty's Stationery Office (HMSO), 1930.

Great Britain, Parliamentary Papers. The Western or Wailing Wall in Jerusalem. Memorandum by the Secretary of State. Cmd. 3229. Cited as White Paper of 1928. London: HMSO, 1928.

—— Report of the Commission on the Palestine Disturbance of August, 1929 (Shaw Commission Report). Cmd. 3530. London: HMSO, 1930.

—— Palestine Commission on the Disturbances of August, 1929 (Shaw Commission, Evidence Heard . . .). London: HMSO, 1930.

—— Report on Immigration, Land Settlement, and Development . . . (Simpson Commission Report). Cmd. 3683–87. London: HMSO, 1930.

—— Statement of Policy by His Majesty's Government . . . (Passfield White Paper). Cmd. 3692. London: HMSO, 1930.

—— Report of the Commission to Determine the Rights and Claims of Moslems

and Jews in Connection with the Western or Wailing Wall at Jerusalem (International Commission). London: HMSO, 1930.
—— *Report of the Palestine Royal Commission* . . . (Peel Commission Report). Cmd. 5479. London: HMSO, 1937.
—— *Statement of Policy* . . . (White Paper of 1939). Cmd. 6019. London: HMSO, 1939.
League of Nations, Permanent Mandates Commission. *Minutes of the Fourteenth Session* . . . C. 568, M. 179, VI. Geneva: League of Nations, 1928.
United States, Department of State. *Foreign Relations of the United States*, Vol. 3, 1958. Washington, D.C.: GPO, 1958.

IV. WORKS IN ARABIC, HEBREW, AND WESTERN LANGUAGES

Abu-Lughod, Ibrahim, ed. *The Transformation of Palestine*. Wilmette, Ill.: Madina University Press International, 1971.
Abu Yasir, Salih Mas'ud. *Jihad Sha'b Filastin Khial Nisf Qarn*. Beirut: Dar al-Fatah, 1968.
American Christian Palestine Committee (ACPC). *The Arab War Effort*. New York: ACPC, 1946.
Andrews, Fannie Fern. *The Holy Land Under Mandates*. 2 vols. Boston: Houghton Mifflin, 1931.
Antonius, George. *The Arab Awakening: The Story of the Arab National Movement*. 3d ed. London: Hamish Hamilton, 1955.
Al-'Awdat, Ya'qub. *Min A'lam al-Fikr wa al-Adab fi Filastin*. Amman: al-Matabi' al-Ta'awuniyya, 1976.
Barbour, Nevill. "Broadcasting to the Arab World." *Middle East Journal* (1951), no. 1.
Ben-Ami, Yitshaq. *Years of Wrath, Days of Glory: Memoirs from the Irgun*. New York: Robert Speller, 1982.
Bentwich, Norman. *England in Palestine*. London: Kegan Paul, 1932.
Bentwich, Norman and Helen Bentwich. *Mandate Memories, 1918–1948*. New York: Schocken Books, 1965.
Caplan, Neil. *Futile Diplomacy: Arab-Zionist Negotiations and the End of the Mandate*. London: Frank Cass, 1986.
Churchill, Winston S. *The Second World War. Vol. 2: Their Finest Hour*. New York: Bantam, 1962.
—— *The Second World War. Vol. 3: The Grand Alliance*. New York: Bantam, 1962.
Cohen, Aaron. *Israel and the Arab World*. Boston: Beacon Press, 1976.
Cooper, Elias. "Forgotten Palestinian: The Nazi Mufti." *American Zionist* (March–April 1978), 68:5–36.
Crossman, R. H. S. and Michael Foot. *A Palestine Munich?* London: Victor Gollancz, 1946.
Darwaza, Muhammad 'Izzat. *Hawl al-Haraka al-'Arabiyya al-Haditha*. 5 vols. Saida: al-Maktaba al-'Asriyya, 1952.

Darwaza, Muhammad 'Izzat. *al-Qaddiyya al-Filastiniyya fi Mukhtalif Marahi-liha*. Vol. 2. Saida: al-Maktaba al-Aniyya, 1951.

Dawn, C. Ernest. *From Ottomanism to Arabism: Essays on the Origins of Arab Nationalism*. Urbana, Ill.: University of Illinois, 1973.

De Luca, Anthony R. "Der Grossmufti in Berlin: The Politics of Collaboration." *International Journal of Middle East Studies* (February 1979), 10:125–38.

Derounian, Arthur. *Cairo to Damascus*. New York: Knopf, 1951.

Elath, Eliahu. "Conversations with Musa al-'Alami." *Jerusalem Quarterly* (Winter 1987), no. 41.

—— *Hajj Muhammad Amin al-Husayni: Mufti Yerushalayim Leshe'avar*. Tel Aviv: Reshafim, 1968.

Elkanah, Shlomo Ben-. " 'Aliyat shel Haj Amin al-Husayni el Rashut he-Hanhaqa ha-Dalit shel he-'Eda ha-Muslimit be-Ertz-Yisrael." In H. Z. Hirshberg, ed., *Sefer H. J. Shapira*. Ramat-Gan: 5732/1971–72.

Elpeleg, Zvi. *The Grand Mufti*. Tel Aviv: Ministry of Defense, Israel, 1989.

ESCO Foundation for Palestine. *Palestine: A Study of Jewish, Arab, and British Policies*. 2 vols. New Haven: Yale University Press, 1947.

Fischer-Weth, Kurt. *Amin al-Husseini, Gross-Mufti von Palestina*. Berlin: Walter Titz Verlag, 1943.

Furlonge, Sir Geoffrey. *Palestine is My Country: The Story of Musa Alami*. New York: Praeger, 1969.

Gensicke, Klaus. *Der Mufti von Jerusalem: Amin al-Husseini, und due National-sozialisten*. Frankfurt: Peter Lang, 1988.

Al-Ghuri, Emile. *Filastin 'Abr Sittin 'Aman*. 2 vols. Beirut: Dar al-Nahar, 1972.

Gibb, Hamilton A. R. "The Islamic Congress at Jerusalem in December 1931." In Arnold Toynbee, ed., *Survey of International Affairs*. London: Oxford University Press, 1935.

Glubb, J. B. *A Soldier with the Arabs*. London: Hodder, 1957.

Great Britain. *Survey of Palestine. Supplement*. Jerusalem: Government Printer, 1946. Reprinted by the Institute for Palestine Studies, 1991.

Grobba, Fritz. *Männer und Mächte im Orient: 25 Jahre diplomatischer Tatigkei-tim Orient*. Gottingen: Muster-Schmidt-Verlag, 1967.

Haddad, 'Uthman Kamal. *Harakat Rashid 'Ali, Sanat 1941*. Sidon: al-Maktaba al-'Asriyya, 1952.

Haim, Sylvia G., ed. *Arab Nationalism: An Anthology*. Berkeley: University of California, 1964.

Hartman, Richard. *Der Mufti Amin el-Husaini*. Berlin: n.p., 1941.

Al-Hasani, 'Abd al-Razzak. *Al-Asrar al-Khafiyya*. Sidon: Matba'at al-'Urfan, 1958.

Hattis, Suzan Lee. *The Bi-national Idea in Palestine During Mandatory Times*. Tel Aviv: Shikmona, 1970.

Hertzberg, Arthur. *The Zionist Idea*. New York: Atheneum, 1975.

Herzl, Theodor. *The Complete Diaries of Theodor Herzl*. Vol. 1. New York: Thomas Yoseloff, 1960.

Hirszowicz, Lukasz. *The Third Reich and the Arab East*. London: Routledge and Kegan Paul, 1966.

Hourani, Albert. *Arabic Thought in the Liberal Age, 1798–1939*. Rev. ed. London: Oxford University Press, 1971.

—— "Ottoman Reform and the Politics of Notables." In William R. Polk and Richard L. Chambers, eds., *Beginnings of Modernization in the Middle East: The Nineteenth Century*. Chicago: University of Chicago Press, 1968.

Hurewitz, J. C. *Middle East Dilemmas*. New York: Harper, 1953.

—— *The Struggle for Palestine*. New York: Greenwood Press, 1968.

Al-Husayni, Muhammad Amin. *Haqa'iq 'an Qadiyyat Filastin*. 2d ed. Cairo: Dar al-Kitab al-'Arabi bi-Misr, 1957.

—— "Mudhakkirat." *Akhbar al-Yawm* (1957–58), nos. 673–90.

—— "Mudhakkirat." *Akhir Sa'a* (1972–74), nos. 1277–2035.

Al-Hut, Bayan Nuwayhid, ed. *Watha'iq al-Haraka al-Wataniyya al-Filastiniyya, 1918–1939: Min Awraq Akram Zu'aytir*. Beirut: Mu'assasat al-Dirasat al-Filastiniyya, 1979.

Ingrams, Doreen. *Palestine Papers, 1917–1922: Seeds of Conflict*. New York: George Braziller, 1973.

Al-Jabarti. *'Aja'ib al-Athar fi al-Tarajum wa al-Athar*. Vol 1, 1904/1322. Cairo.

Jbara, Taysir. *Palestinian Leader: Hajj Amin al-Husayni, Mufti of Jerusalem*. Princeton: Kingston Press, 1985.

Kayyali, 'Abd al-Wahab. *Palestine: A Modern History*. London: Croom Helm, 1973.

Kayyali, 'Ahd al-Wahab, ed. *Watha'iq al-Muqawama al-filastiniyya al-'Arabiyya Did al-Ihtlal al-Britani wa al-Sahyuni (1918–1939)*. Beirut: Mu'assassat al-Dirasat al-Filastiniyya, 1968.

Kedourie, Elie. "Sir Herbert Samuel and the Government of Palestine." *The Chatham House Version and Other Middle-Eastern Studies*. New York: Praeger, 1970.

Khadduri, Majid. *Arab Contemporaries: The Role of Personalities in Politics*. Baltimore: Johns Hopkins University, 1973.

—— *Independent Iraq, 1932–1958*. London: Oxford University Press, 1960.

Khalidi, Rashid. *British Policy Towards Syria and Palestine, 1906–1914*. London: Ithaca Press, 1980.

Khalidi, Walid. "The Arab Perspective," in *The End of the Palestine Mandate*. ed. William Roger Louis and Robert W. Stookey. Austin: University of Texas Press, 1988.

Khalidi, Walid, ed. *From Haven to Conquest: Readings in Zionism and the Palestine Problem until 1948*. Beirut: Institute for Palestine Studies, 1971.

—— *Before Their Diaspora: A Photographic History of the Palestinians 1876–1948*. Washington: Institute for Palestine Studies, 1984.

Khoury, Philip S. *Urban Notables and Arab Nationalism*. Cambridge: Cambridge University Press, 1983.

Kirk, George E. *A Short History of the Middle East*. 5th ed. New York: Praeger, 1959.

Kisch, Frederick H. *Palestine Diary*. London: Victor Gollancz, 1938.

Kurzman, Dan. *Genesis 1948: The First Arab-Israeli War*. New York: New American Library, 1970.

Lesch, Ann Mosely. *Arab Politics in Palestine, 1917–1939: Frustration of a National Movement*. Ithaca: Cornell University, 1979.

Longrigg, Stephen Hemsley. *Iraq, 1900 to 1950*. London: Oxford University Press, 1953.

Lundsten, Mary Ellen. "Wall Politics: Zionist and Palestinian Strategies in Jerusalem, 1928." *Journal of Palestine Studies* (Autumn 1978), 7(1):3–27.

Macdonald, Robert W. *The League of Arab States*. Princeton: Princeton University Press, 1965.

Mandel, Neville J. *The Arabs and Zionism Before World War I*. Berkeley: University of California, 1976.

Al-Mardini, Zuhayr. *Alf Yawm ma'a al-Hajj Amin*. Beirut: Dar al-'Irfan, 1977.

Mattar, Philip. "The Role of the Mufti of Jerusalem in the Political Struggle over the Western Wall, 1928–29." *Middle Eastern Studies* (January 1983), 19(1):104–18.

—— "Amin al-Husayni and Iraq's Quest for Independence, 1939–41." *Arab Studies Quarterly* (Fall 1984), 6(4):267–81.

Meinertzhagen, Richard. *Middle East Diary: 1917–1956*. London: Cresset Press, 1959, New York: Thomas Yoseloff, 1960.

Monroe, Elizabeth. *Britain's Moment in the Middle East, 1914–1956*. Baltimore: Johns Hopkins University, 1963.

Morris, Benny. *The Birth of the Palestinian Refugee Problem, 1947–1949*. Cambridge: Cambridge University Press, 1987.

Nation Associates. *The Arab Higher Committee: Its Origins, Personnel, and Purposes: A Documentary Record Submitted to the United Nations*. New York: n.p., 1947.

Nevo, Joseph. "Al-Hajj Amin and the British in World War II." *Middle Eastern Studies* (January 1984), 22:4–16.

—— "The Renewal of Palestinian Political Activity 1943–1945: (The Shifting of the Pivot of Dissension from the Husayni-Nashashibi Conflict to the Husayni-Istiqlal Rivalry)," in *The Palestinians and the Middle East Conflict*. ed. Gabriel Ben-Dor. Ramat-Gan: Turtledove, 1978.

Nimr, Ihsan. *Tarikh Jabal Nablus wa al-Balqa'*. Vol. 4. Nablus: Matba'at Jami'a 'Ummal al-Matabi' al-Ta'awuniyya, 1975.

Nuwayhid, Ajaj. "Sayyidi al-Fa'iz fi al-Darayn." *Filastin* (August 1974), 16:118–20.

Pearlman, Maurice. *Mufti of Jerusalem: The Story of Haj Amin el-Husseini*. London: Victor Gollancz, 1947.

Plascov, Avi. *The Palestinian Refugee in Jordan*. London: Frank Cass, 1981.

Porath, Yehoshua. "Al-Hajj Amin al-Husayni, Mufti of Jerusalem: His Rise to Power and Consolidation of His Position." *Asian and Africa Studies* (1971), 7:212–56.

—— "Al-Hajj (Muhammad) Amin al-Husseini." In Yaacov Shimoni and Evyatar

Levine, eds., *Political Dictionary of the Middle East in the Twentieth Century.* New York: Quadrangle, 1974.

—— *The Emergence of the Palestinian-Arab National Movement, 1918–1929.* Vol. 1. London: Frank Cass, 1974.

—— *The Palestinian Arab National Movement, 1929–1939: From Riots to Rebellion.* Vol. 2. London: Frank Cass, 1977.

—— "The Political Organization of the Palestinian Arabs Under the British Mandate." In Moshe Ma'oz, ed., *Palestinian Arab Politics.* Jerusalem: Jerusalem Academic Press, 1975.

Qasimiyya, Khayriyya, ed. *Mudhakkirat Fawzi al-Qawuqji, 1914–1932.* Vol. 1. Beirut: Dar al-Quds, 1975.

—— *Filastin fi Mudhakkirat al-Qawiqji, 1936–1948.* Vol. 2. Beirut: Dar al-Quds, 1975.

Al-Sabbagh, Salah al-Din. *Fursan al-'Urba fi al-'Iraq.* Damascus: n.p., 1956.

Safran, Nadav. *From War to War: The Arab-Isralei Confrontation, 1948–1967.* New York: Pegasus, 1969.

Said, Edward. *The Question of Palestine.* New York: Times Books, 1979.

Samuel, Edwin (Second Viscount). *A Lifetime in Jerusalem: The Memoirs of the Second Viscount Samuel.* London: Abelard-Shuman, 1970.

Samuel, Herbert. *Great Britain and Palestine.* The Second Lucien Wolf Memorial Lecture. London, 1935.

Samuel, Horace B. *Beneath the Whitewash.* London: Hogarth Press, 1930.

Samuel, Maurice. *What Happened in Palestine.* Boston: Statford, 1929.

Schechtman, Joseph B. *The Mufti and the Fuehrer: The Rise and Fall of Haj Amin el-Husseini.* New York: Thomas Yoseloff, 1965.

Sheean, Vincent. *Personal History.* Boston: Houghton Mifflin, 1969.

Shlaim, Avi. *Collusion Across the Jordan: King Abdullah, the Zionist Movement, and the Partition of Palestine.* New York: Columbia University Press, 1988.

—— *The Politics of Partition: King Abdullah, the Zionists, and Palestine 1921–1951.* Oxford: Oxford University Press, 1990.

—— "The Rise and Fall of the All-Palestine Government of Gaza," *Journal of Palestine Studies* (Autumn 1990), 77(1):37–53.

Al-Sifri, 'Isa. *Filastin al-'Arabiyya bayn al-Intidab wa al-Sahyuniyya.* Vol. 1. Jaffa: Maktabat Filastin al-Jadida, 1937.

Smith, Charles D. *Palestine and the Arab-Israeli Conflict.* New York: St. Martin's, 1988.

Storrs, Ronald. *Memoirs: Orientation.* New York: Nicholson and Watson, 1937.

Sykes, Christopher. *Crossroads to Israel.* Bloomington: Indiana University, 1973.

Trevor-Roper, H. R. "The Mind of Adolf Hitler." In *Hitler: Secret Conversations, 1914–1944.* New York: Octagon, 1972.

Waters, M. P. *The Mufti Over the Middle East.* London: Barber, 1942.

Wiesenthal, Simon. *Grossmufti—Grossagen der Achse.* Salzburg: Ried-Verlag, 1947.

Wilson, Mary C. *King Abdullah, Britain, and the Making of Jordan*. Cambridge: Cambridge University Press, 1987.

Yasin, Subhi. *Al-Thawra al-'Arabiyya al-Kubra fi Filastin 1936–1939*. Cairo: Dar al-Hana, 1959.

Yasir, Salih Mas'ud Aba. *Jihad Sha'b Filastin Khilal Nisf Qarn*. Beirut: Dar al-Fath li al-Tiba'a wa al-Nashir, 1968.

Yisraeli, David. *Ha-Reich Ha-Germani V'Eretz Yisraeli: B'ayot Eretz yisraeli Be-Mediniyut Ha-Germanit Be-Shanim 1889–1948*. Ramat-Gan: Bar-Ilan University, 1974.

Zeine, Zeine N. *Arab-Turkish Relations and the Emergence of Arab Nationalism*. Beirut: Khayat's, 1958.

V. PERIODICALS AND NEWSPAPERS

Akhbar al-Yawm (Cairo)
Akhir Sa'a (Cairo)
Al-Balagh (Cairo)
Daily Express (London)
Al-Difa'
Filastin (Beirut)
Al-Jami'a al-'Arabiyya (Jerusalem)
Jerusalem Post International
Journal du Caire (Cairo)
Karmil
Manchester Guardian
Mir' at al-Sharq
Al-Misri (Cairo)
The New York Times
Oriente Moderno (Rome)
Palestine Weekly (Jerusalem)
Sirat al-Mustaqim
Suriyya al-Janubiyya
Time Magazine
Times (London)

VI. INTERVIEWS

'Arif al-'Arif with Ann Mosely Lesch, Ramalla, May 21–22, 1971.
Kamil al-Dajani with Muhammad Muslih, Beirut, 1978.
Walid al-Dali with the author, Cairo, 1979.
Muhammad 'Izzat Darwaza with Ann Mosely Lesch, Damascus, 1971.
Ishaq Darwish with Ann Mosely Lesch, Jerusalem, 1971.
Dr. George Farah with the author, 1978.
Amina al-Husayni with the author, Jerusalem and Amman, 1978.

Haydar al-Husayni (close aide, after 1937, and son-in-law of the Mufti) with the author, Beirut, 1978.
Ishaq Musa al-Husayni with Taysir Jbara, Jerusalem, 1978.
Jamal al-Husayni with Ann Mosely Lesch, Beirut, 1971.
Dr. Muhammad Naqib al-Husayni with the author, Jerusalem, 1978.
Munif al-Husayni with Muhammad Muslih, Beirut, 1978.
Su'ad al-Husayni (daughter of the Mufti) with the author, Beirut, 1978.
Zaynab al-Husayni (daughter of the Mufti) with the author, Beirut, 1978.
Kamal al-Din Jalal with the author, Cairo, 1978, 1979.
Ghalib Sa'id al-Nashashibi (former student of Amin at Rawdat al-Ma'arif) with the author, Jerusalem, 1978.
Ahmad Shuqayri with the author, Cairo, 1978.
Ahmad Farraj Tayi' with the author, Cairo, 1978.

Index

'Abd al-Baqi, Ahmad Hilmi, 70, 75, 121, 131
'Abd al-Hadi, 'Awni, 53, 66–67, 70–71, 75–77
'Abd al-Hamid, Sultan, 4–5, 14
'Abd al-Nasir, Jamal, 92, 137
'Abdullah, Amir, 21, 25, 79–81, 113–17, 125; annexation plans for Palestine, 117, 128–31, 135, assassination of, 136; assassination plans for the Mufti, 118; cooperation with British, 117; cooperation with Jewish Agency, 116; and First Palestinian Congress, 133; Greater Syria scheme, 114, 116, 120, 124; negotiations with Israel, 115, 117–18, 136; and 1948 war, 129; and partition, 124; suspicion of, 131
Acre, 30, 81
al-'Alami, 'Abd al-Rahman, 10
al-'Alami family, 6–7
al-'Alami, Musa, 93, 112–13, 130
Alexandria Protocol, 112
All-Palestine Government, 112
Anglo-American Morrison-Grady Committee, 120, 122

Antonius, George, 45, 79
al-Aqsa Mosque, see Haram al-Sharif
Arab Club (al-Nadi al-'Arabi), 13, 15, 23
Arab Covenant, 65
Arab Executive, 30–31, 48, 51, 53, 58, 64, 118
Arab Higher Committee, 70–71, 74–77, 79–84, 93, 121–23; and All-Palestine Government, 131
Arab Higher Front, 121
Arab League, 112–13, 119–21, 123, 128–29, 134, 136; Aley Session, 125; Bludan Session, 121; and civil administration for Palestine, 130; and Amin al-Husayni, 123–25, 129–30; opposition to Amir 'Abdullah, 135; Political Committee meeting in Sufar, 124
Arab Liberation Army, 127
Arab National Fund, 111
Arab Revolt (1916), 5–6, 12
Arab Revolt (1936–39), 68–74, 79, 82–85, 88–89, 99, 147
'Arafat, Yasir, 138
al-'Arif, 'Arif, 15, 17–21, 27

Assassination of Amin al-Husayni, plans, 94–95

Axis (*see also* Germany, Italy, World War II), 90–91, 93–94; radio broadcasts in Arabic, 91, 104, 148

'Azzam, 'Abd al-Rahman (*see also* Arab League), 62–63, 109, 125

Balfour Declaration, 14–16, 17, 20, 22, 38, 52, 71, 80, 82

Ben-Gurion, David, 52, 144, 149

Bentwich, Norman, 26, 28, 32, 54, 142

Bernadotte, Count Folke, 130

Bevin, Ernest, 122, 128

Biltmore Conference, 111

Bludan congress (1937), see National Arab Congress

al-Budayri, Musa, 25

al-Buraq campaign, 38–40

Buraq al-Sharif, see Western Wall

Castel, 127

Chancellor, Sir John, 51, 61, 144, and Western Wall dispute, 40–41, 43–44, 48, 50, 54

Churchill, Winston, 82, 84, 93–95, 100, 104, 113–14; assassination plans for the Mufti, 118, 148

Committee for the Defense of the Buraq al-Sharif, 37

Committee of Seven (Iraq), 93

al-Dajani, 'Arif Pasha, 16

al-Dajani, Hasan Sidqi, 74–75

Darwaza, Muhammad 'Izzat, 20, 35, 66, 83, 143

Deir Yasin, 128

Deutsch-Arabische Lehrabteilung, 104–5

Dome of the Rock, see Haram al-Sharif

Egypt (*see also* 'Abd al-Nasir), 58, 60, 72, 86, 88, 100, 112, 120, 130; and All-Palestine Government, 131, 134; and Amin al-Husayni, 133; and 1948 war, 128

Farraj, Ya'qub, 70

Faruq, King, 110

Faysal, King, 5–6, 12, 15–18, 25, 29, 65, 81

Federal plan for Palestine, 115

First Arab Summit, 120

France, 11, 15, 18, 61–62, 81, 88, 90, 101, 108–9

Fu'ad, King, 59

al-Futuwwa, 125

Galilee, 80–83

Gaza, 77

General Islamic Conference (1931), 58–64, 145

General Muslim Conference (1928), 39, 42, 44–45, 56

Germany (*see also* Axis, World War II), 86, 88, 91–93, 95–96, 99–108; Nazis, 64, 84

Ghuri, Emile, 121

al-Ghusayn, Ya'qub, 70

Great Britain (*see also* Arab Revolt [1936–39], Balfour Declaration), 11, 80; against partition, 117; and All-Palestine Government, 133; and Arab Revolt (1916), 12–15; and Arab Revolt (1936–39), efforts to suppress, 82–83, 85, 90, 100; arrest of Mufti's family, 97; Balfour policy, 153; excludes Mufti, 119, 134; and General Islamic Congress, 60–63; and Iran, 96; and Iraq, 65, 86, 89–96; and Jordanian annexation of West Bank; and Mufti, arrest and assassination plans, 82–83, 85, 87, 94, 107; opposition to Amin al-Husayni, 130; and Palestine delegation (1930), 52–53; Palestine mandate, 30, 35, 38, 80; and Palestine notables, 6; policy, 55–56, 58, 100; and Supreme Muslim Council, 28, 31; and Western Wall dispute, 35, 38, 43–45, 52–54; and World War I, 11; and World War II, 88, 90, 100; and World War II charges against Mufti, 105

Haddad, 'Uthman Kamal, 101

Hagana, 68

Haifa, 15, 30, 48, 69, 128

Haram al-Sharif (*see also* Western Wall), 6–7, 25, 30, 34, 38–40, 56, 69, 82, 143; renovations, 29, 42, 44–45, 56; and Zionist plans, 37, 39–42, 46–47, 78

Hashimites (*see also* 'Abdullah, Arab Revolt [1916], Faysal), 5–6

Hebron, 30, 47–48
Herzl, Theodor, 8, 14
Hilmi, Ahmad Pasha, 75, 132, 134
Hitler, Adolf, 100–104
Hope-Simpson Commission Report, 53, 55
Husayn, Amir, 12, King of Hijaz, 56–57, 71
al-Husayni, 'Abd al-Qadir, 127–28
al-Husayni, Amin, 134, 140–41, 149; and Arab Club, 13; and Arab Executive, 31, 53; Arab Higher Committee chairman, 121; president, 70–71, 74–77; and Arab League, 123–25, 129–30; and Arab Revolt (1916), 12–13; and Arab Revolt (1936–39), 68–72, 74–78, 84–85; arrest plans, 82–83, 107, 110; assassination plans for, 118, 138, 148; and assassination of Amir 'Abdullah, 136–37; and Axis, 93, 99–107; birth, 6; bribe attempts, 82; call for Palestine Government, 125; capture of family, 97; compromise attempt with Jewish Agency, 118–19; cooperation with British, 142, 144, 146, 149; criticized, 66–68; education, 8–9; death of, 139; escape from France, 109, 149; exile, 108–9, 146–48; fund-raising, 29–30, 56–57, 63; and Great Britain, cooperation with, 12–13, 26–27, 32, 43–44, 48, 51–53, 55, 61, 63–64, 66, 68–69, 72, 80–81, 85, 87; negotiations with, 52–55; hajj, 10; and Iraq, 86–96; and Lebanon, 83, 88–89; loss of political power, 134, 137; and military effort for Palestine, 125, 127; Mufti of Jerusalem, campaign and election for, 22–27; and Muslim support for Palestinians, 56–64; and 1948, 128; opposition to Legislative Council, 142; and Palestine government, 132; and Palestine National Council, 132; and Pan-Arabism, 12–18, 80; pardon (1920), 20–21; and partition of Palestine, 80–81; and political violence of 1920, 15–18; rejection of partition, 126, 151; return to leadership, 112; Supreme Muslim Council president, 28–30, 37, 52, 56, 61, 63, 77–78, 88, 117, 142; visits Jerusalem (1967), 138; teaching positions, 10, 14–15; Turkey, escape to, 97; war crimes charges, 105–6, 108–9; and

Western Wall dispute, 35–49, 53–55, 118–19, 122; and World War I, 10–13; and World War II, 88–89, 93, 99–101
al-Husayni, Fakhri, 7, 13, 23
al-Husayni family, 1, 6–7, 13, 23–25, 84, 141, 146; al-Nashashibi rivalry, 20, 22, 24, 31, 45, 66, 79
al-Husayni, Isma'il, 23, 25
al-Husayni, Jamal, 25, 52–53, 55, 57, 69–70, 75–77, 84, 92, 112, 121, 131–32, 144–45
al-Husayni, Kamil, 7–8, 10, 17, 20–23
al-Husayni, Musa Kazim Pasha, 16–17, 21–23, 30–31, 53, 57, 64, 143
al-Husayni, Raja'i, 132
al-Husayni, Tahir (ibn Kamil), 23
al-Husayni, Tahir (ibn Mustafa), 7–8, 13, 56
al-Husayni, Zaynab, 7, 10

Ikhwan al-Qassam (Brothers of Qassam), 64, 68–69
India, 29, 55, 57, 63, 94
Iran, 54, 96–97, 123
Iraq, 29, 63, 65, 86–97, 100–102, 104, 112, 120, 133; and All-Palestine Government, 134; opposition to Amin al-Husayni, 130
Irgun (Zva'i Le'ummi), 95, 109; assassination attempt on Mufti, 118, 148; political violence, 122
al-Istiqlal (Independence) party, 64–67, 69–70, 76, 88, 111
Italy (see also Axis), 61–63, 90, 100–103

Jabotinsky, Zeev (Vladimir), 17–18, 45
Jaffa, 15, 27, 30, 48, 68–69, 74, 78, 83, 128, 141
al-Jami'a al-'Arabiyya, 37, 42, 62
Jaralla family, 6–7
Jaralla, Husam al-Din, 24–25, 27
Jaysh al-Jihad al-Muqaddas, 132, 136–37
Jews (see also White Paper [1939], Zionists), and election of Amin al-Husayni as mufti, 25; immigration, 7–8, 10, 31, 53, 55, 62, 64, 67, 71–72, 74, 79–81, 84, 88, 120, 122–23, 135, 145, 147, 149, 153; land purchases, 31, 40–41, 53, 62, 67, 72, 149, 153; and Western Wall, 34–39, 41–42, 45, 54

Jewish Agency, 32, 38, 46, 79, 81, 105–6

Keith-Roach, Edward, 35
al-Khalidi family, 7
al-Khalidi, Husayn Fakhri, 70, 74–76, 121
al-Khalidi, Khalil, 24–25
al-Kilani, Rashid 'Ali, 91–95, 103
King-Crane Commission, 15
Kisch, Colonel Frederick, 37, 40–41, 45

League of Arab States, *see* Arab League
League of Nations, 30, 36–37; Wailing
    Wall Commission, 54, 57–58, 62
Lebanon, 56, 83, 86, 88, 103, 112, 120; and
    All-Palestine Government, 134
Legislative Council, 30–31, 48, 142, 150
Literary Club (al-Muntada al-Adabi), 13, 23
London Round Table Conference on Pales-
    tine, 84, 89, 122
Luke, Sir Harry, 36–37

MacDonald letter ("Black Letter" [1931]),
    55, 58
Meir, Golda (Meyerson), 117, 128
Mufti: definition, 3; election, 25–26; role
    under British rule, 22
Muslim Brothers (Ikhwan al-Muslimun), 9
Muslim-Christian Association (al-Jam'iyya
    al-Islamiyya al-Mashihiyya), 13
Mussolini, Benito, 102, 104

Nablus, 30, 69, 77, 141
al-Nashashibi, Fakhri, 69, 76, 83
al-Nashashibi family, 7, 13, 20, 22, 24, 81,
    84, 110; al-Husayni rivalry, 20, 22, 24,
    31, 45, 66, 79
al-Nashashibi, Raghib (*see also* Opposi-
    tion), 22–23, 25, 27–28, 31, 53, 70, 75–
    76, 79, 81–82, 110; British attempts to
    bribe, 82
National Arab Congress (1937), 82
Nazis, 64, 84, 112, 148
Notables, 1–6, 121; politics of, 2

Opposition (Mu'aridun), 28, 30–32, 41,
    44–45, 51, 66, 70, 76, 81, 87–88, 90
Ottoman Empire: and *awqaf* administra-
    tion, 27; and European presence, 4, 8;
    and mufti of Jerusalem, 22; and Pales-

tine, 1–8; Tanzimat, 3–4; and Western
    Wall, 34; World War I, 10–12; Young
    Turks, 4

Palestine, 7, 11–14, 110–14; civil adminis-
    tration, plans for, 130; civil war (1948),
    126–28; Declaration of Independence,
    132; exodus of Palestinians, 128; land
    sales to Jews, 7–8, 53, 63; (May 15,)
    1948 war, 130; opposition to British (*see
    also* Arab Revolt [1936–39]), 49–50, 59,
    63, 66–68, 82, 84–85, 89, 122; under
    Ottomans, 1–5, 8; partition plans, 80,
    83; refugees, 135
Palestine Arab Executive, 143
Palestine Arab party, 69–70, 111, 125
Palestine Liberation Organization (PLO),
    138
Palestine National Charter, 138
Palestine National Congress (1919), 13
Palestine National Council, 132; and Amin
    al-Husayni, 132
Palin Commission Report, 17, 75
Pan-Arabism, 5, 9, 11–13, 15, 65, 82, 86,
    93
Pan-Islamism (*see also* General Islamic
    Congress), 5, 9, 56–57
Partition plans for Palestine, 80–83, 113–
    16, 122–24, 126, 128, 147, 150–51
Passfield White Paper (October 1930), 53,
    55, 145
Peel Commission (*also known as* Royal
    Commission), 80–81, 114, 124, 150
Plumer, Lord, 43
Porath, Yehoshua, x, 8, 28, 31, 35–36, 143
Puaux, Gabriel, 85, 88

Qalqilya, 15
al-Qassam, 'Izz al-Din (*see also* Ikhwan al-
    Qassam), 30, 67–68

Rawdat al-Ma'arif al-Wataniyya, 10, 14,
    29, 62
Revisionist Zionism, 17, 45, 109
Richmond, Ernest, 25–26, 29
Rida, Rashid, 9, 12, 18, 62
Rock, Alfred, 70, 75

Rutenberg, Pinhas, 38, 52, 86–87, 144; assassination plans for Amin al-Husayni, 118, 148

Safad, 48
Safwat, General Isma'il, 125
al-Sa'id, Nuri, 79, 89–93, 96
Salah, 'Abd al-Latif, 70
Samuel, Sir Herbert, 30, 32, 43, 142; and mufti's election and appointment, 25–27; and pardon of al-Husayni, 19–21; and Supreme Muslim Council, 28–29
Sasson, Eliahu, 115–16
Sa'udi Arabia, 54, 59–60, 63, 79, 94, 96, 112, 120, 130; and All-Palestine Government, 134
Schechtman, Joseph, ix–x, 3, 20, 68, 141
Seychelles, 83, 109–110
Shaw Commission, 46, 48, 53, 55, 75, 144
al-Shuqayri, Ahmad, 66, 113, 138
Society for the Defense of al-Masjid al-Aqsa, 42
Storrs, Ronald, 15, 17, 24–25, 27, 40–41
Supreme Muslim Council, 27–29, 31, 40, 52, 58, 62–63, 66–67, 69, 77, 80
Syria, 11, 13–18, 56, 72, 80–83, 88, 90, 101–3, 112, 120, 130; and All-Palestine Government, 134

Tel Aviv, 68, 73
Tiberias, 128
Transjordan (*see also* 'Abdullah, Jordan), 12, 17–19, 56, 80, 88, 104; Transjordan, 112, 114–15, 120; opposition to Amin al-Husayni, 130
Truman, Harold S., 120–22
Turkey, 1, 3, 11, 14, 18, 60, 96–97, 100
Turkification, opposition to, 5, 9, 11–12

UNSCOP Majority Report, 123–24

Va'ad Le'ummi, 37
Violence, political, 122, 143, 145, 147, 149; Arab Revolt (1936–39), 68–74, 82–85, 88–90; executive general strike (1933); Iraq pogrom (June 1941), 95–96; May Day (1921), 27; al-Nabi Musa (April 1920), 16–17; Western Wall (August 1929), 33, 36, 40, 46–50, 57

Wailing Wall, *see* Western Wall
War of 1948, 126–34
Wauchope, Sir Arthur, 69, 71, 74–80, 82, 145
Weizmann, Chaim, 38, 40, 52, 55, 73, 81, 144, 149
Western Wall (al-Buraq) (*see also* League of Nations, Shaw Commission), 33–43, 45–49, 52, 56–59, 61, 143; British role in dispute, 35, 38, 43–45, 48, 50; legal proceedings, 53–54; violence, 45–48
White Paper (1928), 43–44
White Paper (1930), *see* Passfield White Paper
White Paper (1939), 84, 90, 93, 113, 147, 151–52
World War I, 5, 10, 80
World War II, 88, 90–91, 93
World Zionist Organization, 8, 14, 36–38

Zionists (*see also* Jews, Israel), 14, 110–11, 116, 119; and 'Abdullah; and Great Britain, 84; and Mufti, 16, 105–6; and Palestine (*see also* Western Wall), 58–60, 78; and violence, 90